Also, the blades and discs suggested can be changed if you like a different texture or if that disc is not available. The reason these points are brought up here is because we do not want you to pass over a recipe because the disc or a certain ingredient are missing in your kitchen. Use your imagination and let the recipe come alive.

PURCHASING A FOOD PROCESSOR

We cannot let this book go to press without making a few comments on the quality of various food processors. We have found that machines that are belt driven are loud and break down more quickly than machines that have a direct drive motor. Those with a direct drive motor will last much longer. When purchasing a food processor check on the type of warranty that is available. Find out if additional accessories can be purchased and where they may be purchased. The size of the feedtube and the capacity of the machine can vary from brand to brand. Pick the features that suit your needs best. If the machine requires service find out where it is available and how easy it is to contact the food processor company.

Talk to other food processor owners to see what brand they like. Buying a better machine from the beginning pays off in the long run. You will probably find that the people who own a high quality food processor and one with more features will use the processor more often.

We tested all the recipes in this book on various machines. There is a definite difference in the way food processors perform. Some machines process quickly while others take twice as long to process the same food item. This is the reason why there is always a variable in the times in our cookbook recipes.

You will also note that we mention different quantity capacities for the recipes. It is possible to process small amounts in any size processor but you cannot increase the capacity of the processor once you buy it. It is less expensive to buy the size you need than to replace it with a larger one in just a few years. Plan ahead, buy a good food processor to begin with and buy one to fit your needs now and in the future.

KEY TO COOKBOOK SYMBOLS

In this book the recipes may appear long to you but that is because we teach you exactly how to prepare each step IN the food processor. We know you know how to chop an onion or slice a carrot by hand but we want you to discover the ease and speed of doing these preparations in the food processor.

To eliminate confusion over which disc or blade to use at each step we have inserted a tiny symbol representing the disc or blade to be used. You will only see a different symbol if you need to change to a different disc or blade.

Each symbol used is listed next to the commonly used name or names. The first name listed is the way we refer to that blade or disc in this cookbook.

    =   METAL BLADE, Steel Blade, Chopping Blade, Metal or Steel Knife, S-Blade, Knife Blade.

    =   SHREDDING DISC, Grater Blade, Shredding Blade.

    =   DOUGH BLADE

    =   SLICING DISC, Slicing Blade, Slicer.

    =   FRENCH-FRY DISC, French-fry Blade, 6 x 6mm Cutter

THE FIRST DAY WITH YOUR FOOD PROCESSOR

"So Now You Own a FOOD PROCESSOR". What do you do? Where do you start? The first thing you must do is take it out of the box! This may sound funny, but there are a lot of people who are afraid of it and will not take it out of the box. We are going to make this a fun day for you. The family will love your meals and you will love the extra time you have for yourself.

The second thing you must do is go to the grocery store and buy fresh fruits and vegetables to cut up, cheese to shred, and meat to slice or chop. Don't forget to pick something up like a cake mix for dessert. All this preparation of food will take just a few minutes, so buy a lot of items. For your first experience with your food processor we want you to get comfortable using the machine. The only way you can do this is to spend time doing some food preparation.

SUGGESTED GROCERY LIST

Produce—
Tomatoes-2
Lettuce
Cucumber
Dry onion-1
Green onions-1 bunch
Carrots-1 bunch
Rutabaga-1
Green pepper
Radishes
Garlic bulb-1

Dairy—
1/2 pint whipping cream
8 oz. cheddar cheese

3 oz. pkg. cream cheese
1/2 pint sour cream

Bagels or English Muffins
Walnuts-8 oz.pkg.
1-1/2 pounds round steak
1 (18-1/2 oz.) yellow cake mix
1 env. onion soup mix
8 oz. can tomato juice

Staples—
Oil
Vinegar
Rolled oats
Almond flavoring

Now you are home with all the groceries. To make food preparation easier in the food processor put the round steak and cheddar cheese in the refrigerator. With all the other groceries in front of you, you are now ready to play. With food processor out of the box, let's get started.

Electricity is not the only answer. Plugging in the food processor doesn't make the machine run. Put on your home engineer's hat and *ASSEMBLE* your food processor. Read, Read, Read, your instruction booklet until you can assemble your food processor properly. The machine will *NOT* start until the lid is locked properly in place. This is a safety feature built into the food processor.

We know that assembling the food processor for the first time is harder than picking up a knife, but after you learn to use your food processor it will be your most valuable kitchen tool. Besides you will never have shredded knuckles again.

If you have any questions about assembling your food processor do not be afraid to ask your spouse or children. You will be amazed how interested they are in your new "toy". Or ask friends or neighbors who own a food processor about the "mysteries" of this machine and have a nice social afternoon. There is nothing like combining food and friends. But just in case you are out there all by yourself, we are here to help you.

Let us go over the basic parts of the food processor. Food processors come with a metal knife or blade, shredding disc, and slicing discs. Some machines offer additional pieces such as: a dough blade, whipping blade, French-fry blade, julienne blade or extra slicing and shredding discs in various thicknesses. Some of these items come with the machine and with some machines the extra blades are an additional cost.

WORKBOWL & BASE

STEP 1—This bowl must be set on the base first; then rotate the bowl to lock it in place.Check the owners manual.

The workbowl is used to hold all the food that you will process. The capacity of the workbowl varies with the type of food being processed.It can be filled to within one inch from the top when slicing or shredding. Generally, when using the METAL BLADE, filling the workbowl no more than half full gives more even chopping results. A full bowl of fruit or vegetable pieces may result in a "blender effect" where the bottom pieces are chopped very finely and the upper-most pieces are coarse.

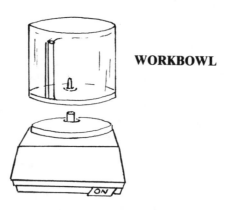

WORKBOWL

METAL BLADE

STEP 2—This is the most versatile blade in your machine. Set it on the shaft in the bottom of the workbowl.

Generally, all food is placed in the workbowl when using the METAL BLADE. The important thing to remember about this blade is to PULSE-CHOP every food item that is put into the workbowl. Pulse-chopping means turning the machine on and off. You do this for two reasons: 1. You will not over process the food. You are checking the coarseness of the food by stopping the machine, checking, and if necessary pulse-chopping again until food reaches proper consistency. 2. The on-off motion moves the food around and the food gets chopped more evenly.

Remember, with the metal blade, *THE LONGER THE MACHINE RUNS THE FINER THE FOOD GETS*. It doesn't take more than a few SECONDS to make onions into mush or turn peanuts into peanut butter. *REMEMBER*—pulsing or pulse-chopping means to turn the machine on and off. Each pulse or pulse-chop is about one second. Pulsing is the *KEY* to success when using the METAL BLADE. Some of the food items you will use the metal blade for are the following:

1. Mixing cakes
2. Mixing cookie dough
3. Mixing quick breads
4. Cutting fat into pastries and pie crust
5. Making cheese cakes
6. Kneading bread dough (when using 3 cups flour)
7. Chopping meat, raw or cooked (for hamburger, sausage, etc.)
8. Chopping nuts
9. Making peanut butter or any nut butter
10. Making ice cream and sherbet
11. Whipping cream
12. Whipping egg whites
13. Grating parmesan cheese
14. Preparing mayonnaise
15. Chopping any fruit or vegetable, e.g. onions, carrots, parsley, cabbage, garlic, apples, cranberries, etc.
16. Grating any fruit or vegetable
17. Grating citrus rinds
18. Purees, e.g. soups, pates, and baby foods

SLICING DISC

This disc is used to slice all foods that need slicing. In order to use this disc, place food in feedtube, resting on the slicing disc, and process using the pusher to guide the food. For more detailed instruction about placement of food in the feedtube look under SLICING in TIPS. SLICING DISCS vary in thicknesses. Most processors have as standard equipment a slicing disc about 3-4mm thick (1/8 inch). As you become familiar with the machine you may want to get a very thin slicing disc or the thickest one available. Some foods that you might slice are—

Pepperoni (frozen)
Meat (frozen but partially thawed)
Lunch meats (very cold)
Fruits and vegetables e.g. lettuce, French style green beans,
    cabbage, potatoes, carrots,
    onions, celery, mushrooms, strawberries,
    apples, bananas, pineapple, lemons, limes,
    oranges, olives, pickles, etc.
You may also use the SLICING DISC to cut foods twice and achieve a julienne cut.See the JULIENNE TIP in TIPS.

SHREDDING DISC

This disc is used to shred all foods that require shredding. In order to use this disc, place food in the feedtube, resting on the shredding disc, and process using the pusher to guide the food. For more detailed instruction about shredding of food, look under TIPS for that food. Sometimes the shredding disc can take the place of thin cut julienne strips. Some foods that you might shred are—

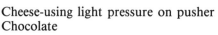

Cheese-using light pressure on pusher
Chocolate
Nuts
Fruits and vegetables eg. carrots, cabbage, beets, coconut, broccoli stems, squash, celery, apples, pears, potatoes, zucchini, celery, radishes, etc.

DOUGH BLADE

Available with some machines. This blade is used to make bread when more than 3-1/2 cups of flour are being used. Check the instruction booklet to see if this blade comes with the machine.

PLASTIC KNIFE

Available on some machines. Do not confuse this blade with the dough blade. The only thing this blade has in common with a dough blade is that they are both plastic. It does not have the same strength or function as the dough blade.

Some people use this blade often while others use it seldom. It could be used for making mayonnaise, salad dressings, sauces, gravies, whipping cream and egg whites. Because these items can be done just as successfully with the METAL BLADE, this plastic knife gets put away. The choice is yours if you want to use it or not.

COVER with FEEDTUBE

STEP 3—The feedtube is attached to the cover. Place the cover on the workbowl and rotate to lock in place. When the cover is locked in place the machine will start. If the cover is not locked in place properly the machine won't start.

The food is placed into the feedtube when using the slicing, shredding, French-fry or julienne discs. The bottom of the feedtube is a little larger than the top. If, for example, a lemon won't fit in the top of the feedtube, try placing it in the bottom of the feedtube.

In a Cuisinart® food processor with a large feedtube place the food in the large feedtube BEFORE locking the sleeve of the pusher assembly in place. The pusher will expand upward to accommodate the food when the sleeve is locked in place. Food is always placed in the feedtube when using the slicing, shredding, French-fry or julienne disc. The food rests on the disc surface before processing. For best results have the feedtube packed with food rather than loosely filled. Always stop the machine before refilling the feedtube.

(When discussing placing food in the feedtube, we will refer to the height, width and length of the feedtube as diagrammed below.)

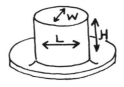

FOOD PROCESSOR EYE

TIP: Try to buy food that will fit in the feedtube. EXAMPLE- if you need round whole lemon slices buy a smaller lemon that you're sure will fit the feedtube. If it's too big you will have to cut the lemon in half.

PUSHER

STEP 4—Place the pusher in the feedtube. Place palm of hand over pusher. Be ready to push BEFORE you turn on machine. Start to push gently, turn on machine, and follow pusher down all the way through.

This may not seem like much but it is a very important little item. The food that is in the feedtube is guided by the pusher. If the food is not guided properly it will not process nicely. For nice even slices or shreds do not stop pushing halfway in between—follow food all the way through. If you want to slice just part of a cucumber then only put what you want in the feedtube. It is very difficult to stop processing halfway through the piece of food. The pusher is to the food processer as the steering wheel is to the car.

On a Cuisinart® food processor the pusher sleeve assembly must be locked into place before the machine will start. When using the large feedtube in the Cuisinart® food processor the food must not exceed 3-1/2 inches in height. You must place the food in the large feedtube *BEFORE* putting the pusher sleeve assembly in place. The pusher sleeve assembly expands upward to accommodate the food; if the food goes above the rim of the feedtube the pusher sleeve assembly will not lock in place.

ON-OFF SWITCH, PULSE OR MOMENTARY SWITCH

STEP 5—To use the pulse or momentary button; hold the button or switch and the machine stays on until you release your finger. Once the pulse button or momentary switch is released by your finger the machine turns off. The ON BUTTON continuously runs the machine until the off button is pushed. The pulse button or momentary button may also say OFF so you will push that button just once to turn off the machine if you have been using the ON button.

To pulse or pulse-chop means to turn the machine on and off. Each pulse should be equal to one second. This method is used when processing with the metal blade. When you first begin operating the food processor use the pulse button or momentary switch and time yourself with a second hand watch until you are familiar with the length of a second.

You should be ready to begin now. If you read all of the previous material you know a lot about the uses of the food processor and you have a completely assembled food processor in front of you. Now it is time to see if this machine will run. If the machine will not operate by pressing the on, pulse or momentary switch, *CHECK THE ASSEMBLY INSTRUCTIONS AGAIN.* For safety reasons all food processors have interlock mechanisms which must be in place properly or the machine *WILL NOT RUN.*

Let's make some lunch now. The menu is—

Cheese Walnut Broiler Buns

Fresh Vegetable Tray

Beverage

We'll prepare the vegetables first, today, as it may take you longer. Remember you are learning and that takes time. But once you have your learner's permit—watch out! You will love how quickly you can do these things. As you finish each of the vegetables arrange them on a serving tray.

CARROT STICKS OR DIPPERS

2 Dozen Sticks

Use the largest, fattest carrots that you purchased. Fat carrots make the best dippers. Peel 2 carrots, remove root and stem end. Cut the carrots in three or four even lengths that will fit horizontally in the feedtube. Insert the ⌣ (3-4 mm). Position the cutting edge of the slicing disc opposite the spot the feedtube locks in place. This produces a clean even first cut. Place the cover on the workbowl. Place the carrots on their sides in the feedtube resting on the disc surface. Alternate the narrow and wide ends of the carrots to make an even layer. Put pusher in feedtube and make sure cover is locked in place. Place palm of hand on pusher and press with a firm pressure. Use the pulse switch to turn the machine on and continue pressing evenly on the pusher. Release the switch when all the carrots are processed. This stops the machine. One or two pieces may remain on the disc. This is acceptable as you don't want to process the lid. Yes, it is very fast and a little noisy because carrots are a hard root vegetable. This is also the reason your machine may have moved a little. But wasn't it easy?

CUCUMBER SLICES

1 Cucumber

Leave ⌣ in place. Stripe cucumber skin with a fork or citrus stripper for a decorative effect. Check to see if it fits in the feedtube. Cut in half vertically for a small feedtube or cut whole cucumber in half horizontally to fit two pieces side by side in a large feedtube. Follow same technique as above but use a medium pressure on the pusher. If you don't use a continuously even pressure on the pusher the vegetable will cut into slices of various thicknesses.

RUTABAGA HALF MOONS   1 Rutabaga

Try it first before you turn up your nose. It's better uncooked! Peel and cut in half vertically. Be sure to cut both ends flat. The flat surface starts the slices evenly and the pusher presses evenly on the upper flat surface. Insert the ⌒. Process both half pieces together if the feedtube is big enough or one half at a time. Use a firm pressure on the pusher.

GREEN PEPPER RINGS   1 Green Pepper

Cut off stem end. Remove seed pod, but don't cut pepper. If the whole pepper doesn't fit in the feedtube then cut off the blossom end and cut through one side of the pepper. Roll this pepper piece like a jellyroll to fit the feedtube. Place the whole pepper with the flat side down, or prepared pepper roll in the feedtube, resting on the ⌒, and process using medium pressure on the pusher.

Remove the slicing disc, wipe out workbowl and processor cover with a paper towel. When using the food processor plan the order of work so dry foods are processed first and then moist or liquid foods last. You should be able to prepare most meals in the processor and only wash the workbowl after all the preparation is over. Even though the vegetables are moist it is easy to wipe out the bowl with a paper towel and continue processing.

The CHEESE WALNUT BROILER BUNS have mayonnaise in them so we put that preparation last. Several of the items for the sandwich could be processed in continuous order but we want you to learn many skills today so we are doing the foods separately.

CHOPPING NUTS

1 Cup Walnuts

Insert ⬤. Add 1 cup walnut pieces to workbowl, lock cover in place. Pulse-chop for 1 second, again, and again. These nuts will be coarsely chopped. Reserve 1/3 cup in a small mixing bowl. Save remainder for cakes, cookies or ice cream sundaes. It is NOT necessary to clean the workbowl.

SHREDDING CHEESE

1 Cup Cheese

Insert ⬤. Cut a piece of very cold cheese to fit the feedtube and place in the feedtube resting on the shredding disc. One half of the 8 ounce piece should fit in most feedtubes. Always use a light pressure when shredding cheese. "Push-release" is the very best technique to keep the cheese from getting gummy and not shredding properly. You may use the "ON" button or push the "PULSE" button and hold it until you finish. Press moderately on the pusher—release (lift up pusher), press pusher—release, press and release to let the last little piece of cheese bounce through.

You can now process your own mayonnaise by following the recipe in SALADS. This MAYONNAISE is lovely and light—please try it. Leave about three tablespoons in the workbowl. You could use commercially prepared mayonnaise if you wish. Remember you are learning to use the food processor and we want you to make as many foods as possible.

CHEESE WALNUT BROILER BUNS   4-6 Sandwiches

4 oz. cheddar cheese (1 cup shredded)
1/3 cup walnut pieces
1/4 onion (2 Tbsp. chopped)
3 Tbsp. MAYONNAISE
Split bagels or English muffins

Insert ⚒ in workbowl. Add shredded cheese, chopped nuts and onion (cut in quarters) to mayonnaise in workbowl. Pulse-chop three times to combine and chop onion. Spread mixture on split bagels or English muffins and broil until brown and bubbly. *DO NOT WASH WORKBOWL*; the next recipe has similar flavors and it will blend well with the residue in the workbowl.

After lunch rearrange any remaining vegetables, cover and refrigerate to use as munchies with the dip for tonight.

CALIFORNIA ONION SOUP DIP   1-1/2 Cups

1-3 oz. pkg. cream cheese
1 cup sour cream
1/2-1 pkg. Onion Soup mix

Insert the ⚒. Cut cream cheese in four pieces and put in workbowl. Pulse-chop 4 times, then process until creamy. Add sour cream and soup mix to taste. Pulse-chop 3-4 times to blend. Remove workbowl from processor base. Some processors have openings in the bottom of the ⚒. Insert the index or middle finger through the outside center of the workbowl into this opening while the ⚒ is in the workbowl. Hold tightly with the finger and place thumb around bottom outer side of workbowl. Fan out the rest of the fingers over the bottom of the workbowl. If your finger won't fit in bottom of ⚒ opening, or if workbowl has no opening then remove blade and place on wax paper. Scrape dip into serving dish.* Refrigerate dip to let flavors blend.

*METAL BLADE, CLEANING

TIP: To easily remove creamy, sticky dips, spreads or batters from the blade, first scrape most of the mixture from the workbowl. Put METAL BLADE and workbowl back on base, cover and lock machine. Pulse machine 2-3 times. The food clinging to the blade will spin off leaving a clean blade. Then remove the clean blade and scrape out any remaining mixture from the workbowl. Most blades have a knob or special notch to hold onto when the blade is soiled or slippery.

About 1-1/2 hours before dinner; begin dinner preparations. Place the meat in the freezer to firm slightly.

MENU

Fresh Vegetables and California Onion Dip
Everybody's Favorite Meatloaf
One Bowl Salad
Yellow Cake with Almond Cream
Beverage of Your Choice

ALMOND WHIPPED CREAM   2 Cups Topping

Use a clean workbowl, insert ⬥ and prepare as directed in DESSERTS. Keep chilled until serving time. Without washing out workbowl proceed with cake mix. At serving time place mound of whipped cream on cake square and sprinkle with leftover chopped nuts.

CAKE MIX

1-18.5 oz. pkg. yellow cake mix
Water and egg as required in recipe

Insert ⏣, add cake mix. Add eggs and water, and oil if required. Pulse-chop 2-3 times, just until cake mix is blended. Remove cover and scrape down sides of workbowl, pulse twice more. *DO NOT OVERPROCESS.* Four to five pulses are ample to mix a cake. Hard to believe isn't it? Do not process a cake for two minutes like you would in a mixer. Bake at 350° in a prepared 9x13 inch pan for time directed on the box. Use previous tip to clean metal blade. Prepare meat loaf and bake at the same time.

EVERYBODY'S FAVORITE MEATLOAF
4-6 Servings

An old favorite as adapted from The Quaker Oats Company recipe.

1-1/2 pounds boneless round steak
1/2 of small onion,
    quartered (1/4 cup chopped)
1 egg
1 cup tomato juice
1 tsp. salt
1/4 tsp. pepper
3/4 cup rolled oats, quick or regular

Remove meat from freezer, 30-60 minutes freezing time is long enough. You should be able to cut it with a knife. Cut into 2 inch squares. Remove gristle as necessary, but do not remove fat. Insert ⏣. Process meat in 3 batches if you have a standard size food processor, or all at once for a medium or large capacity workbowl. If you are unsure of the capacity of the workbowl just use this general rule of thumb. Fill the workbowl no more than half full when processing raw meat to chop evenly and without straining the machine.

19

Pulse-chop 4-8 times. Check the consistency after 4 pulses. With larger capacity bowls, which hold all the meat, add onion pieces, eggs, tomato juice and seasonings. Pulse 3 times more. Add oats and pulse twice to combine. In smaller workbowls pulse-chop 2 separate batches to the desired consistency and remove to mixing bowl. Process the third batch as described for larger machines. Then combine with meat in mixing bowl. Place meat mixture in 8 or 9 inch loaf pan. Bake at 35 ° for 1 hour. Prepare salad.

EASY ONE BOWL SALAD   4-6 Servings

Insert ⬚, add 1 clove garlic, 1/4 cup red wine vinegar, 1/2 cup salad oil, 1 tablespoon water, 1/2 tsp. salt, 1/2 tsp. oregano, and 1/4 tsp. pepper. Process until well blended and garlic is chopped. Pour half of VINAGRETTE DRESSING in a container for another salad. Leave remaining dressing in workbowl. Remove ⬚. Each ingredient will be left in the workbowl as it is processed.

SHREDDED CARROTS   1/2 Cup

Insert ⬚. Peel one carrot. Cut the carrots in lengths to fit horizontally in the feedtube. Process using a firm pressure on the pusher. This gives long shreds. It's O.K. if a piece remains on top of the disc. *EAT IT!!* You don't want to shred the top of the processor cover so a piece will remain. Leave carrots and disc in bowl and continue.

SHREDDED RADISHES   1/4 Cup

Place 3-4 cleaned radishes in the feedtube. Process using firm pressure on pusher.

CUCUMBER HALF MOONS   1 Cucumber

Remove ⊘ and insert ⌣ (3-4mm). Use quantity of cucumber desired and peel if you wish. Cut cucumbers in half vertically so you get half circles which are easier to eat. Place cucumber to farthest side of feedtube from the blade. This helps prevent the cucumber from falling over. Pack the feedtube with cucumber if possible. Process using medium pressure on pusher.

TOMATO SLICES   1 Tomato

Core tomatoes, cut in half vertically. Use (4-8mm) ⌣ , depending on the thickness desired. Process the whole or half tomato depending on the feedtube size. Use a quick medium-light pressure on the pusher.

LETTUCE SLICES   2-3 Cups

Insert ⊝ of desired thickness (4-8mm). Pull apart large pieces
of iceberg lettuce to fit in feedtube. Process using firm pressure on
the pusher. A light pressure on the pusher will result in very thin
slices of lettuce. Slice desired quantity—about one half of a medium
head of lettuce. Invert workbowl over serving bowl and toss.
Refrigerate until serving time.

It's been a busy day. Yes, you did work hard at food preparation
but you were learning every minute and you prepared two complete
meals. Always take the time to try new ideas in the food processor
and you are on your way to a whole new world of easy and enjoyable
food preparation. The next section will show you how to convert
recipes from your old favorites or any new recipes that are suddenly
no trouble with the food processor's help. Kick off your shoes, get
another cup of coffee or tea, relax and read RECIPE CONVER-
SION and browse through the recipes. Read BREADS also to see
how easily bread is made in the food processor. You'll almost be
able to smell it baking.

RECIPE CONVERSION

As you become familiar with the food processor's capabilities you
will soon see how easily you can adapt recipes to use in the processor.
Recipes that have ingredients that need to be sliced, chopped or
shredded are just calling to you to process them in the food processor. Look for these terms in the ingredient list or in the body of
the recipe—chopped, sliced, creamed, crumbled, combined, minced, grated or sifted.
Examples:
1 cup chopped onion
1 cup graham cracker crumbs
2 cups sifted flour
Grate the peel of one lemon and combine with the sugar

Also remember that you may change the preparation order to process all the "dry" ingredients first, set them aside and then process
the "moist" steps. Often with a food processor chopping some ingredients may be done as other ingredients are being mixed. The
following recipe is in its "pre-processor" form so you can see where
conversions are made. As you prepare old favorites you may want
to note on the recipe card the order and techniques for processing
you used when you prepared the recipe.

Read the following recipe and see if you note the same changes we did.

CELERY PARMIGIANA   6 Servings

4 cups celery, cut in 1 inch pieces
1/4 tsp. salt
1/4 tsp. basil
2/3 cup consomme or bouillon
1 Tbsp. cornstarch
1/4 cup grated parmesan cheese
1/4 cup shredded cheddar cheese

Reserve 3 tablespoons of consomme.Cook celery with salt, basil and remaining consomme in a 2 quart saucepan for 8-10 minutes until tender-crisp. Combine cornstarch and reserved consomme and stir into cooked celery; cook and stir about 2 minutes until consomme thickens.
Place celery mixture in a shallow ovenware casserole.Sprinkle with parmesan and cheddar cheese. Broil until nicely browned.

These would be notes on that recipe.
NOTE 1—Use METAL BLADE to grate parmesan cheese.
NOTE 2—Shred or chop cheddar cheese and set aside on wax paper.
NOTE 3—Slice 8 stalks celery — be sure to pack feedtube.
NOTE 4—Remove slicing disc. Use METAL BLADE to combine cornstarch and consomme.

This is the same recipe as written in this cookbook so you can compare the procedures used.

CELERY PARMIGIANA   6 Servings

1 oz. parmesan cheese (1/4 cup grated)
2 oz. cheddar cheese (1/2 cup chopped)
8 stalks celery (4 cups sliced)
1/4 tsp. salt
1/4 tsp. basil, crushed
1 Tbsp. cornstarch
2/3 cup consomme

Using ⚒, process parmesan cheese by adding 1 inch pieces through the feedtube while the machine is running. Replace pusher. Process for 1 minute or until fine. Set aside on wax paper. Cut cheddar in 4 quarters and pulse-chop 6-8 times until finely chopped. Remove and reserve with parmesan cheese. Insert ⌣. Cut celery in even vertical lengths the height of the feedtube. Pack celery tightly into the feedtube and slice using a medium pressure on the pusher. Reserve 3 tablespoons of consomme. Cook celery with salt, basil and remaining consomme in a 2 quart saucepan for 8-10 minutes or until tender crisp. Insert ⚒; add cornstarch and reserved consomme, pulse twice to combine. Stir mixture into cooked celery; cook and stir about two minutes until consomme thickens. Place celery mixture in a shallow ovenware casserole. Sprinkle with parmesan and cheddar cheese. Broil for 2-3 minutes or until nicely browned.

Let's look at a dessert recipe.

LEMON PIE BARS

30-40 Bars

3/4 cup butter or margarine,
  softened
1/2 cup sifted confectioners' sugar
1-1/2 cups flour
3 eggs, slightly beaten
1 tsp. grated lemon peel
1-1/2 cups sugar
3 Tbsp. flour
3 Tbsp. lemon juice
2 Tbsp. confectioners' sugar, sifted

Mix butter, confectioners' sugar and the 1-1/2 cups flour together and press into a 13x9x2 inch baking pan. Bake at 350° for 20 minutes. While baking, mix eggs, sugar, flour and lemon juice. Pour mixture over hot crust and bake 20-25 minutes longer. Cut while warm. When cool, sprinkle top with about 2 tablespoons confectioners' sugar. Makes 30 to 40 bars.

These are the notes you might make on the recipe card.

NOTE 1—Sifting confectioners' sugar is a snap with the food processor. Use METAL BLADE in a clean, dry workbowl and add confectioner's sugar. Pulse-chop 4-6 times until lumps disappear. Now you can throw the flour sifter away! Store any extra sugar.

NOTE 2—Use FROZEN butter to make the base and be sure to pulse-chop it just to coarse crumbs. Use METAL BLADE.

NOTE 3—Grate the lemon peel in the processor using the METAL BLADE while the machine is running. Use some of the sugar from the recipe to help the METAL BLADE "catch" all the pieces of lemon peel.

NOTE 4—Mix all the ingredients for the filling with the METAL BLADE.

This is the same recipe as it is written in this cookbook so you can compare the methods used.

LEMON PIE BARS

40 Bars

3/4 cup butter or margarine,
  refrigerated or frozen
1/2 cup confectioners' sugar
1-1/2 cups flour
1 lemon, peeled and juiced*
Reserved lemon juice (3 Tbsp.)
3 eggs
1-1/2 cups sugar
3 Tbsp. flour
Confectioners' sugar for garnish

Cut butter into four even pieces. Insert ⬤, add butter, confectioners' sugar and 1-1/2 cups flour. Pulse-chop 4-6 times until butter is finely cut into flour. It should be the consistency of coarse crumbs. Pat this mixture into a 13x9x2 inch baking pan. Bake at 350° for 20 minutes. Insert ⬤. With machine running add lemon peel through the feedtube. Process until finely chopped, 1-2 minutes.

Add eggs, remaining flour, sugar and three tablespoons of lemon juice from the reserved juice. Process 20 seconds or until well blended. Pour this mixture over the hot crust and bake 20-25 minutes longer. Cut while warm into bars. When cool, sprinkle top with about 2 tablespoons confections' sugar.

*NOTE: Roll the lemon on the counter top to soften and release the juices. Use a vegetable peeler to remove thin slices of lemon peel for the lemon zest. Do not cut into the white membrane as this is the bitter part. Then cut the lemon in half and juice, reserving the juice.

The food processor eliminates a lot of work and only uses one bowl and blade for all the preparation of this recipe. Aren't you glad you took it out of the box?!!

APPETIZERS

| METAL BLADE | SHREDDING DISC | DOUGH BLADE | SLICING DISC | FRENCH-FRY DISC |

HOT BEEF CHEESE ROLLUPS   16 Appetizers

2 oz. cheddar cheese (1/2 cup)
1 (2-1/2 oz.) jar dried chipped beef (3/4 cup chopped)
1 tsp. horseradish
1 tsp. Worcestershire sauce
1-8 oz. pkg. refrigerated crescent rolls
2 Tbsp. melted butter or margarine

Insert ⬚, cut cheese into four even pieces and place in workbowl. Cut or tear through the roll of beef so it is in four smaller pieces. Add beef and pulse-chop 4-6 times or until cheese and beef are evenly grated. Add horseradish and Worcestershire sauce and pulse twice. Separate crescent rolls into four rectangles. Pinch center perforations together. Brush each with melted butter and spread mixture evenly on the four rectangles. Roll up each piece and cut into four slices using a serrated knife. Place seam side down on greased baking sheet. Bake at 375° for 12 to 14 minutes.

CRAB DABS   20 Appetizers

1/2 cup dry bread crumbs (1-1/2 slices)
1-1/2 oz. cream cheese (1/2 of a 3 oz. pkg.)
1-1/2 Tbsp. lemon juice
1 tsp. MSG
1/2 tsp. dry mustard
6-8 pitted black olives (1 Tbsp. chopped)
1 cup crabmeat (6-1/2 oz. can or 6 oz. pkg. frozen)
10 slices bacon cut in half crosswise

Insert ⬚, break bread into 6-8 pieces and place in workbowl. Pulse-chop 6-8 times or until finely crumbed. Add cream cheese and lemon juice and process for 2 seconds. Add MSG, mustard, olives and crabmeat, pulse-chop 4-6 times until blended and olives are chopped. Form into one inch balls. Wrap each with half a bacon slice, fasten with toothpick. Broil 6-8 inches from the source of heat 5-7 minutes, then turn and broil on second side 5-7 minutes more.

NOTE: One can (6 oz.) tuna fish may be substituted for the crab meat for TUNA DABS.

NOTE: Dry each bread slice in microwave for one minute on HIGH power.

NUTTY CHEESE PUFFS   3-4 Dozen Appetizers

2 oz. Swiss cheese (1/2 cup shredded)
1 cup loose macadamia, pecans, or cashews
1/4 cup butter or margarine (frozen or refrigerated)
1 cup biscuit mix
1 egg

Shred cheese with ⊙ using push-release method,* set aside. Insert ⟁, add butter** and biscuit mix. Pulse chop 4-6 times or until biscuit mix and butter resemble coarse crumbs. Add cheese, nuts, and egg; pulse 2-3 times or until blended. Drop by teaspoonfuls on an ungreased baking sheet. Bake in a preheated 400° oven for 8 minutes.

*CHEESE, SHREDDING—PUSH-RELEASE METHOD
TIP: Place piece of very cold cheese in the feedtube. Set pusher in feedtube and lock cover. Turn on the machine, press moderately on the pusher, release pressure by pulling up on the pusher. Repeat pressing and releasing of pusher until last piece is processed.

**CUTTING IN BUTTER
TIP: Always cut butter or margarine into 4-6 equal pieces before adding to workbowl. It will process more evenly.
TIP: Use frozen butter or margarine when you want to cut the butter into the flour to make a crumb mixture.

MEXICAN LAYERED DIP

30-40 Servings

2 (10-1/2 oz.) cans plain or jalapeno flavored bean dip
1/2 cup MAYONNAISE
3 medium ripe avocados
2 Tbsp. lemon juice
1/2 tsp. salt
1/4 tsp. pepper
1 cup sour cream
1/4-1/2 pkg. (1-1/4 oz.) taco seasoning mix
1 bunch green onions, sliced
3 medium tomatoes (2 cups coarsely chopped)
1-6 oz. can pitted jumbo black olives, drained
8 oz.sharp cheddar cheese(2 cups shredded)
Tortilla chips, corn chips, or nacho chips

Spread bean dip evenly over the bottom of a round 14-16 inch glass dish or 2-8 inch round dishes. Insert ⚒. If necessary prepare MAYONNAISE recipe in SALADS. Leave about 1/4 cup in workbowl. Continue without cleaning workbowl.* Peel and pit avocado; add in chunks to workbowl with lemon juice, salt and pepper. Pulse-chop 4-6 times. Spread over the bean dip. Do not wash bowl. Add sour cream, 1/4 cup mayonnaise, and taco seasoning to taste. Pulse-chop 3-4 times until mixture is blended. Spread onto avocado layer. Scrape out workbowl well. Clean with a paper towel.

Insert thin ⊖ (2-3mm) and slice green onions by "dancing."** Sprinkle onions over sour cream mixture. Place whole olives *** upright in feedtube and slice using a light pressure on pusher. This is easier if you have a machine with a large feedtube. (You may also use the ⚒ and pulse-chop the olives 5-6 times.) Sprinkle olives over onions. Insert ⚒ or ⌇. If using the metal blade, quarter tomatoes and pulse-chop 3-4 times or until the tomatoes are coarsely chopped. If using the French fry disc to cube the tomatoes, process using light pressure on pusher. Remove tomato from workbowl and drain liquid from tomatoes, layer over olives.

Insert ⊙, shred cheese using push-release method **** with pusher. Sprinkle cheese over all of appetizer. Refrigerate 2-3 hours or overnight.

NOTE: The layers are 1)Beans 2)Avocado 3)Sour cream 4)Onions 5)Olives 6)Tomatoes 7)Cheese.

NOTE: Buy avocados that are very soft or buy ahead and let soften in a brown paper bag. Hard avocados are not ripe and will not taste good.

NOTE: This recipe may be made the day before. Make sure the tomatoes are well drained or they will make this dip "runny"

NOTE: The workbowl does not need to be washed in between steps except as noted. We have written the steps to avoid this.

*METAL BLADE, CLEANING
TIP: To easily remove creamy, sticky dips, spreads or batters from the blade, first scrape most of the mixture from the workbowl. Put METAL BLADE and workbowl back on base, cover and lock machine. Pulse machine 2-3 times. The food clinging to the blade will spin off leaving a clean blade. Then remove the clean blade and scrape out any remaining mixture from the workbowl. Most blades have a knob or special notch to hold onto when the blade is soiled or slippery.

WORKBOWL, CLEANING BETWEEN STEPS
TIP: Often all that is necessary is to wipe out the workbowl with a paper towel. Plan your steps to work from dry to liquid ingredients and leave odorous items like onion and garlic until last if possible.

**SLICES—EVEN SLICES OF LONG SLENDER VEGETABLES OR "DANCING"
TIP: Hold onto UNTRIMMED tops and insert in feedtube. With the machine running move the vegetable up and down in the feedtube and stop slicing when the tops of the vegetable reach the top of the feedtube. DO NOT try to process your fingers.

***OLIVES, SLICED
TIP: Pack the feedtube with one layer of pitted olives, standing the olives upright for perfect slices. Larger olives are easier to handle. Insert pusher and process using light pressure.

****CHEESE, PUSH-RELEASE METHOD
TIP: Place piece of very cold cheese into the feedtube. Set pusher in feedtube and lock cover. Turn machine on, press moderately on the pusher, release pressure by pulling up on the pusher. Repeat pressing and releasing of pusher until last piece is processed.

OLIVE CHEESE NUGGETS   2 to 2-1/2 Dozen

3/4 cup flour
1/8 tsp. salt
1/2 tsp. paprika
4 oz. cheddar cheese (1 cup shredded)
1/4 cup butter or margarine
24-30 medium sized stuffed green olives

Insert ⬥, add dry ingredients and pulse twice. Remove to wax paper. Insert ⬤ and shred cheese using push-release method,* leave cheese in workbowl. Place ⬥ in workbowl, being careful that blade is resting on bottom of workbowl. Add butter, pulse-chop butter and cheese until well blended and soft. Add flour mixture and pulse-chop 2-4 times or just until blended. Shape dough around olives using about a teaspoonful of dough for each. Place on an ungreased baking sheet and bake at 400° for 12-15 minutes or until light golden brown.

*CHEESE, PUSH-RELEASE METHOD
TIP: Place piece of very cold cheese into the feedtube. Set pusher in feedtube and lock cover. Turn machine on, press moderately on the pusher, release pressure by pulling up on the pusher. Repeat pressing and releasing of pusher until last piece is processed.

NOTE: Dough may be covered and refrigerated before baking. This dough also freezes well; baked or unbaked.

VARIATION: Cheese mixture may be formed in 1-1/2 inch roll and sliced about 1/8 inch thick. Place on baking sheet, top with olive slice** and bake at 400°, 6-8 minutes.

**OLIVES, SLICED
TIP: Insert (2-6mm) SLICING DISC. Put cover in place. Pack the feedtube with one layer of pitted olives, standing the olives upright for perfect slices. Larger olives are easier to handle. Insert pusher and process using light pressure.

KAHLUA FRUIT DIP

1-8 oz. pkg. cream cheese
2 Tbsp. confectioners' sugar
1/4 cup kahlua
1/4 cup almonds
2-3 Tbsp. milk or cream

Insert ⌒. Add cream cheese, cut evenly into 8 pieces, and pulse 4-6 times (depending on softness of cheese). Add sugar and pulse 2 times. Add almonds and pulse twice. Add kahlua and cream, pulse 2-3 times. Refrigerate over night. Serve with fresh fruit such as whole strawberries, grapes (light and dark), sliced bananas,* sliced apples,** cantaloupe, pineapple, pears, oranges, or whatever fruit that is in season. If you have a 6 or 8mm slicing disc use it as these fruits will slice beautifully for this dip. See SALADS for FRUIT TRAY tips.

*SOFT FRUITS
TIP: When slicing soft fruits such as bananas, strawberries or kiwis in a food processor use a light, quick pressure on the pusher.
TIP: Soft fruits and vegetables (such as strawberries, bananas, mushrooms) will slice well in a food processor as long as they are firm and not over ripe.

**NOTE: To keep apples, bananas,and pears from turning brown; sprinkle thoroughly with lemon juice. Grapefruit juice or orange juice will work also, plus they give the fruit a good flavor.

NOTE: Lemon juice enhances the flavor of fruit and vegetables. If you have an apple that doesn't have a great flavor, sprinkle with lemon juice and let sit for awhile. It should taste better.

PINEAPPLE CREAM FRUIT DIP

2 Cups

1/4 fresh pineapple, peeled and cored
1 cup sour cream
1 Tbsp. maraschino cherry juice
1/8 tsp. ground ginger
1/2 cup nuts

Insert ⚒. Cut pineapple in 1-1/2 inch chunks, add to workbowl. Pulse-chop 3-4 times. Add remaining ingredients. Pulse-chop 3-4 times, scrape down sides, check consistency and pulse once more if necessary. Chill several hours or overnight before serving with fresh fruit tray. See SALADS.

VARIATION: Prepare PINEAPPLE CREAM SPREAD using an 8 oz. pkg. cream cheese instead of sour cream. Use on a variety of breads or crackers for a fruity cheese spread.

LEMON FRUIT DIP

2 Cups

1 lemon, zested
1-1/3 cups sour cream
1/4 cup confectioners' sugar

Insert ⚒ in dry workbowl. Peel whole lemon with vegetable peeler. With machine running drop pieces of lemon peel through feedtube. Replace pusher. Process lemon zest about two minutes or until fine. Add 2 tablespoons granulated sugar if lemon peel is still chunky. Process one minute more. Scrape down workbowl when necessary. Add sour cream and confectioners' sugar. Pulse-chop 3-4 times, scrape down workbowl and pulse 1-2 times more until mixture is blended. Chill several hours or overnight before serving with fresh fruit tray. See SALADS.

ORANGE SUNSHINE FLUFF   2-1/2 Cups

1 orange, zested
1-8 oz. pkg. cream cheese
1/4-3/4 tsp. ground ginger
1/2 of a 7 oz. jar marshmallow fluff

Insert ⟨⟩ in dry workbowl. Peel whole orange with vegetable peeler. With machine running, drop orange peel through feedtube. Replace pusher. Process 1-2 minutes until finely grated. If not finely grated after 2 minutes continue by adding cream cheese cut in 8 pieces. Pulse-chop 3-4 times to blend mixture then continue to process until orange is finely grated. Add ginger and marshmallow fluff, pulse-chop 5-6 times until blended. Chill, if desired, or you may serve immediately with a fresh fruit tray. See SALADS.

CLAM CHEESE DIP   1-1/4 Cups

1-8 oz. pkg. cream cheese
1 tsp. Worcestershire sauce
2 tsp. lemon juice
1 Tbsp. clam juice (reserved from can)
1 green onion
1/4 of a green pepper
1-7 oz. can minced clams, drained (reserve juice)

Insert ⟨⟩. Add cream cheese, Worcestershire sauce, lemon juice, and clam juice. Pulse chop 3-4 times to blend ingredients. Process until light and fluffy. Add onion* to workbowl, pulse-chop 4-5 times. Add pepper*; pulse-chop 2-3 times, and add clams. Pulse-chop 2 times or until clams are just blended in. Serve with crackers.

NOTE: You may substitute 1-7 oz. can tiny, cleaned shrimp for clams to make SHRIMP CHEESE DIP.

*EVEN CHOPPING
   TIP: Important—cut vegetables into 4-6 equal pieces and add to workbowl so they will chop evenly.

CHILI CHEESE LOG

1-10 Inch Cheese Log

1 small clove garlic
8 oz. cheddar cheese (2 cups shredded)
1-3 oz. pkg. cream cheese
1 Tbsp. lemon juice
3 dashes hot pepper sauce
1/3 cup loose pecans (1/4 cup chopped)
1 tsp. chili powder
1 tsp. paprika

Insert ⌐⊾. With machine running drop garlic through the feedtube to finely chop. Remove blade but leave garlic in workbowl and insert ⊙. Shred cheese using push-release method.* Remove disc, leaving cheese in workbowl. Place ⌐⊾ back in workbowl being careful that blade is resting on the bottom of the bowl and that there is no food under the blade. Add cream cheese,** lemon juice, and hot pepper sauce. Pulse-chop 5-6 times. Add nuts and pulse-chop 5-6 times or until nuts are finely chopped. Shape in a roll about 1-1/2 inches in diameter. Combine chili and paprika; place on wax paper. Roll log in mixture and chill several hours. Let stand at room temperature 15 minutes before serving. Serve with crackers.

*CHEESE, PUSH-RELEASE METHOD
TIP: Place piece of very cold cheese into the feedtube. Set pusher in feedtube and lock cover. Turn machine on, press moderately on the pusher, release pressure by pulling up on the pusher. Repeat pressing and releasing of pusher until last piece is processed.

**CREAM CHEESE, SOFTENING
TIP: Cream cheese does not need to be softened when using a food processor. Cut cheese into 6-8 even pieces and pulse in workbowl using METAL BLADE until creamy. Remember the colder the cream cheese the longer it will take to process. The friction of the blade does the softening of the cream cheese.

PHILLY PECAN SPREAD

2/3 cup loose pecan pieces
2 Tbsp. butter
1/2 tsp. salt
1-8 oz. pkg. cream cheese
1/2 tsp. garlic salt
1/2 cup sour cream
1-2 Tbsp. mayonnaise (optional: adds creaminess)
1 (2-1/2 oz.) jar dried beef (3/4 cup chopped)
1/4 wedge of onion
1/4 wedge of green pepper

Insert ⚒, add pecans and pulse-chop 3-4 times until coarsely chopped. Melt butter in skillet, add pecans and salt, saute lightly. Add cream cheese to workbowl and pulse-chop 4-6 times. Add garlic salt, sour cream, and mayonnaise and pulse-chop 3 times or until mixture is creamy. Cut or tear through the roll of beef so it is in four smaller pieces. Put in workbowl and pulse-chop 3-4 times until coarsely chopped. Add onion and green pepper, pulse-chop 3-4 times until pepper and onion are chopped and ingredients are well blended. Spread into a 9 inch pie pan. Sprinkle with prepared pecans. Bake at 350° for 20 minutes. Serve hot with crackers or melba toast.

PATE UNDER ASPIC

40 Servings

This is very elegant looking yet very easy to prepare with the food processor. It's a special treat for a New Year's buffet or a cocktail party.

1 env. unflavored gelatin
1/4 cup sherry (optional but lovely flavor)
1 (10-1/2 oz.) can condensed beef consomme
1/2 pound mushrooms
1/2 cup butter or margarine
1-1/2 pounds chicken livers
3 strips crisply cooked bacon
1-3/4 tsp. salt
1/8 tsp. pepper
6-8 sprigs parsley (1/4 cup chopped)
Crackers for serving

Soften gelatin in sherry or 1/4 cup cold water. In small saucepan, heat undiluted consomme with 3/4 cup water and bring to a boil. Remove from heat and stir in softened gelatin, making sure it is dissolved. Pour about 1/4 cup of this mixture into a 1-1/2 quart mold or mixing bowl. Cut one side off 5-6 mushrooms caps. Put these mushrooms in the feedtube with the flat side on the ⊖. If the feedtube is small it may be easier to rest the mushrooms on the blade and then place the feedtube over them. Use the medium ⊖ (3-4mm) and process the mushrooms using a light pressure on pusher. Place 6 or 8 of the perfect slices over the consomme in a circle. Process remaining mushrooms, set aside on wax paper. (It is not necessary to trim sides of remaining mushrooms.) Refrigerate mold with mushroom slices until set. Pour the remaining consomme into the mold and refrigerate until firm, about two hours.

While mold is chilling saute livers and mushrooms. In a large skillet, melt 1/4 cup butter, saute chicken livers until tender with 1-1/4 teaspoons salt and 1/8 teaspoon pepper. Cool slightly. Insert ⟲, add chicken livers to workbowl. In same skillet with remaining 1/4 cup butter saute mushroom slices with 1/2 teaspoon salt. Cool and add to chicken livers in workbowl. Add parsley and bacon pieces, pulse-chop until coarse. Continue processing until fine and smooth. Spread mixture over aspic in mold and chill overnight. Before serving, dip mold in warm water for about a minute. Run a spatula around the edges to loosen. Place serving dish over mold and then invert mold onto it. Garnish with parsley or watercress sprigs.

TOASTY ONION STICKS   5 Dozen Sticks

1 cup butter
1 env. onion soup mix
12 slices white bread

Insert ⌐. Add butter to workbowl and pulse-chop 4-6 times. Process until smooth and soft, about 1-2 minutes. Add soup mix and pulse 2-3 times until blended. Spread mixture on bread slices. Trim crusts from bread and reserve*. Cut each slice of bread into 5 strips. Bake strips on ungreased baking sheet at 400° for 5 minutes or until golden. These store well in a dry place.

*BREAD CRUSTS, LEFTOVER TRIMMED - FROM TEA SAND-WICHES, APPETIZERS, ETC.
TIP: Without washing workbowl, insert METAL BLADE. Add trimmed crusts. Pulse chop 4-6 times until crusts are crumbed. Use crumbs for vegetable or casserole toppings. Freeze if you can't use that day. When ready to use it is not necessary to thaw out, just remove what you need. Gives a great flavor to casseroles, meatloaves, etc.

NOTE: Prepare ONION CROUTONS by cutting the baked strips into cubes.

ZUCCHINI APPETIZERS 4 Dozen

4 small zucchini, unpeeled
1 clove garlic
2 oz. parmesan cheese (1/2 cup grated)
3 sprigs parsley (2 Tbsp. chopped)
1 small onion (1/2 cup chopped)
1/2 tsp. salt
1/2 tsp. dried oregano
Dash of pepper
4 eggs
1/2 cup oil
1 cup biscuit mix

Insert ⊙. Pack feedtube with zucchini standing up. Process using medium pressure on pusher. Remove zucchini and set aside. Insert ⌐. With machine running add garlic through feedtube. Continue running machine while adding parmesan cheese which has been cut in small pieces. Replace pusher. Stop machine, add parsley and continue processing until cheese and parsley are finely chopped. Scrape down sides of workbowl and add quartered onion, spices and eggs. Pulse-chop 2 times. Add oil and pulse once. Add baking mix, pulse once. Add shredded zucchini and pulse twice. Grease a 12x7x1-1/2 inch baking pan. Spread mixture in pan and bake for 25 minutes at 350° or until golden brown. Cut into 2x2 inch squares. Serve warm or reheat just before serving.

NOTE: The squares will be thinner if you use a 13x9 inch baking dish.

BEVERAGES

| METAL BLADE | SHREDDING DISC | DOUGH BLADE | SLICING DISC | FRENCH-FRY DISC |

Use the food processor to prepare delicious milkshakes and drinks. The metal blade swirls together fresh fruit and ice cream with ease, whips cream and crushes ice. But don't stop here, turn to the BABY chapter for some other delicious drink ideas. Listed below are some tips that apply to many drink recipes.

LIQUIDS, PROCESSING

TIP: After processing hold the middle of the metal blade in place with a finger tip until you pour the liquid into another container. Leaving the blade in place keeps the liquids from running out through the center of the workbowl.

TIP: Some processors have openings in the bottom of the METAL BLADE. Insert the index or middle finger through the outside center of the workbowl into this opening while the METAL BLADE is in the workbowl. Hold tightly with the finger and place thumb around bottom outer side of workbowl. Fan out the rest of the fingers over the bottom of the workbowl. Then pour out the liquid while holding onto the blade. You may find this a convenient way to hold the workbowl whether or not it has liquid in it.

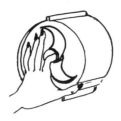

MILK SHAKES

TIP: Insert METAL BLADE and place ice cream in the workbowl, pulse-chop 2-3 times. With machine running add milk and flavorings through the feedtube. This order of food placement prevents the liquid from "running out" the center workbowl opening. This makes a super creamy shake.

See ICE CUBES, CRUSHED TIP also.

STRAWBERRY MILK SHAKES   3 Drinks

1 pt. strawberry or vanilla ice cream
1-10 oz. pkg. frozen strawberries, partially thawed
    or 1 cup whole (8-10) fresh strawberries
1-1/2 cups milk

Insert ⚙ add ice cream and pulse-chop 5-6 times. Add strawberries and pulse-chop another 5-6 times depending on the consistency of the strawberries. With the machine running add milk through the feedtube. Process until all ingredients are well mixed, about 5-10 seconds.

CHOCOLATE MILK SHAKES   3 Drinks

1 pt. chocolate or vanilla ice cream
1/4 cup chocolate syrup
1-1/2 cups milk

Insert ⟨🔪⟩, add ice cream and pulse-chop 5-6 times. Add chocolate syrup. With machine running add milk through the feedtube. Process until all ingredients are well mixed, about 5-10 seconds.

BANANA MILK SHAKES   3 Drinks

1 pt. vanilla ice cream
1 whole ripe banana
1-1/2 cups milk

Insert ⟨🔪⟩, add ice cream and pulse-chop 5-6 times. Add banana, pulse-chop 3-4 times. With machine running add milk through the feedtube. Process until all ingredients are well mixed, about 5-10 seconds.

ORANGE MILK SHAKES   3-4 Drinks

Zest from 1/2 of an orange
1 pt. vanilla ice cream
1-6 oz. can frozen orange juice concentrate
1-1/2 cups milk
1/4 tsp. almond flavoring

Insert ⟨🔪⟩. With machine running, drop zest through feedtube and process until finely chopped. Add ice cream and pulse-chop 5-6 times. Add orange concentrate and pulse-chop another 5-6 times depending on the consistency of the juice. With machine running add milk and almond flavoring through the feedtube. Process until all ingredients are well mixed, about 5-10 seconds.

STRAWBERRY SURPRISE

4-5 Drinks

1 pt. vanilla ice cream
4 oz. fresh or fresh-frozen strawberries
or 6-8 fresh, whole strawberries
6 oz. almond liqueur

Insert ⚒, add ice cream and pulse-chop 5-6 times. Add strawberries and pulse 2-3 times. With machine running add liqueur through feedtube. Process until ingredients are well mixed, about 5-10 seconds.

GRASSHOPPER

3-4 Drinks

1 pt. vanilla ice cream
4 oz. creme de cacao
4 oz. creme de menthe, green
1/4 cup milk or cream

Insert ⚒, add ice cream and pulse-chop 5-6 times. With machine running add liqueurs and milk through feedtube. Process until ingredients are well mixed, about 5-10 seconds. Garnish with whipped cream and shaved chocolate or a fresh strawberry.

NOTE: Shave the chocolate* and whip the cream** before preparing the drinks if you wish to use the garnishes.

*CHOCOLATE SHAVINGS
TIP: Insert SHREDDING DISC. Have chocolate at room temperature. Place chocolate in the feedtube and with very little pressure on the pusher, process the chocolate. Do not process chocolate into a warm workbowl or it will melt the shaved chocolate.

**WHIPPING CREAM, WHIPPED
TIP: A clean cold bowl and cold blade speed the processing. Insert METAL BLADE. With machine running, add cream slowly through feedtube. Process 1 minute. With machine running add sugar and vanilla, if desired, through the feedtube. Process an additional minute or until stiff. Do not overprocess unless you want to make butter!

HUMMERS

4-5 Drinks

1 pt. vanilla ice cream
6 oz. rum
4 oz. kahlua

Insert ⚗, add ice cream and pulse-chop 5-6 times. With machine running add liquors through feedtube. Process until ingredients are well mixed, about 5-10 seconds.

DONA'S SPECIAL

4-5 Drinks

1 pt. vanilla ice cream
4 oz. creme de banana
4 oz. creme de cacao
4 oz. creme de almond

Insert ⚗, add ice cream and pulse-chop 5-6 times. With machine running add liqueurs through feedtube. Process until ingredients are well mixed, about 5-10 seconds.

PEACHES'N CREAM

4-5 Drinks

1 pt. vanilla ice cream
10 oz. peach flavored brandy

Insert ⚗, add ice cream and pulse-chop 5-6 times. With machine running add brandy through feedtube. Process until ingredients are well mixed, about 5-10 seconds.

BRANDY ALEXANDER

4-5 Drinks

1 pt. vanilla ice cream
6 oz. creme de cacao
4 oz. brandy

Insert ⬙, add ice cream and pulse-chop 5-6 times. With machine running add liquors through feedtube. Process until ingredients are well mixed, about 5-10 seconds. Garnish with shaved chocolate.*

*CHOCOLATE SHAVINGS
TIP: Insert SHREDDING DISC. Place chocolate in the feedtube and with very little pressure on the pusher, process the chocolate. Do not process chocolate into a warm workbowl or it will melt the shaved chocolate.

IRISH CREAM

8-12 Drinks

For after dinner drinks this recipe is a winner!! Take as a special treat to give your hostess. You may adjust the amount of whiskey to your taste and also use regular whiskey.

1 cup whipping cream
1-14 oz. can sweetened condensed milk
2-4 Tbsp. chocolate syrup
2-4 Tbsp. coconut milk
2/3-1 cup Irish whiskey

Insert ⬙. With machine running pour cream slowly through feedtube.* Stop machine when cream is fluffy, 1-2 minutes. Add remaining ingredients and run machine for 8-10 seconds or until ingredients are well combined. Let chill overnight to allow the flavors to blend. Keeps up to six weeks in refrigerator.

*WHIPPING CREAM, WHIPPED
TIP: A clean cold bowl and cold blade speed the processing. Process 1 minute or until stiff. Do not overprocess unless you want to make butter!

MAIN DISHES

METAL   SHREDDING   DOUGH   SLICING   FRENCH-FRY
BLADE   DISC   BLADE   DISC   DISC

AUTUMN SOUP

6 Servings

1 pound round steak, chopped
1 Tbsp. cooking oil
1 large onion (1 cup chopped)
2 large carrots (1 cup sliced)
2 stalks celery (1 cup sliced)
2 medium potatoes (1 cup sliced)
4 cups water
2 tsp. salt
1/2 tsp. pepper
1 bay leaf
3 bouillon cubes
1/4 tsp. basil
1 clove garlic
6 whole tomatoes

Insert ⌐, cut meat into 10-12 pieces, remove gristle as necessary. Add to workbowl filling no more than half full. Pulse-chop 8-10 times or until finely chopped (like hamburger).* Repeat as necessary. Brown beef in shortening in a large kettle. Cut onion in quarters and pulse-chop 6-8 times or until coarsely chopped. Add onions to beef and cook five minutes longer. Meanwhile cut carrots and celery in even lengths to fit the feedtube. Insert ⌐ (4-8mm) and pack feedtube tightly with lengths of carrots and celery. Slice carrots and celery using medium pressure on pusher. Leave in workbowl. Quarter potatoes to fit in feedtube. Process using medium pressure on the pusher. Add sliced vegetables, water and seasonings to kettle, stir well. Bring to a boil, cover and simmer for 20 minutes. While soup simmers, cut tomatoes in quarters and place in workbowl with ⌐. Pulse-chop tomatoes until coarse. (The tomatoes may also be cubed** using the ⌐. Process tomatoes in 2 batches depending on size of workbowl.) Add tomatoes to kettle, cover and simmer 10 minutes longer.

NOTE: It is not necessary to wash out workbowl between steps as all the food will be cooked together.

*GROUND MEAT
   TIP: Meat that is partially frozen will chop more evenly than meat that is cold from the refrigerator.

**TOMATOES, CUBING

TIP: Depending on the size and firmness of the tomato make three or four vertical cuts not quite through the tomato. If the cuts are made all the way through the tomato will not cube nicely. Insert the FRENCH FRY DISC. Place the tomato, cut side down, with the cuts going across the feedtube. Pack the feedtube as full as possible. Process using a quick, firm pressure on pusher.

EVERYDAY DRUMSTICKS   8 Servings

1 cup cornflakes
1-1/2 pounds round or chuck steak, partially frozen
1/4 wedge of a green pepper
1/2 of a small onion
1 egg
2 tsp. MSG
8 wooden skewers
4 slices bacon

Insert ⟨blade⟩, add corn flakes and process 10 seconds or until finely crumbed. Set aside on wax paper. Remove gristle from meat and cut into 12-16 even pieces. Add meat to workbowl filling no more than half full. Pulse-chop 4-6 times. Stop machine, scrape down sides of workbowl. Add green pepper,* onion, egg, and MSG to meat. Pulse-chop an additional 4-6 times or until mixture is evenly ground. Set aside in a mixing bowl. Process any remaining meat. Add to bowl and mix together. Divide mixture into eight portions. Shape each portion around a skewer to look like a drumstick. Roll in reserved crumbs and place in a greased baking pan. Cut each bacon slice crosswise into four pieces. Cross two pieces on each drumstick. Bake in a preheated 425° oven for 25 minutes.

*EVEN CHOPPING

TIP: Important-cut vegetables into 4-6 EQUAL pieces and add to workbowl so they will chop evenly.

VEAL SCALLOPINE

4-6 Servings

1-1/2 lbs. loin or round of veal (cut to fit
  feedtube and frozen but partially thawed)
1/4 cup flour
1-1/2 tsp. salt
1/4 tsp. pepper
2 Tbsp. butter
1/4 cup beef broth
1/2 cup sweet sherry

Insert ⌒ (4-6mm). In order to slice meat in the food processor
it must be frozen but slightly thawed.* Process using medium-light
pressure on the pusher. Mix flour, salt, and pepper together. Coat
veal with flour mixture. In a skillet melt butter until hot, fry veal
slices quickly on both sides. Arrange on heated platter. Stir broth
and sherry into meat juices in skillet. Heat through and pour over
veal. Serve immediately with hot, cooked noodles.

*MEAT, SLICING RAW
*TIP: Insert SLICING DISC. In order to slice meat in the food processor
it must be frozen but slightly thawed. Thaw the meat enough so the point
of a knife can go into the meat. If you cannot cut the meat with a knife
then neither can the food processor. If the meat is too soft the meat will
not slice properly. The meat should be firmly packed into the feedtube. It
should also be set in the feedtube so it will slice against the grain. Process
using medium-light pressure on the pusher. Machine may make loud noises
when slicing partially thawed meat. Some processors may not slice the whole
loin of veal when it is very firmly frozen. If not, you will need to slice by
hand.*

PEPPER STEAK

1 pound round steak, frozen but partially thawed
3 Tbsp. sherry
3 Tbsp. soy sauce
1 Tbsp. cornstarch
1/2 tsp. salt
1 clove garlic, minced
2 green peppers, thinly sliced
1 medium onion, cut in rings
3 Tbsp. oil

Insert ⌣ (3-4mm). In order to slice meat in the food processor it must be frozen but slightly thawed. Thaw the meat enough so the point of a knife can go into the meat. If the meat is too soft the meat will not slice properly. The meat should be firmly packed into the feedtube. It should also be set in the feedtube so it will slice against the grain. Process using medium-light pressure on the pusher. Marinate steak pieces with sherry, soy sauce, cornstarch and salt for ten minutes. Insert ⌇. With machine running, add garlic through feedtube and process until finely minced. Leave garlic in workbowl. Insert ⌣ (2-4mm). Core green peppers. Leave whole if they will fit in the feedtube or cut in half and place pieces upright, wedging them into the feedtube. Process using medium pressure on pusher. Leave green pepper in workbowl. Peel and cut onion to fit in feedtube. Slice, using a medium-firm pressure on the pusher. Add two tablespoons of the oil to a saute pan and heat over medium temperature. Stir-fry garlic, green pepper, and onion until pepper is tender-crisp. Remove and set aside. Add remaining oil to pan and stir-fry meat mixture until meat is cooked. Add vegetables and stir until hot and mixture is thick and clear. Serve over cooked rice.

EASY SUKIYAKI   4-6 Servings

1 pound round steak, frozen but partially thawed
3 stalks celery, (1-1/2 cups diagonally sliced)
6-8 fresh mushrooms (2/3 cup sliced)
1 small onion (1/2 cup sliced)
1/2 pound fresh spinach, cleaned and dry
2 Tbsp. salad oil
1 (10-3/4 oz.) can beef gravy
2 Tbsp. soy sauce
3 cups hot cooked rice or chow mein noodles

Insert medium (4mm) ⌒ . In order to slice meat in the food processor it must be frozen but slightly thawed. Thaw the meat enough
so the point of a knife can go into the meat. If the meat is too soft
the meat will not slice properly. The meat should be firmly packed
into the feedtube. It should also be set in the feedtube so it will slice
against the grain. Process using medium-light pressure on the pusher.
Remove meat from workbowl and set aside. Insert (2-4 mm) ⌒ .
Cut celery pieces in even lengths to fit the feedtube. Fill the feedtube loosely with celery.* Process using a light pressure on pusher.
Trim mushrooms and cut one side flat. Lay the mushrooms on their
sides. Process using a light pressure on pusher. Place onion in feedtube and process using a medium pressure on pusher. Remove all
vegetables from workbowl and set aside. Insert (4-6 mm) ⌒ . Fill
the feedtube with spinach and process using medium pressure. Repeat
with any remaining spinach. In a large skillet heat oil until hot. Brown
beef. Remove any excess oil. Stir in gravy and soy sauce, heat well.
Add celery, mushrooms and onion. Cook over low heat 5 minutes.
Add spinach and cook 2-3 minutes longer. Serve over rice or chow
mein noodles.

*DIAGONALLY CUT VEGETABLES
   *TIP: Vegetables that are not quite tightly packed in the feedtube will pro-
cess on the diagonal when using the SLICING DISC. If they are too loosely packed they will fall on their sides.*

CHICKEN CACCIATORE

4-6 Servings

This is a wonderful company dish for last minute entertaining. Your family will love it too! The blend of flavors is delicious with a side dish of rice or a loaf of homemade FRENCH BREAD and a crisp green salad.

1-1/2 Tbsp. each butter and salad oil
2-1/2 to 3 lb. broiler-fryer, cut-up
1 clove garlic, minced
1/4 wedge of a green pepper
1 medium onion (1 cup sliced)
1-29 oz. can tomatoes (3-1/2 cups)
1-8 oz. can tomato sauce
1 tsp. salt
1/4 tsp. pepper
1/4 tsp. allspice
1 bay leaf
1/2 cup Chianti or red wine

About 1 hour before serving put oil and butter in a large skillet. Saute chicken over medium heat until golden on all sides. While chicken is cooking, process the vegetables for the sauce. Insert ⚓. With the machine running drop the garlic through the feedtube and process until finely minced. Add green pepper* and pulse-chop 3-4 times. Remove blade and put in ⌒ (2-4mm). Slice onion using medium pressure on the pusher. Remove the ingredients to the frying pan and brown lightly. (Without wiping out the work bowl, prepare a salad of your choice.) Add remaining ingredients to the frypan; simmer, uncovered, for 30-40 minutes or until chicken is fork tender. Be sure to pass the tomato sauce to spoon over the chicken or rice. Go Italian-style and dip fresh homemade bread in the sauce, too!

*EVEN CHOPPING
TIP: Important-cut vegetables into 4-6 EQUAL pieces and add to workbowl so they will chop evenly.

EGG ROLLS

8 Egg Rolls

2-3 green onions (1/3 cup sliced)
6-7 small mushrooms (1/2 cup chopped)
4 stalks celery (2 cups chopped)
1/2 pound pork (very cold or partially frozen)
8 oz. cooked shrimp (cleaned)
3 Tbsp. oil
1 Tbsp. dry sherry
1 Tbsp. soy sauce
2 tsp. salt
1/2 tsp. sugar
1/2 pound fresh bean sprouts
1-8 oz. can bamboo shoots
1 Tbsp. cornstarch
2 Tbsp. water
1 pkg. egg roll skins
3 cups oil for frying

Insert medium (3-4mm) . With machine running "dance"* green onions, set aside on wax paper. Insert , add mushrooms. Pulse-chop 3-4 times, set aside with onions. Cut celery stalks in 3 inch lengths, add to workbowl. Pulse-chop 5-6 times until chopped. Set aside. Cut pork into 6-8 pieces, add to workbowl and pulse-chop 4-5 times. Set aside. Pulse-chop small shrimp 2-3 times or larger ones 3-4 times until coarsely chopped. Add 2 tablespoons oil to wok, heat until oil sizzles when you add a drop of water. Add pork and stir-fry until cooked, 3-4 minutes. Add shrimp, sherry, soy sauce, salt, sugar, mushrooms and onions. Stir-fry 2 minutes more. Set aside in a large mixing bowl. Add 1 tablespoon oil and stir-fry celery for 3-5 minutes. Add bean sprouts and bamboo shoots. Blend in pork mixture with vegetables, stir pan liquid until it boils. Combine cornstarch and water in small dish. Add cornstarch mixture to wok and cook until mixture thickens and is clear. Return mixture to mixing bowl and cool.

Wash wok to use for frying egg rolls. Add 1/4 cup cooled filling to each skin. Bring bottom point of skin to center, fold each side towards center and roll skin to top. Moisten top point of skin with water and press to roll to seal. Heat 3 cups of oil to 375 ° in wok. Place 2-3 egg rolls in oil and fry for 3-4 minutes or until brown. Keep warm at 250° or cool and freeze for future use. Heat frozen egg rolls at 400° for 10 to 15 minutes or until heated through.

NOTE: Egg roll skins are available in the produce section of the grocery store.

NOTE: Tiny packaged frozen salad shrimp are fine in this recipe. These are so small it is not necessary to chop them.

*EVEN SLICES OF LONG SLENDER VEGETABLES—"DANCING"
TIP: This tip applies especially to celery and green onions. Insert SLIC-ING DISC. Lock the cover in place. Hold on to untrimmed tops and insert in feedtube. With the machine running move the onions up and down in the feedtube and stop slicing when the tops of the onions reach the top of the feedtube.

CHICKEN RATATOUILLE

6 Servings

2 whole chicken breasts skinned, boned,
  split, and frozen
1 small eggplant
2 small zucchini, unpeeled
1/2 pound mushrooms
1 large onion (1-1/2 cups sliced)
1 medium green pepper (1 cup chopped)
2 medium tomatoes
1 garlic clove
1/4 cup corn or salad oil
1 tsp. salt
1 tsp. MSG (optional)
4 sprigs fresh sweet basil (1 Tbsp.)*
3 sprigs parsley (1 Tbsp.)
1/2 tsp. black pepper

Chicken should be firmly frozen but you should be able to pierce it with the tip of a knife. In order to slice meat in the food processor it must be frozen but slightly thawed. If the meat is too soft the meat will not slice properly. The meat should be firmly packed into the feedtube. Using thickest SLICING DISC available, insert chicken breasts tightly and vertically in feedtube. Process using medium-light pressure on the pusher. Set aside. Quarter the eggplant to fit the feed-tube. Insert (−) (4 mm) and slice eggplant, zucchini, mushrooms and onion. You may slice the onion with a thinner blade if you wish. Use a (ᨏ) to process the green pepper.** (You may also slice the green pepper.)*** Remove all vegetables from the workbowl. Set aside.

Process the tomatoes with the (ᨏ),**** set aside. (You may also pulse-chop the tomatoes using the ⬥ so you have coarse chunks.) Wipe the workbowl. Insert ⬥ and with machine running, mince the garlic by dropping it through the feedtube.

Heat the oil in a large skillet, add the minced garlic and saute the chicken pieces about 4 minutes. Use ⬥ to pulse-chop fresh parsley and basil while the chicken is cooking. Add eggplant, zucchini, mushrooms, onions, and green pepper to skillet. Cook about 15 minutes, stirring occasionally or until vegetables are tender but crisp. Add tomatoes, salt, MSG, basil, parsley and black pepper. Stir together carefully. Simmer about 5 minutes or until chicken is tender. Serve over rice or noodles.

*NOTE: Substitute 3/4 teaspoon each of dry basil and parsley if desired.

**GREEN PEPPERS, CHOPPED

TIP: The FRENCH FRY DISC will also cube green peppers evenly. Slice the top and bottom off the green pepper and then cut it into fourths. Stand up in the feedtube so the round side of the pepper is across the width of the feedtube. The feedtube must be tightly packed. In a large feedtube it takes 2 green peppers to pack the feedtube. Process using a quick firm pressure on the pusher.

***GREEN PEPPER RINGS

TIP: Insert SLICING DISC of desired thickness. Cut off stem. Remove seed pod, but don't cut pepper. If the whole pepper doesn't fit in the feedtube then cut off the blossom end and cut through one side of the pepper. Roll this pepper piece like a jelly roll to fit the feedtube. Place the whole pepper, cut side down, or prepared pepper roll standing up in the feedtube and process using medium pressure.

**** TOMATOES, CUBING

TIP: Depending on the size and firmness of the tomato make three or four vertical cuts not quite through the tomato. If the cuts are made all the way through the tomato will not cube nicely. Insert the FRENCH FRY DISC. Place the tomato, cut side down, with the cuts going across the feedtube. Pack the feedtube as full as possible. Process using a quick, firm pressure on pusher.

NOTE: You may omit the chicken in this recipe and serve as VEGETABLE RATATOUILLE.

COMPANY BEEF STROGANOFF 6-8 Servings

Adapted from a recipe by a well known cooking instructor from the Detroit area this stroganoff is very elegant and flavorful. An excellent company dish as preparation can be done ahead. The liquors give a very special flavor.

2 pounds flank or round steak (marinated)
1 clove garlic, minced
1 medium onion (1 cup sliced)
1/2 pound fresh mushrooms (2 cups sliced)
3 Tbsp. flour
2 Tbsp. tomato paste (no substitute!)
1 tsp. salt
Pepper to taste
1 cup beef stock (1 cup water and 1 beef bouillon cube)
1/4 cup white wine
3-8 Tbsp. oil
1/4 cup brandy
1 to 1-1/2 cups sour cream
1 tsp. dillweed (optional)

SHERRY MARINADE:
This is an all-purpose marinade. Try it for shish kabob, pork, chicken or even shrimp.

1/4 cup dry sherry
1-1/2 Tbsp. lemon juice
2 Tbsp. soy sauce
1 tsp. Worcestershire sauce
1 tsp. salt
Dash of pepper

Insert ⌒ (3-4mm). In order to slice meat in the food processor it must be frozen but slightly thawed. Thaw the meat enough so the point of a knife can go into the meat. If the meat is too soft the meat will not slice properly. The meat should be firmly packed into the feedtube. It should also be set in the feedtube so it will slice against the grain. Process using medium-light pressure on the pusher. Combine marinade ingredients in a suitable container. Remove meat from workbowl and marinate for 2 hours or overnight.

Insert ⊖ (3-4mm). Slice onions and mushrooms, set aside. Wipe workbowl dry with a paper towel. Insert ⬤ . With machine running drop garlic through feedtube. Continue processing until finely minced, stopping machine and scraping down sides as needed. Set aside. Add flour, tomato paste, salt, and pepper to workbowl. Pulse-chop 3-4 times. Add beef stock and wine. Pulse quickly 2-3 times. Leave in workbowl.

Heat 2 tablespoons of the oil in a large skillet. Drain meat from marinade. Brown small portions of meat at a time to get nice even browning, adding oil as necessary. Remove meat as it is browned and set aside. In the same skillet brown garlic, onions and mushrooms for 3-5 minutes. Remove from skillet and set aside with meat. To the same pan that has not been washed out add the brandy and heat until warm. Stir to break up any particles on the bottom of the pan. This will give a good flavor to the sauce. Light the warm brandy with a match. It will burn off in only a few seconds with a very low, blue flame. Keep on low heat and pour in the flour mixture from the workbowl. Stir with a whisk until smooth and bubbly. Simmer* for 10 minutes.

At this point you may ''hold''dinner until 15 minutes before you are ready to serve. At that time heat sauce over low heat to a simmer. Stir in sour cream. Do not add it to a very hot mixture. Do not let sour cream come to a boil or it will separate. Add vegetables and beef to sauce. Let mixture simmer* for 10-15 minutes or until heated through. Sprinkle with dill if desired. Serve over cooked rice or noodles.

*NOTE: To simmer means to cook just below the boiling point.

NOTE: Substitute apple juice or beef broth for the liquors if desired.

TROUT WITH WILD RICE
AND MUSHROOM STUFFING

6 Servings

Use trout or any other favorite pan-dressed fish for this recipe. Try the foil wrap method, even in the oven, for a very tender, moist baked fish.

1-6 oz. pkg. long grain and wild rice
6 slices bacon
6 small pan-dressed fish or 2 large
    fish, thawed if necessary
2 tsp. salt
1/4 tsp. pepper
8 sprigs parsley (1/4 cup chopped)
1 small onion (1/2 cup chopped)
2 stalks celery (1 cup sliced)
6 fresh mushrooms (2/3 cup sliced)
1/4 cup salad oil or butter
1 lemon, sliced
Extra parsley sprigs

Cook rice according to package directions. Partially cook bacon on range top or 4 minutes on HIGH in microwave. Drain and set aside. Clean and pat fish dry, sprinkle with salt and pepper. Insert ⟱. Cut onion in quarters, add to workbowl with parsley. Pulse-chop 5-6 times. Remove metal blade, but leave food in workbowl.

Insert medium (3-4mm) ⊝. Pack feedtube with short even lengths of celery. Process using medium pressure on pusher. Cut off one side of mushroom caps, lay mushrooms in feedtube with cut side on slicing disc. Process using light pressure on pusher.

Heat oil in large skillet and saute onion, parsley, celery, and mushrooms until tender. Add cooked rice to skillet and mix well. Insert medium (3-4mm) ⊖. Slice off one end of lemon and place in feedtube with cut side on slicing disc. Process using medium pressure on pusher. Remove lemon slices. Sprinkle any lemon juice in workbowl onto the fish. Stuff fish loosely with rice mixture. Close sides of fish with skewers or toothpicks. Place fish in a buttered baking dish large enough to lay them in one layer. Lay bacon strips on individual fish or three on each large fish. Bake at 350° for one hour. The six small fish will take less time to bake. Cook until fish flakes easily when tested with a fork.

Heat any remaining stuffing and place on platter to make bed for fish. Garnish with parsley sprigs and lemon slices.

VARIATION: For CHARCOAL BARBECUED TROUT use the following method. Tear enough pieces of heavy duty foil to wrap each fish double. Use the sandwich wrap method to keep all the moisture in the foil packet. Place fish on foil pieces and add bacon. Wrap tightly by bringing two edges together and folding over and over until fold is tight to fish. Then fold each end in several times until it is tightly folded to fish. Place over hot coals and cook about 45-60 minutes or until fish flakes easily. Take the size of the fish into consideration when timing the fish.

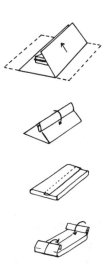

ROAST BEEF IN SPICY BARBECUE SAUCE

6-8 Servings

2-3 pound rump roast

Cook roast at 325° until cooked to medium degree of doneness. Chill overnight. Cut cold roast beef* in pieces to fit the feedtube. Insert ⌒ (2-4 mm) and process meat using medium light pressure. Pour SPICY BARBECUE SAUCE over sliced meat and refrigerate over night. Two hours before serving, heat in a covered casserole at 250° until heated through. Serve this warm in homemade buns for a delicious casual supper when entertaining. Needs no last minute attention.

*MEAT, SLICING COOKED

TIP: Rare and medium rare cooked meats must be frozen but partially thawed so the meat surface can be pierced with the tip of a knife. Rare cooked meat is not firm enough to slice well unless frozen. Medium and well done cooked meats are firm enough when refrigerated to slice but some freezing time will improve the slicing ease. Insert SLICING DISC of desired thickness. It is best to use a slicing disc of 4mm or thicker when slicing cooked meat. Pack feedtube firmly and slice using a medium-light pressure.

FISH 'N CHIPS

6 Servings

1 oz. parmesan cheese (1/4 cup grated)
4 oz. potato chips (1 cup crumbled)
1/4 tsp. thyme
1/2 tsp. salt
1/3 cup evaporated milk
1/4 cup melted butter or margarine
2 lbs. frozen fish, cut in six pieces
    while partially thawed
Paprika

Insert ⬤. Cut cheese in four pieces. With machine running add cheese through feedtube, replace pusher and process until finely grated. Leave cheese in workbowl. Add chips, thyme and salt to workbowl, pulse-chop 5-6 times until coarsely ground. Place mixture on wax paper. Dip fish pieces in evaporated milk, then in potato chip mixture and place in buttered baking dish. Sprinkle any extra crumbs on top and drizzle with melted butter. Shake paprika on all pieces and bake in a preheated 500° oven for 12-15 minutes.

SPICY BARBECUE SAUCE   2 Cups

2 Tbsp. brown sugar
1 Tbsp. paprika
2 cloves garlic
1 tsp. salt
1 tsp. dry mustard
1/4 tsp. chili powder
1/8 tsp. cayenne pepper
1/4 cup catsup
2 Tbsp. Worcestershire sauce
1/4 cup vinegar
1-1/4 cups tomato sauce
1/4 cup water

Insert ⚙, add all ingredients except last three. Pulse 5-6 times to combine and mince garlic well. Add vinegar, tomato sauce and water; pulse-chop 5 seconds until smooth. Pour* ingredients into saucepan and simmer 15-20 minutes or until slightly thickened. Use on barbecued spareribs, chicken, pork chops, or beef.

*PROCESSING LIQUIDS
TIP: Hold the metal blade in place with a finger tip until you pour the liquid into another container. The blade keeps the liquids from running out.
TIP: Use only half the liquid in a recipe if the processor workbowl has a small capacity. The remaining liquid, like milk or water, can usually be stirred in easily by hand.

*WORKBOWL, HOLDING
TIP: Some processors have openings in the bottom of the METAL BLADE. Insert the index or middle finger through the outside center of the workbowl into this opening while the METAL BLADE is in the workbowl. Hold tightly with the finger and place thumb around bottom outer side of workbowl. Fan out the rest of the fingers over the bottom of the workbowl. Then pour out the liquid while holding onto the blade. You may find this a convenient way to hold the workbowl whether or not it has liquid in it.

QUICHE LORRAINE   6 Servings

9 inch unbaked pastry shell in pie pan*
4 oz. Swiss cheese (1 cup shredded)
1/2 small onion (1/4 cup chopped)
6-8 slices bacon, cooked crisp and drained
4 eggs
2 cups whipping cream
  or 1 cup whipping cream
  plus 1 cup evaporated milk
1/2 tsp. salt
1/4 tsp. sugar
1/8 tsp. red or cayenne pepper

Insert ⊙, process Swiss cheese using push-release method.**
Sprinkle cheese in bottom of pie shell. Insert ⚓, add onion and
pulse-chop 4 times. Add bacon broken in half, eggs, cream, salt and
red pepper. Pulse-chop 4 times or until bacon is coarsely chopped
and eggs and cream are combined. Pour egg mixture over cheese,
keeping metal blade securely in place in workbowl. Bake in a
preheated 425° oven for 15 minutes: reduce heat to 300° and bake
30 minutes longer or until knife inserted 1 inch from edge comes
out clean. Let stand 10 minutes before cutting into six pieces.

NOTE: See DESSERTS for BASIC PASTRY DOUGH. Prepare the pie
crust or try the SAVORY CRUST QUICHE before proceeding to other steps
in quiche recipe.

VARIATIONS: Vary the flavor of the pie crust by adding a wedge of onion,
piece of cheese (parmesan or cheddar) or an herb like parsley or basil for
SAVORY CRUST QUICHE. Add desired savory to flour. Pulse-chop 6-8
times or until finely blended with the flour. The metal blade chops the food
so finely that the flavor is delicious but no large pieces in the pie crust. You
may want to decrease the amount of water in the crust recipe depending
on how much moisture was added by the flavoring. Try this delicious crust
with any of the quiches.

NOTE: Using half evaporated milk and half cream reduces the cost and
calories without affecting flavor.

NOTE: Use different cheeses or meats like ham, turkey, chicken or seafood
to vary flavor.

**CHEESE, PUSH-RELEASE METHOD
TIP: Place piece of very cold cheese into the feedtube. Set pusher in feedtube and lock cover. Turn machine on, press moderately on the pusher, release pressure by pulling up on the pusher. Repeat pressing and releasing of pusher until last piece is processed.

VARIATIONS: Use either of the following recipes for a different flavored quiche.

ZUCCHINI-CHEDDAR QUICHE   6 Servings

Insert ⊙ . Using medium pressure on the pusher, shred 2 cups zucchini and stir in 1/2 teaspoon salt. Let rest 30 minutes, then drain. Substitute 1 cup shredded cheddar for Swiss cheese, place cheddar and zucchini in pie shell and proceed, reducing recipe by 1 egg and 1/2 cup cream.

NOTE: Fresh vegetables with a high water content like broccoli, spinach or zucchini need to be partially precooked to reduce the amount of liquid in the vegetable before adding to quiches.

NOTE: During summer months shred extra zucchini and package in 2 cup quantities. Freeze—no blanching is necessary. Defrost, drain off extra liquid and use in ZUCCHINI-CHEDDAR QUICHE. Salting the zucchini is not necessary if this method is used. You can also use the thawed zucchini, without draining off the liquid, in any cake or bread recipe in the cookbook as the liquid from the zucchini is part of those recipes.

HAM-MUSHROOM QUICHE   6 Servings

Pulse-chop 4 ounces of ham with ⌐ and slice 6 medium mushrooms with ⌒ . Place in bottom of pie shell. Proceed, reducing recipe by 1 egg and 1/2 cup cream.

NOTE: Quiches are based on one egg for each 1/2 cup of cream. If you desire a more substantial filling with vegetables or meat then reduce the custard by one egg and 1/2 cup cream.

BEEF SUPREME

6 Servings

1/2 lb. beef round steak, frozen but partially thawed
1 medium onion (1 cup sliced)
1 green pepper (1 cup sliced)
2 stalks celery(1 cup sliced)
6 mushrooms (2/3 cup sliced)
1/3 pound green beans
2 Tbsp. vegetable oil
3/4 tsp. salt
2 Tbsp. cornstarch
1 Tbsp. soy sauce
1-1/3 cups water
Pimiento strips for garnish

Insert medium (3-4mm) ⌒. In order to slice meat in the food processor it must be frozen but slightly thawed. Thaw the meat enough so the point of a knife can go into the meat. If the meat is too soft the meat will not slice properly. The meat should be firmly packed into the feedtube. It should also be set in the feedtube so it will slice against the grain. Process using medium-light pressure on the pusher. Heat the oil in a large skillet and brown meat. Slice the onion, pepper, celery, and mushrooms using the same slicing disc.* Use a thin (1-2mm) ⌒ to French cut** the green beans by laying whole beans in the feedtube on the slicing disc. Add onion, green pepper, celery, mushrooms, and beans to the skillet. Cover and simmer 8-10 minutes. Blend the cornstarch, soy sauce, and water; pour into the mixture. Cook until sauce becomes thick and clear and until beans are tender. Garnish with pimiento strips and serve over cooked rice.

*SLICING, EVEN
TIP: Always cut the ends of fruit, vegetables, meat, etc. flat for a more even cut. Lay the food flat side down on the SLICING DISC. Use the palm of hand with an even pressure on pusher to guide the food through the feedtube. Always stop the machine to refill the feedtube. Pack the feedtube evenly and as fully as possible.

**GREEN BEANS, FRENCH-CUT
TIP: Use the SLICING DISC, preferably a thin (2 mm) slicing disc. Cut the beans in lengths to fit horizontally in the feedtube. Stack them horizontally in the feedtube and apply medium pressure on pusher. Green beans may be blanched before processing. The blanching makes it easier for some processors to slice the beans.

BEEF BOURGUIGNONNE

6-8 Servings

4 slices bacon
1-1/2 lbs. boneless beef stew meat
1/3 cup flour
1 clove garlic, finely chopped
3 small onions (1-1/2 cups sliced)
1 large carrot (1/2 cup sliced)
1 tsp. salt
1 tsp. chopped parsley
1/4 tsp. pepper
1 bay leaf
1 can (10-3/4 oz.) condensed beef consomme
1/2 cup burgundy wine

Cook bacon in a 12 inch skillet until crisp, drain and cool.* Leave drippings in skillet; coat meat cubes with flour, add to hot drippings and brown on all sides. While meat is browning insert ⬳ and mince garlic by dropping through feedtube while machine is running. Leave garlic in workbowl but remove metal blade. Insert ⊖ (4-6mm). Pack feedtube with onions and carrots and slice using medium pressure on pusher. Add garlic, onions and carrots to skillet and cook until onion is tender. Insert ⬳, break bacon into workbowl and pulse-chop 4-6 times until coarsely chopped. Add bacon and remaining ingredients including any flour to skillet. Bake in covered skillet or Dutch oven at 325° for 1-1/2 to 2 hours or until meat is tender. Remove bay leaf. Serve with boiled potatoes or noodles.

*NOTE: Bacon may be microwaved using a bacon dish. Be sure to reserve bacon drippings for frying meat.

MACARONI AND CHEESE

6-8 Servings

1-3/4 cups uncooked elbow macaroni (3-1/2 cups cooked)
10 oz. cheddar cheese (2-1/2 cups shredded)
1/4 cup cornstarch
1-1/2 tsp. salt
Dash of pepper
2-1/4 cups milk
1/2 small onion (1/4 cup chopped)

Cook elbow macaroni in 5 cups boiling salted water until tender; drain. While macaroni is cooking insert ⬚ in workbowl, add cheese which has been cut in 1 inch cubes and pulse-chop 4-6 times. Continue processing 20-30 seconds or until cheese is well chopped. Add cornstarch, salt, and pepper. Pulse 2 times. Heat milk in microwave on HIGH 2-4 minutes or until very hot, or in a saucepan until very hot. With machine running add milk through the feedtube in a steady stream. Stop machine and scrape down sides of the workbowl when necessary. Add quartered onion and pulse-chop 3-4 times. Add cooked macaroni to a 2-quart casserole. Pour cheese mixture on top of macaroni. Stir to mix well, bake in 350° oven for 50 minutes or until top is nicely browned and bubbling.

NOTE: Place 3/4 cup of buttered bread crumbs* on top of casserole before baking, if desired. One slice of fresh bread will make 2/3 to 3/4 cup of crumbs.

*BREAD CRUMBS, BUTTERED AND SEASONED
TIP: Butter a slice of bread. If desired sprinkle on seasonings like garlic powder or salt, celery salt or parsley flakes. Insert METAL BLADE, tear or cut bread in quarters. Pulse-chop until desired consistency. You can do at least three slices at a time. If you have a larger workbowl you may do more.

VEGETABLES

| METAL BLADE | SHREDDING DISC | DOUGH BLADE | SLICING DISC | FRENCH-FRY DISC |

Chop onions, double-cut carrots, shred fresh beets, or julienne zucchini!! These are just a few of the ways to add excitement to fresh vegetables all year round. Liven up your meals with any of our recipes in VEGETABLES. The tips listed below are ones that you can use in everyday vegetable preparation.

JULIENNE STRIPS - VEGETABLES SUCH AS CARROTS, ZUCCHINI, BROCCOLI STEMS, BEETS, POTATOES

TIP: Insert the SLICING DISC. The thickness of the julienne will be decided by the thickness (2-8mm) of the slicing disc used. To achieve "picture perfect" julienne strips, first place the food horizontally and cut one side flat. Cut the food in lengths to fit the feedtube. Fill the feedtube with one layer of food that has the flat side on the slicing disc. Process using medium to firm pressure on the pusher, depending on the firmness of the vegetable. Repeat first three steps until all vegetables are processed. Take slices out of workbowl and stack them like a deck of cards. Replace the SLICING DISC. Pack the slices in the feedtube vertically so they are standing on edge. Make sure the feedtube is TIGHTLY packed. Use up the slice you cut off by hand, if necessary, to pack the feedtube tightly. If the feedtube is only half full the slices will fall over and not julienne correctly. The final length of the julienne depends on whether you slice the width or the length of the food.

ONIONS, CHOPPED

TIP: Insert METAL BLADE. Cut onion in 4-6 even pieces. Pulse-chop 4-6 times. Count out each second for each pulse. Pause for 1 second after each pulse so that you DO NOT OVERPROCESS or you will have onion mush!!

SLICES, "PICTURE PERFECT"

TIP: Always cut the ends of fruit, vegetables, meat, etc. flat for a more even slice. Place cutting edge of disc opposite the feedtube when the cover is locked in place. Lay the food flat side down on the SLICING DISC. Pack the feedtube evenly and as fully as possible. Place pusher in feedtube. Use the palm of hand with an even pressure on pusher to guide the food through the feedtube. Be ready to push BEFORE the machine is started for "picture perfect" slices. Start the machine, pressing pusher through with palm of hand. Always stop the machine to refill the feedtube. If the feedtube is refilled while the machine is running when using the slicing, shredding or French fry disc it could be dangerous and the processed food will be uneven and unattractive.

JULIENNE
STRIPS

STUFFED TOMATOES

4 Servings

4 medium tomatoes
1 Tbsp. grated parmesan cheese
Salt
4 Tbsp. butter or margarine, divided
1/2 tsp. basil
2 cups CHEESE GARLIC CROUTONS
or dry herb seasoned stuffing mix

Cut off the tops of tomatoes; discard. Carefully scoop out the pulp and reserve. Sprinkle insides of tomatoes with salt and set aside, upside down on a rack for about 30 minutes. Insert ⌇, process cheese* by adding small pieces through feedtube while machine is running. Replace pusher. Process 1 minute or until fine. Measure 1 tablespoon for recipe and freeze remainder for later use. No need to wash bowl. Add tomato pulp and process 4-6 times until smooth. Measure 2/3 cup of puree. Reserve remainder for another use. Put puree, basil and 2 tablespoons butter in workbowl, process 3-4 times. Add tomato mixture to stuffing and stir just to moisten croutons. Spoon stuffing into tomato shells. Place on baking sheet. Dot with remaining butter and sprinkle with grated cheese. Bake in a 350° oven, 15-20 minutes or until heated through.

*CHEESE,PARMESAN
TIP: Cut the parmesan cheese in 1 inch pieces. Room temperature cheese is easier to cut. If you cannot cut it with a knife then the food processor can't either. With the machine running add the pieces one at a time through the feedtube. Cover feedtube with hand or replace pusher to eliminate small pieces of cheese from coming out. After adding all cheese continue to process until cheese is finely grated, about 30-60 seconds more.

NOTE: Use the remaining tomato puree for spaghetti sauce, chili, or meatloaf—freeze if desired. May strain puree and add lemon juice, pepper and salt for a delicious FRESH TOMATO JUICE.

SWEET CARROTS

4-6 Servings

1 pound carrots (4 cups sliced)
1/4 cup butter
1/4 cup brown sugar, packed

Insert ⊖. Cut carrots in lengths to fit the feedtube. Pack carrots* vertically in feedtube. Using medium pressure, process the carrots. Cook carrots in covered saucepan with 1/4 cup water until tender or microwave in covered 2 quart casserole with two tablespoons water on HIGH for 5-7 minutes. Drain. Add butter and stir until melted. Stir in brown sugar and mix until blended.

*EVEN CIRCULAR SLICES - CARROTS, CELERY, RHUBARB ETC.
TIP: To slice long slender fruits or vegetables evenly be sure the feedtube is packed tightly or the produce will fall over and slice diagonally. Cut the vegetables in short EVEN lengths to pack the feedtube rather than using long pieces in an unpacked feedtube.

DILLED GREEN BEANS

4 Servings

6 sprigs parsley (2 Tbsp. chopped)
1 small clove garlic
1 small onion (1/2 cup sliced)
2 Tbsp. butter or margarine
1/2 lb. cleaned green beans
1/4 tsp. salt
1/2 tsp. dill seed
1 tsp. lemon juice
1 Tbsp. pimento

Using ⊛, pulse-chop parsley, set aside. Mince garlic by dropping through feedtube while the machine is running. Remove ⊛ and insert thinnest ⊖ available. Slice onion using medium pressure on pusher. Melt butter in 1 quart saucepan, add onion and garlic. Cut or snap beans to fit length of feedtube. Lay on sides in feedtube, stack to within one inch of the top of feedtube. Slice, using light pressure. Place beans on onion and garlic; cover, and simmer 20 minutes or until beans are tender. Add dill seed, parsley, lemon juice and pimento. Heat through and serve.

SPANISH CORN

2 slices buttered bread (1-1/3 cups crumbs)
1/2 pound fresh green beans
2 Tbsp. butter or margarine
1 egg
1 cup evaporated milk
6 springs parsley (2 Tbsp. chopped)
Quarter wedge of onion (1/4 cup chopped)
1/2 tsp. salt
1/2 tsp. dillweed
3 Tbsp. flour
1 tsp. sugar
1-12 oz. can Mexicorn, undrained

Insert ⟨knife⟩. Tear bread into four quarters, add to workbowl. Pulse-chop 5-6 times until crumbed. Remove blade and crumbs, set aside. Insert ⊝ (2-4mm). Place green beans horizontally in feedtube. Process using a medium pressure. Cook beans in 1/4 cup water in a covered saucepan until tender-crisp, drain. You may cook in microwave on HIGH power for 5-7 minutes in a covered casserole, drain. Stir with butter. Insert ⟨knife⟩, add egg, milk, parsley, onion, salt, dillweed, flour and sugar to the workbowl. Pulse-chop 4-6 times until onion and parsley are finely chopped. Add egg mixture and can of Mexicorn to beans, mix well. Place in a greased 9 inch round casserole. Top with buttered crumbs. Bake at 350° for 30 minutes.

CHEDDAR CARROTS

8 Servings

12 round butter crackers (1/2 cup crushed)
4 oz. cheddar cheese (1 cup chopped)
1-1/2 to 2 pounds carrots
1/2 tsp. salt
Dash pepper
1 small onion (1/2 cup chopped)
1/4 cup butter

Insert ⤸, break crackers into workbowl. Pulse-chop 5-6 times until crackers are crushed. Remove metal blade and insert ⊙. Process cheese using push-release method.* Add salt and pepper to crackers and cheese, stir with a spoon, set aside on wax paper. Insert medium ⌒, julienne carrots as directed in JULIENNE STRIPS.** Cook carrots in boiling salted water 15-20 minutes or microwave on HIGH for 10 minutes with 1/4 cup water. Insert the ⤸, pulse-chop onion 6-7 times until fine. Melt butter in skillet, add onion and saute until tender. Drain carrots and combine with onions. Place 1/2 the carrots in a two quart casserole, then 1/2 the cheese-cracker mixture. Repeat. Bake at 350° 20 to 25 minutes.

*CHEESE, PUSH-RELEASE METHOD
TIP: Place piece of very cold cheese into the feedtube. Set pusher in feedtube and lock cover. Turn machine on, press moderately on the pusher, release pressure by pulling up on the pusher. Repeat pressing and releasing of pusher until last piece is processed.

**JULIENNE STRIPS - VEGETABLES SUCH AS CARROTS, ZUCCHINI, BROCCOLI STEMS, BEETS, POTATOES
TIP: To achieve "picture perfect" julienne strips, first place the food horizontally and cut one side flat. Cut the food in lengths to fit the feedtube. Fill the feedtube with one layer of food that has the flat side on the slicing disc. Process using medium pressure on the pusher. Repeat first three steps until all vegetables are processed. Take slices out of workbowl and stack them like a deck of cards. Replace the SLICING DISC. Pack the slices in the feedtube vertically so they are standing on edge. Make sure the feedtube is TIGHTLY packed. Use up the slice you cut off by hand, if necessary, to pack the feedtube tightly. If the feedtube is only half full the slices will fall over and not julienne correctly. The final length of the julienne depends on whether you slice the width or the length of the food.

YAMS AND APPLES

8-10 Servings

6 yams, cooked and peeled
6 large apples, peeled and cored
1/2 cup butter or margarine
3 Tbsp. cornstarch
1/2 cup sugar
1/2 cup brown sugar, packed
2 cups water
Dash of salt

Insert thickest ⌣ available. Cut yams* to fit and place in feed-tube, slice using a medium pressure on pusher. Leave yams in workbowl. If a whole apple doesn't fit in feedtube cut in half. Process. Place yams and apples in a 13x9 inch greased baking dish** or a large covered casserole. Insert ⬤, cut butter into 4 even pieces. Pulse-chop 4-6 times. Add cornstarch, both sugars, and salt. Pulse-chop 6-8 times. Add water and pulse-chop 2-3 times. Butter mixture may separate. Pour over yams and apples. Bake, covered, for 45 minutes at 375°.

*SLICING, EVEN

TIP: Always cut the ends of fruit, vegetables, meat, etc. flat for a more even cut. Lay the food flat side down on the SLICING DISC. Use the palm of hand with an even pressure on pusher to guide the food through the feed-tube. Always stop the machine to refill the feedtube. Pack the feedtube evenly and as fully as possible.

NOTE: Cover a 13x9 inch casserole with aluminum foil.

JULIENNE STRIPS

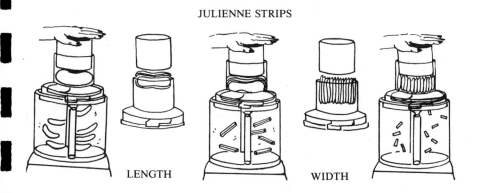

LENGTH   WIDTH

BROCCOLI PUFFS

6-8 Servings

1-1/2 pounds fresh broccoli
1-1/2 slices buttered bread
1-2 oz. parmesan cheese
1 (10-3/4 oz.) can cream of mushroom soup
1/2 cup MAYONNAISE
1/2 cup sour cream
2 eggs
1 small onion (1/3 cup chopped)

Cook whole pieces of clean broccoli until tender-crisp on the rangetop or microwave on HIGH power 5-7 minutes with 5 minutes of standing time. Use the same casserole in the microwave that you will use to cook this dish. While broccoli cooks, insert ⬙, add bread which is cut or torn into 6 pieces. Pulse-chop 4-5 times or until crumbs. Remove from workbowl and reserve for topping. Cut cooked broccoli stems in 3-4 pieces, leaving flowers* whole. Add stems to workbowl, pulse-chop 4-5 times THEN add the flowers and pulse 2 times. Place chopped broccoli in a casserole dish. Leave blade in place, no need to clean workbowl. With machine running, drop small pieces of parmesan cheese through the feedtube. Process until fine, about 20-30 seconds. Stop machine, scrape down sides of workbowl and add remaining ingredients. Pulse-chop 5-6 times, making sure onion is chopped in small pieces. Stir this mixture into broccoli. Top with reserved bread crumbs. Bake at 350° for 30 minutes.

*BROCCOLI STEMS
TIP: If a recipe calls for just the flowers of broccoli, use the SHREDDING DISC, FRENCH FRY DISC, JULIENNE DISC or the SLICING DISC (4-6mm) and the JULIENNE TIP to make fine shreds or matchstick julienne pieces of the stems. Processing with one of these discs will make the stem more tender. You can stir-fry or steam the stems. If stem is very tough peel the outside skin.

BROCCOLI-RICE CASSEROLE

6-8 Servings

1 pound broccoli
1 small onion (1/2 cup chopped)
1 (10-1/2 oz.) can condensed cream of chicken soup
1-8 oz. jar processed cheese spread
1/2 cup milk
2 Tbsp. butter
1 cup uncooked rice

Cook broccoli with 1/4 cup water in a covered saucepan over medium heat or 5 minutes on HIGH in a covered microwave container until tender crisp, drain.* Insert ⬩, add quartered onion and pulse chop twice. Cut cooked broccoli stems in 3-4 pieces, leaving flowers whole. Add stems to workbowl, pulse-chop 4-5 times *THEN* add the flowers and pulse 2 times. Place chopped broccoli and onion in a buttered 13x9 inch baking dish or 3 quart casserole. Add soup, cheese, milk and butter to workbowl. Pulse-chop 4 times to blend ingredients. Add rice and pulse once.** Add this mixture to broccoli, stirring to mix. Bake uncovered for 35 minutes at 350°.

NOTE: Save vegetable water in a container in the freezer. Keep adding to it whenever you cook vegetables. Use this water as the base for homemade soups. If there is a baby in the house, you may add the water to puree vegetables for baby food. You can also just drink it or put it in gravy. Since this water is rich in vitamins try not to feed it to your kitchen sink.

**METAL BLADE, CLEANING
TIP:** *When processing dips, spreads or batters that cling to the metal blade, scrape most of the food out of the workbowl leaving the metal blade in place. Put the bowl with the blade back in place on the base, cover and process for about 2 seconds. The food clinging to the blade will spin off leaving a clean blade.*

FRIED CABBAGE

6 Servings

2 cloves garlic
1 medium red onion (1 cup sliced)
1 small head cabbage (red or green - 4 cups shredded)
1 medium tart apple
3 Tbsp. oil
1/2 cup chicken broth
1/2 tsp. salt
1-1/2 tsp. caraway seeds (optional)
1 bay leaf
3 Tbsp. red wine vinegar
1 Tbsp. sugar

Insert ⚓. With machine running add garlic through feedtube and process until finely minced. Remove metal blade but leave garlic in bowl. Insert thin* (1-2mm) ◡, place onion in feedtube and process using light pressure on pusher. Remove food from workbowl and set aside. Insert ⊙, place cabbage pieces in feedtube. Process using firm pressure on pusher. Leave cabbage in workbowl. Core apple; cut to fit feedtube, if necessary. Shred apple by applying firm pressure on pusher. Heat oil in a large skillet; add garlic and onion, saute 3-4 minutes. Stir in cabbage and apple. Add remaining ingredients, cover and cook 10-15 minutes stirring occasionally. Add more broth if liquid evaporates before cabbage is cooked. If cabbage is cooked but liquid remains, uncover the skillet and boil off the liquid, stirring to prevent the cabbage from burning. May be made ahead and reheated just before serving.

*SLICES, THIN
TIP: Not all machines have thin slicing discs or you may not have this disc for the processor. To produce thinner slices pack the feedtube very tightly and apply a light pressure on the pusher. The slices should be thinner. It is the next best technique to owning a 1-2 mm slicing disc.

CELERY PARMIGIANA

6 Servings

1 oz. parmesan cheese (1/4 cup grated)
2 oz. cheddar cheese (1/2 cup chopped)
8 stalks celery (4 cups sliced)
1/4 tsp. salt
1/4 tsp. basil, crushed
1 Tbsp. cornstarch
2/3 cup consomme

Using ⬩, process parmesan cheese by adding 1 inch pieces through the feedtube while the machine is running. Replace pusher. Process 1 minute or until fine. Set aside on wax paper. Cut cheddar in 4 quarters and pulse-chop 6-8 times until finely chopped. Remove and reserve with parmesan cheese. Insert ⌣. Cut celery in even vertical lengths the height of the feedtube. Pack celery tightly into the feedtube and slice using a medium pressure. Reserve 3 tablespoons of consomme. Cook celery with salt, basil and remaining consomme in a 2 quart saucepan for 8-10 minutes or until tender crisp. Insert ⬩, add cornstarch and reserved consomme, pulse twice to combine. Stir mixture into cooked celery; cook and stir about two minutes until consomme thickens. Place celery mixture in a shallow ovenware casserole. Sprinkle with parmesan and cheddar cheese. Broil for 2-3 minutes or until nicely browned.

EGGPLANT CREOLE

4-6 Servings

2 slices buttered bread
1 medium-large eggplant
1 medium onion (3/4 cup chopped)
1 medium green pepper (1 cup chopped)
3 large tomatoes (3 cups chopped)
3 Tbsp. butter
3 Tbsp. flour
1 Tbsp. brown sugar
1 tsp. salt
1 small bay leaf
2 cloves
Parmesan cheese

Season buttered bread as desired with garlic, basil, or parsley. Insert ⬖, process bread until coarsely crumbed. Set aside. Peel eggplant, cut in fourths. Insert ⌒ (4-6mm). Place eggplant in feedtube, process with medium pressure on pusher. Cook for 10 minutes in boiling salted water. Drain it well and place in the bottom of a 2 quart casserole, greased lightly with butter. Insert ⬖, chop* onion, green pepper, and tomatoes (cube each vegetable instead using the ⬒ if available-see CUBING TIP). In a saucepan, melt butter; add the flour, stir until bubbly and blended. Add onions, green pepper and tomatoes to flour mixture in saucepan. Add brown sugar, salt, bay leaf, and cloves. Cook over low heat for 5-7 minutes stirring occasionally. The mixture will be quite thick. Spread over the eggplant. Sprinkle bread crumbs on top of casserole with a sprinkling of freshly grated parmesan cheese. Bake at 350° for about 30 minutes until the top is golden brown.

*CHOPPING, VARYING CONSISTENCIES
TIP: The order ingredients are added to the workbowl when chopping with the METAL BLADE will give different consistencies. For example, three vegetables pulse-chopped all together will be the same fineness while chopping celery and green pepper first and onions last will produce coarser onions. The other variable is the hardness of the vegetable or fruit. In the above example if celery and carrots had been chopped together the carrots would be a little coarser then the celery. If the same consistency is desired for a hard and soft vegetable first pulse-chop the hard vegetable a few times and then add the softer vegetable. Pulse-chop to desired consistency.

NOTE: Double this recipe when using a 13x9 inch dish. Give this recipe a try, it's delicious, even people who don't like eggplant will like this.

HASH BROWN POTATOES

4 large potatoes (2 pounds)
1 small onion (1/2 cup chopped)
1 tsp. salt
1/3 cup oil or bacon drippings

Scrub potatoes well. Place them in a 3 quart saucepan with enough cold water to cover. Heat to boiling; cover, and boil gently 12-15 minutes. The potatoes should be slightly underdone. Drain water, process immediately or refrigerate potatoes until needed. Peel potatoes if desired. Insert ⊙, place potato in feedtube. Process using medium pressure on pusher. Repeat until all potatoes are shredded. Place onion in feedtube. Shred using light pressure on pusher. Gently mix potatoes and onions by hand.

Heat oil or fat until it just sizzles. Form 4 patties and place in skillet. Pat down to uniform thickness, if desired. Cover and cook over moderately high heat until beautifully browned on bottom. Turn and cook other side. Serve immediately.

NOTE: Undercooked potatoes will hold together well. It is not necessary to add cream to hold these potatoes together while cooking.

OVEN HASH BROWNS
10-12 Servings

1 cup potato chips (1/2 cup crushed)
10-12 small potatoes
8 oz. cheddar cheese (2 cups shredded)
Lemon juice
1/2 cup butter or margarine
2 cups sour cream
1 (10-1/2 oz.) can cream of mushroom soup
1 small onion (1/2 cup chopped)
Salt and pepper to taste

Insert ⟲, add potato chips. Pulse-chop 3-4 times until coarsely crumbed, set aside. Remove metal blade and set aside. *Insert ⟲. Cut each potato in half or thirds, place pieces standing up in feedtube being careful that feedtube is packed. Process using a medium pressure on pusher. Stop machine each time you reload feedtube. Sprinkle lemon juice over potatoes in workbowl to prevent potatoes from browning. Add potatoes to greased 13x9 inch baking dish or 3 quart casserole. Continue without washing workbowl. Insert ⟲. Place cheese in feedtube. Use the push-release method** of shredding cheese with a light pressure. Set cheese aside. Insert ⟲, cut margarine in 6 pieces. Pulse-chop 4-6 times until softened. Add sour cream, soup and onion cut in quarters. Pulse-chop 4-5 times. Add half of the cheese and pulse-chop 3-4 times. Add mixture to potatoes. Sprinkle remaining cheese over the casserole and top with potato chip crumbs. Bake 1 hour at 350°.

*CUBING POTATOES
TIP: For "picture perfect" cubes process as directed. Insert SLICING DISC of desired thickness. Use at least a 4-8mm thick blade. The thicker blade will, of course, make larger cubes. Slice the vegetable using a firm pressure on the pusher. Remove disc, take slices out of workbowl. Insert FRENCH FRY DISC. Pack slices upright, tightly and across the width of the feedtube. If slices are packed parallel to the length of the feedtube, you will produce French fries. Process using a quick, firm pressure on pusher.

**CHEESE,PUSH-RELEASE METHOD
TIP: Place piece of very cold cheese into the feedtube. Set pusher in feedtube and lock cover. Turn machine on, press moderately on the pusher, release pressure by pulling up on the pusher. Repeat pressing and releasing of pusher until last piece is processed.

POTATO PANCAKES

Baking powder makes these potato pancakes light and fluffy. A little onion adds just enough flavor contrast.

3 large potatoes (2 cups chopped)
1/2 small onion (1/4 cup chopped)
2 Tbsp. flour
1 tsp. baking powder
1-1/4 tsp. salt
2 eggs
Oil for frying

Insert . Cut potatoes in 4-6 pieces, add to workbowl. Pulse-chop 6-8 times. Cut onion in half, add to workbowl and pulse-chop 3-4 times. Add remaining ingredients and pulse-chop 3-4 times or until desired consistency. Heat enough fat to cover skillet to a depth of 1/4 inch. Drop pancake mixture by heaping tablespoons into hot fat, flattening out to form pancakes. Fry until golden brown on both sides, adding fat as needed. Serve with applesauce or sour cream.

NOTE: The longer chopped potatoes sit, the more they "weep".

CUBING

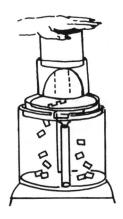

OR

SNOWY MASHED POTATOES

10 Servings

12 medium potatoes
2 cups potato chips (1 cup crushed)
1 clove garlic
Green onion tops, chives or parsley
1-8 oz. pkg. cream cheese
1 cup sour cream
Salt and pepper to taste
Butter

In a large covered saucepan cook unpeeled potatoes in water to cover until soft. Meanwhile insert ⚒ and put potato chips in workbowl. Pulse-chop 3-4 times until coarsely crushed. Set aside. With machine running add garlic through feedtube and process until garlic is finely minced. Scrape down sides of workbowl and add pieces of onion tops or chives and a few sprigs of parsley. Pulse chop 3-4 times. Cut cream cheese in 6-8 pieces, add to workbowl and pulse chop 6-8 times.* Add sour cream and pulse until creamy. Place mixture in a large mixing bowl. Do not wash workbowl. Remove metal blade and insert ⊚. Peel potatoes. Fill feedtube with potatoes. Process using a light pressure. If workbowl becomes full add potatoes to cream mixture. Stop the machine each time you fill the feedtube. Mix shredded potatoes with cream mixture. Spoon into a lightly greased 13x9 inch baking dish or a 3 quart casserole. Dot with butter. Sprinkle with potato chips. Bake uncovered for 30 minutes at 350°

NOTE: Use this recipe with leftover mashed potatoes (6 cups.)

*CREAM CHEESE, SOFTENING
TIP: Cream cheese does not need to be at room temperature when using a food processor. In fact, the cream cheese may break down into a liquid if too soft before processing. Remember the colder the cream cheese the longer it will take to process. The friction of the blade against the cream cheese does the softening.

ZUCCHINI ROUNDS

Terrific light vegetable patties to take advantage of a large zucchini harvest.

2 medium unpeeled zucchini (2 cups shredded)
1 small clove garlic
1 oz. parmesan cheese (1/4 cup grated)
1/3 cup biscuit mix
1/8 tsp. pepper
1/4 tsp. basil
2 eggs
2 Tbsp. butter or margarine

Insert ⊙ , shred zucchini using medium pressure on pusher. Remove and set aside on wax paper. Insert ⌒.With machine running drop garlic and cheese through feedtube and process until finely minced. Add biscuit mix, seasonings, eggs and shredded zucchini. Pulse-chop 5-6 times just until mixture is blended. In a large skillet, melt one tablespoon butter over medium heat. Use 2 tablespoons of the mixture for each round and cook four rounds at a time, about 2-3 minutes on each side. Repeat. Serve as a side dish; or cover with spaghetti sauce and mozarella cheese, bake at 350° for 15 minutes for a vegetarian ZUCCHINI PARMIGIANA.

NOTES

SALADS

| METAL BLADE | SHREDDING DISC | DOUGH BLADE | SLICING DISC | FRENCH-FRY DISC |

Food processors and salads go hand-in-hand. A "picture-perfect" salad bar can be prepared in minutes. Finish off the salad bar with several homemade salad dressings. The following list of tips apply to many processing steps for salad and salad dressing preparations.

METAL BLADE, CLEANING

TIP: When processing dips, spreads or batters that cling to the metal blade, scrape most of the food out of the workbowl leaving the metal blade in place. Put the bowl with the blade back in place on the base, cover and process for about 2 seconds. The food clinging to the blade will spin off leaving a clean blade.

SLICES, "PICTURE PERFECT"

TIP: Always cut the ends of fruit, vegetables, meat, etc. flat for a more even slice. Place cutting edge of disc opposite the feedtube when the cover is locked in place. Lay the food flat side down on the SLICING DISC. Pack the feedtube evenly and as fully as possible. Place pusher in feedtube. Use the palm of hand with an even pressure on pusher to guide the food through the feedtube. Be ready to push BEFORE the machine is started for "picture perfect" slices. Start the machine, pressing pusher through with palm of hand. Always stop the machine to refill the feedtube. If the feedtube is refilled while the machine is running when using the slicing, shredding or French fry disc it could be dangerous and the processed food will be uneven and unattractive.

SLICING, THIN

TIP: Not all machines have thin slicing discs or you may not have this disc for the processor. To produce thinner slices pack the feedtube very tightly and apply a light pressure on the pusher. The slices should be thinner. Use this technique for thin slices of carrots, celery, cabbage, cucumber, potatoes, etc. It is the next best technique to owning a 1-2mm slicing disc.

CUCUMBER CREAM SALAD

8 Servings

This is just a lovely light salad for a summer luncheon or to accompany a ham or pork dinner menu. It practically melts in your mouth. Be sure to seed the cucumber.

1-3 oz. pkg. lime gelatin
1 env. unflavored gelatin
1 tsp. salt
1 cup very hot water
2 Tbsp. cider vinegar
1 small wedge fresh onion
1 medium cucumber, peeled and
    seeded, (2 cups chopped)
1/2 cup MAYONNAISE
1 cup sour cream

Insert ⟨blade⟩. Pour gelatins, salt and water in workbowl. Pulse-chop 6-7 times until gelatins are dissolved. Cut cucumber into 8 even pieces. Add vinegar, onion and cucumber to workbowl. Pulse-chop 6-7 times or until cucumber is finely chopped. Hold metal blade* in place and pour mixture into a mixing bowl. Chill until slightly thickened. Prepare MAYONNAISE according to recipe in SALADS, if needed. Reserve 1/2 cup in workbowl, add sour cream and pulse twice to combine. Place thickened gelatin in workbowl and pulse-chop 2-3 times to combine with sour cream. Pour into a six cup mold or individual molds. Chill until firm. Unmold on salad greens and serve. Garnish with cucumber slices and pimiento strips.

*WORKBOWL, HOLDING METAL BLADE WITH
TIP: Some processors have openings in the bottom of the METAL BLADE. Insert the index or middle finger through the outside center of the workbowl into this opening while the METAL BLADE is in the workbowl. Hold tightly with the finger and place thumb around bottom outer side of workbowl. Fan out the rest of the fingers over the bottom of the workbowl. Then pour out the liquid while holding onto the blade. You may find this a convenient way to hold the workbowl whether or not it has liquid in it.

NOTE: To unmold salad, use a small knife and loosen around all edges of mold. Fill sink with medium warm water. Place mold in water just to upper edge, hold in water for about a minute. Place greens over mold, center plate over mold and then invert mold.

COLESLAW

If for no other reason, people buy a food processor to eliminate the tedious task of making coleslaw. Coleslaw is as American as apple pie and a required food at church suppers, graduation parties, and backyard barbecues. The textures that are deemed appropriate are also as varied as our American heritage. We give you three possibilties to suit your family and friends' tastes.

Sliced Coleslaw:
1 head cabbage
2-3 medium carrots, peeled and cut in 1-1/2 inch chunks
1 small onion, cut in quarters (whole green onions are good also)
1 green pepper, cut in quarters(optional)

Insert ⬛ in workbowl. Add carrots to workbowl, pulse-chop 4-5 times. Add onion to workbowl with carrots, pulse-chop 3-4 times. To this mixture add green pepper, pulse 2-3 times. This should give you finely chopped carrots, medium chopped onion and coarsely chopped green pepper. Leave in the workbowl but remove metal blade.

A thin (1-2mm) slicing disc will give you finely sliced coleslaw like Grandma used to make. Use the medium (3-4mm) slicing disc for a coarser slaw. Insert the ⬡. Cut cabbage in thirds across the core. Use the center section and remove 3-4 layers of leaves. Roll cabbage leaves jelly roll style to fit in feedtube. Insert cabbage roll standing up in feedtube and slice using a medium pressure on pusher. Continue removing and rolling leaves until you have sliced as much as you desire. Remove ingredients from workbowl and toss with DONA'S COLESLAW DRESSING.

Shredded Coleslaw:

Place the quartered onion in the workbowl with the ⚒ and pulse-chop 3-4 times. Add pepper and pulse-chop 2-3 times more. Remove metal blade. Insert ⊙ and process the cabbage using firm pressure on the pusher. You will get longer shreds if you place the cabbage in the feedtube with the direction of the leaves running with the shredding disc. Pack carrots* tightly in feedtube and shred using medium pressure. Remove mixture and toss with DONA'S COLESLAW DRESSING.

*LENGTH OF SHRED
TIP: For longer shreds of cheese, fruit, or vegetables like carrots, zucchini, potatoes, etc. lay the food or vegetable horizontally in the feedtube. Shorter shreds are produced by standing the food or vegetable vertically and tightly in the feedtube.

Chopped Coleslaw:

Chopping is perhaps the easiest method of processing cabbage because only the ⚒ is used. Beginners often use this blade and get cabbage soup by over processing. You will know that you have the pulse-chop technique mastered if this slaw has the proper consistency. Insert ⚒, add carrots to workbowl, pulse-chop 3-4 times. Add onions and pulse-chop 2-3 times, add cabbage which has been cut into 2-3 inch chunks. Fill workbowl only half full of cabbage for best results. Pulse-chop 3-4 times or more depending on the coarseness you desire. The quartered green pepper is pulse-chopped last, about 2-3 pulses will get it coarsely chopped. If this consistency is too fine pulse-chop less next time or for finer slaw pulse-chop the cabbage more.* You can also vary the fineness of each ingredient by when it is added to the workbowl, i.e. add the carrot at the same time as the cabbage and you will have larger pieces of carrot.

*VARYING CONSISTENCIES
TIP: The order ingredients are added to the workbowl when chopping with the METAL BLADE will give different consistencies. Example: Three vegetables pulse-chopped all together will be the same fineness while chopping celery and green pepper first and onions last will produce coarser onion pieces and finer pieces of celery and green pepper. The other variable is the hardness of the vegetable or fruit. In the above example if celery and carrots had been chopped together the carrots would be a little coarser then the celery.

CHICKEN STACKED UP SALAD   6-8 Servings

A clear glass bowl will show this salad as a work of art and you can thank the food processor for making it a short work of art!

2 cups cubed cooked chicken
1/2 tsp. curry powder
1/4 tsp. salt
1/4 tsp. paprika
Dash pepper
1/2 head lettuce
Small bunch romaine
1 medium red onion
1 medium cucumber, peel if desired
1 cup cooked macaroni
2 medium tomatoes
1 medium green pepper
1-1/2 cups salad dressing
2 Tbsp. lemon juice
2 Tbsp. milk

Combine chicken, curry, salt, paprika, and pepper in a mixing bowl. Insert medium (3-4mm) ⊝. Fill feedtube with large wedges of lettuce and process with medium pressure on pusher. Place lettuce in clear glass salad bowl. Insert thick (6-8mm) ⊝ if available. Place romaine leaves upright in feedtube, process using a medium-firm pressure on pusher. Place in bowl, layer chicken mixture over this. Whole slices are most attractive but if the feedtube will not accommodate them then process the vegetables in half slices. Slice onion and cucumber using a thin (1-3mm) ⊝.

Layer vegetables on chicken, then layer macaroni over vegetables. Slice the tomato* using the medium (4 mm) ⊝ and add to salad bowl. Slice the green pepper and leave it in the workbowl. Insert the ⌒ and pulse-chop 3-4 times. This will give you coarsely chopped green pepper. (You may also use the ⌒ to process the green pepper.**) Add to the salad. Process salad dressing, lemon juice and milk together with ⌒. Spread mixture over salad and refrigerate covered several hours or overnight. Each serving should have all the layers included. May be tossed before serving.

*SLICING TOMATOES
TIP: A slightly firm tomato will process best.
TIP: Apply quick light pressure when processing soft vegetables and fruits like tomatoes.

**GREEN PEPPERS, CHOPPED
TIP: The FRENCH FRY DISC will also cube green peppers evenly. Slice the top and bottom off the green pepper and then cut it into fourths. Stand up in the feedtube so the round side of the pepper is across the width of the feedtube. The feedtube must be tightly packed. In a large feedtube it takes 2 green peppers to pack the feedtube. Process using a quick firm pressure on the pusher.

GREEK SALAD   8-10 Servings

1 large or 2 medium heads of lettuce
1 medium red onion (1 cup sliced)
6-8 fresh mushrooms, one side cut flat
6 slices bacon, cooked crisp
2 oz. cold feta cheese (1/2 cup crumbled)
1 cup CHEESE GARLIC CROUTONS

Use a thick (6-8mm) ⌒ to slice the lettuce.* Fill the feedtube with quarter sections of lettuce and process using a medium pressure on the pusher. Empty workbowl into serving bowl as necessary. You may also tear the lettuce into a serving bowl. Insert the thin (1-2mm) ⌒ , place the onion in the feedtube and slice the onion using medium pressure on the pusher. Place the mushrooms in the feedtube with the flat side on the slicing disc, process using a light pressure on pusher. Place in serving bowl. Insert METAL BLADE, add bacon and feta cheese and pulse-chop about 3-4 times until bacon is finely chopped. Add to salad. Do not wash bowl. Make SWEET WINE VINEGAR DRESSING. See page 107.

*SHREDDED LETTUCE
TIP: Lettuce is shredded in a food processor by slicing it. A thin slice will produce long thin strands while a thick slice will produce slices that are good for tossed salads. Break iceberg lettuce in pieces to fit the feedtube, insert SLICING DISC of desired thickness and process using a medium pressure. Using the shredding disc will produce lettuce puree. Chopping lettuce with the metal blade will bruise it.

TABBOULEH SALAD

4-6 Servings

This recipe is good as a salad, appetizer, or in pita bread as a sandwich. For an unusual appetizer, serve in a bowl garnished with cherry tomatoes and a basket of crackers or quartered pita bread.

1 cup fine bulgar or cracked wheat
3-1/2 inch bunch of parsley
2/3 cup mint leaves
1 medium onion (1 cup chopped)
3-4 green onions including the tops
1 tsp. salt
1/4 tsp. freshly ground black pepper
1/3-1/2 cup lemon juice
1/2 cup olive or salad oil
2 medium tomatoes

Put bulgar wheat in a bowl. Add warm water until it just covers wheat. Let stand for about one hour or microwave 3-5 minutes on HIGH power until all the water is soaked into the wheat. Insert ⟨⟩ in workbowl, add parsley.* Pulse-chop 4 times. Add mint leaves, pulse chop 2-3 times. Cut dry onion in quarters and green onion in short lengths, add to workbowl and pulse 4-5 times. Add salt, pepper, lemon juice, and oil, pulse 2- 3 times. Add quartered tomatoes and drained wheat, pulse twice until tomatoes are in small chunks. Be very careful not to over process the tomatoes. (You may also pulse in the wheat, remove metal blade and dice the tomatoes** using the ⟨⟩. Use a quick, firm pressure on the pusher when processing the tomatoes.)

NOTE: Tastes best if made the day before or let stand 2-3 hours. Keeps up to a week.

*PARSLEY, CHOPPED
TIP: Use stems of parsley since they contain all the vitamins. Pulse-chop the stems first 5-6 times. Add parsley flowers and pulse-chop 4 times. Continue with the recipe.

**TOMATOES, CUBING
TIP: Depending on the size and firmness of the tomato make three or four vertical cuts not quite through the tomato. If the cuts are made all the way through the tomato will not cube nicely. Insert the FRENCH FRY DISC. Place the tomato, cut side down, with the cuts going across the feedtube. Pack the feedtube as full as possible. Process using a quick, firm pressure on pusher.

ITALIAN DELI SALAD

6-8 Servings

ITALIAN DELI DRESSING:
1 clove garlic
2 sprigs parsley (1 Tbsp. chopped)
1/2 cup salad oil
1/3 cup red wine vinegar
1 tsp. salt
1/2 tsp. pepper
1/4 tsp. dried basil
1/4 tsp. dried oregano

Salad:
1 green pepper (1 cup chopped)
1 red pepper (1 cup chopped)
1 small onion (1/2 cup chopped)
1-6 oz. can pitted jumbo black olives
4 oz. fresh mushrooms (1 cup sliced)
1/2 large head cauliflower

Insert ⬩. With machine running drop garlic through feedtube. Continue processing until finely minced, scraping down sides as needed. Add parsley and pulse-chop 4-6 times. With machine running add remaining dressing ingredients through the feedtube. Replace pusher. Process 5-10 seconds longer. Remove ⬩, leave dressing in workbowl.

Insert ⬩, pack feedtube with peppers.* Process using medium pressure on pusher. Place onion in feedtube, process using medium pressure. Remove disc and insert medium (4-6mm) ⬩. Lay mushrooms on sides in feedtube. Process using light pressure on pusher. Place olives standing upright and packed in feedtube, process using light pressure on pusher. The cauliflowerets may also be sliced using the 6mm SLICING DISC. If you wish, break the cauliflower into small flowerets and add to salad. Invert workbowl over serving bowl. Toss and refrigerate salad 4 hours or overnight.

*GREEN PEPPERS, CHOPPED
TIP: The FRENCH FRY DISC will also cube green peppers evenly. Slice the top and bottom of the green pepper and then cut it into fourths. Stand up in the feedtube so the round side of the pepper is across the width of the feedtube. The feedtube must be tightly packed. In the large feedtube it takes 2 green peppers to pack the feedtube. Process using a quick firm pressure on the pusher.

*NOTE: If FRENCH FRY DISC isn't available then remove dressing and pulse-chop peppers and onion coarsely with METAL BLADE. Follow remaining directions and add dressing over salad.

EASY POTATO SALAD

6-8 Servings

Using frozen French fries is a real shortcut for this tasty potato salad. The food processor takes the work out of the remaining chopping of fresh vegetables which make this salad so delightful.

2-9 oz. pkg. frozen French fried potatoes (4 cups)
1-1/2 tsp. salt
8 sprigs fresh parsley (2 Tbsp. chopped)
1/2 medium cucumber, unpeeled(2/3 cup chopped)
6-8 radishes (1/2 cup sliced)
1 stalk celery (1/2 cup sliced)
2 green onions (2 Tbsp. sliced)
1-2 Tbsp. cider vinegar
1 cup MAYONNAISE (see INDEX)
2 tsp. to 1 Tbsp. Dijon mustard (to your taste)
Hard cooked eggs, sliced*
Paprika

Add 4 cups of water to a large saucepan and bring to a boil. Carefully add frozen potatoes to water. Remove from heat immediately; cover and let stand 4-5 minutes. Drain potatoes at once and spread on paper toweling. Sprinkle with salt; cool. Insert ⚙, add parsley. Pulse-chop 6-7 times, add cucumber cut in 4 pieces. Pulse-chop 3 times more or until cucumber is coarsely chopped. Leave vegetables in workbowl, remove metal blade. Insert thin ⊝ (2-4mm). Cut off root and stem end of radishes. Place flat side down on slicing disc. Process using medium pressure on pusher. Hold onto celery stalks at the top, insert in feedtube. "Dance" celery up and down on slicing disc while machine is running. Stop when top of celery reaches top of feedtube. Process green onion in same manner. Do not trim off the onion tops so you have enough to hold while processing the onions. Combine mayonnaise, vinegar and Dijon mustard in a large serving bowl. Add potatoes and vegetables from workbowl, toss together and chill. Garnish with hard cooked egg slices and paprika.

NOTE: This salad has a wonderful flavor due to the Dijon mustard. Dijon mustard is a good addition to any potato salad.

*EGGS, HARD COOKED—CHOPPED AND SLICED
TIP: Use the METAL BLADE to pulse-chop hard cooked eggs in the food processor. Hard cooked eggs do not slice well in a food processor because the yolks are very soft.

SOUR CREAM CUCUMBER SALAD   4 Servings

1 medium cucumber, peeled
1 tsp. salt
2 green onions
1/2 cup sour cream
4 tsp. vinegar
2-3 drops hot pepper sauce
1/2 tsp. dillweed
Dash black pepper
1 small onion

Use thin (1-2mm) ⌒ to slice cucumber using light to medium pressure on the pusher. If the feedtube will not accommodate a whole cucumber cut it in half vertically and then process. Sprinkle with salt and let stand 30 minutes. Use ⌇ and pulse-chop green onions including tops, add sour cream and seasonings, process 2-3 seconds until blended. Insert thin ⌒ and slice whole onion into workbowl. Drain cucumbers; pour dressing and onions over cucumbers. Place in a serving bowl and chill about 30 minutes before serving.

CARROT APPLE RAISIN SALAD   3-4 Servings

1 red apple, unpeeled and cored
1 Tbsp. lemon juice
2-3 carrots
1/2 cup raisins, or more to your taste

Insert ⊙, put red apple in feedtube. If the processor has a small feedtube then cut the apple in half to fit the feedtube. Process with medium pressure on pusher. Add lemon juice to workbowl and toss lightly with a spoon to prevent apple from browning. Wedge carrots into feedtube and shred using medium pressure on pusher. Place apples and carrots in a serving bowl, add raisins, toss and refrigerate until serving time. No dressing is needed.

HOT SPINACH SALAD

4-6 Servings

4 slices bacon
1/4 cup vinegar (wine)
1/2 tsp. Worcestershire sauce
2 Tbsp. sugar
1/2 tsp. salt
1 green onion
1 stalk celery (1/4 cup sliced)
1 pound spinach,clean, dry and torn
1 oz. blue cheese (2 Tbsp. crumbled)

Cook bacon until crisp in microwave or use a skillet reserving bacon drippings. Add vinegar, Worcestershire sauce, sugar and salt to drippings. Heat on MEDIUM power 3-4 minutes in microwave or in skillet until sugar is melted. Insert ◁◮, add crisp bacon slices, pulse-chop 4-6 times. Leave bacon in workbowl. Insert thin to medium ⟨—⟩ (2-4mm) depending on desired thickness. Lock cover in place. With machine running, process onion by holding it at the top and "dance" it on slicing disc by moving onion up and down in the feedtube. Stop slicing when your hand reaches the top of the feedtube. Process celery the same way. Remove disc, place ingredients over spinach in salad bowl. Insert ◁◮, add cheese* and pulse-chop 2-3 times or until cheese is crumbly, scraping sides of bowl. Pour hot dressing over salad just before serving and toss lightly. Top with blue cheese.

*CRUMBLED BLUE CHEESE
TIP: Place inch cubes of well chilled or partially frozen blue cheese in workbowl, pulse-chop 2-3 times until cheese is crumbled. If cheese is at room temperature it will cream together instead of crumbling.

POSH SALAD

6-8 Servings

Garnish:
2 oz. blue or Roquefort cheese (1/4 cup crumbled)

RED WINE MARINADE:
4 Tbsp. red wine or tarragon vinegar
6 Tbsp. salad oil
1/2 tsp. salt
1/4 tsp. pepper

Salad:
1/2 head cauliflower (3-4 cups sliced)
1 small mild red onion (1 cup sliced and separated)
10-12 jumbo pitted black olives
1 Tbsp. sliced pimiento
Small head of iceberg lettuce or romaine

Insert ⚥. Cut blue cheese* in four pieces and add to workbowl. Pulse-chop 3-4 times and store in refrigerator. Add vinegar, oil, salt, and pepper to workbowl, pulse-chop 3-4 times to combine. Remove metal blade. Insert medium(4-6mm) ◡. Break cauliflower into flowerets and fill feedtube. Slice using medium pressure on the pusher. Insert onion in feedtube. Slice using medium pressure on the pusher. Remove slicing disc, separate onion into rings. Leave onion in workbowl. Use same ◡. Place olives** upright in feedtube and process with a gentle pressure on pusher. Place RED WINE MARINADE, sliced ingredients, and pimiento in a covered bowl; let marinate for at least 1/2 hour or overnight.

When ready to serve insert medium (4-6mm) ◡. Fill feedtube with lettuce or romaine. Slice, using a medium pressure on the pusher. Place lettuce in a salad bowl. Pour marinated mixture over lettuce. Sprinkle with crumbled blue cheese, toss lightly and serve.

*BLUE CHEESE, CRUMBLED
TIP: Insert METAL BLADE. Place inch cubes of well chilled or partially frozen blue cheese in workbowl, pulse-chop 2-3 times until cheese is crumbled. If cheese is at room temperature it will cream together instead of crumbling.

**OLIVES, SLICED
TIP: Insert (2-6mm) SLICING DISC. Put cover in place. Pack the feedtube with one layer of pitted olives, standing the olives upright for perfect slices. Larger olives are easier to handle. Insert pusher and process using light pressure.

FRESH FRUIT TRAY

10-12 Servings

Everyone seems to be diet conscious these days so a fresh fruit tray or salad is good for you as well as a spectacular offering to serve your guests. It's such an easy thing to do with the food processor! Use any or all of these fruits.

Apple—Use red or golden Delicious, Granny Smith or Spartan apples depending on the color you want. Buy apples that will fit whole in the feedtube. Use a (3-4 mm) SLICING DISC. Cut off blossom end of apple so it sits flat on disc in feedtube. Apply medium pressure on pusher. The seeds will fall out of the apple as it is sliced. Dip in lemon juice and water to prevent browning.

Banana—Peel and cut in half horizontally. Fill feedtube with enough pieces so they hold one another up. Slice using (4-8mm) SLICING DISC and light pressure on the pusher. Dip in lemon juice and water to prevent browning.

Kiwi fruit—Use a moderately ripe kiwi. If it is too soft it will not slice nicely. Peel, cut off blossom and stem ends. Place kiwi closest to the side of the feedtube that the disc slices toward to keep the kiwi from falling over. Slice whole, using (4-6mm) SLICING DISC with light pressure on the pusher.

Jicama—This is a root vegetable that comes from Mexico. It is usually available in winter and early spring. Peel off fibrous exterior. Cut in pieces to fit the feedtube. Use a 4-8mm SLICING DISC. Slice using medium pressure on the pusher. Refer to the JULIENNE STRIPS-VEGETABLES in TIPS if you wish to make matchstick pieces of this or use the FRENCH FRY DISC. The kids think it tastes like coconut and it doesn't brown after it is peeled.

Orange—Don't peel the orange if it will be a finger food. Oranges make delightful "Smiley Faces" by cutting in half and then slicing. Cut off stem and blossom end. Use (4-8mm) SLICING DISC. Cut the orange in half. Pack the two orange halves together in the feedtube or process one at a time depending on the size of the feedtube and the oranges. Use medium quick pressure on the pusher when processing.

Pear—Slice off blossom and stem end. Do not peel. Cut in half vertically, if needed, to fit feedtube. Use (4-8mm) SLICING DISC and a medium pressure on pusher. You may also cut in half vertically, core and process with the FRENCH FRY DISC by laying the flat side of the pear on the disc.

Pineapple—Don't peel the pineapple if it will be a finger food. It looks prettier, gives your guests something to hold on to and is less work for you. Cut off stem and base. Cut circular sections the height of the feedtube. Cut the section in pie-shaped thirds or fourths which will fit in the feedtube. Use (4-8mm) SLICING DISC and slice each section using a medium pressure on the pusher.

Add seedless grapes, wedges of watermelon, honeydew or canteloupe and whole berries to finish a spectacular tray. Of course you can use only two or three fruits if you wish. Refer to any of the APPETIZER or SALAD recipes that have fresh fruit trays for dips and marinades.

PICTURE-PERFECT SLICES
TIP: Remember, for picture perfect results each time you slice, always place the cutting edge of the SLICING DISC opposite where the feed tube locks before you start to process.

FRESH FRUIT SALAD

6-8 Servings

If making a fresh fruit salad process fruits according to the directions given before for the FRESH FRUIT TRAY. Quarter the fruits like apple, orange, pear, etc. Of course, remove the skin from the orange and pineapple; and core the fruits as needed. When in season add canteloupe, seeded watermelon and strawberries. They all slice beautifully. Try slicing seedless grapes too! Fill the feedtube with grapes and apply medium pressure on pusher. In seconds, you will have created a marvelous fruit salad. Use any of the FRUIT MARINADES or thin one of the FRUIT DIPS with juice, milk, mayonnaise, or yogurt to use as a salad dressing.

FRESH FRUIT ORANGE MARINADE

1-1/4 Cups

1-6 oz. can grapefruit juice concentrate*
1/4 cup orange marmalade
2 Tbsp. orange liqueur

Prepare desired fruits as directed under FRESH FRUIT SALAD. Combine the above ingredients with the ⚙ and stir gently into fruit. Chill at least 2 hours before serving.

*NOTE: May use orange or lemonade concentrate also.

CRANBERRY RELISH

3 Cups

1 pkg. cranberries (3-4 cups)
1 orange, unpeeled
1 cup sugar

Insert ⚙ in workbowl, add cranberries and pulse until medium coarse. Cut orange into eighths and add to workbowl. Do not remove the peel from the orange, just the seeds. Pulse-chop six times. Add sugar, pulse-chop 4-6 times or until sugar is mixed in. Let stand for 1 hour in refrigerator or may be frozen for later use.

NOTE: Cranberries may be processed fresh or frozen.

ORANGE WALNUT TOSS

6-8 Servings

FRESH LEMON DRESSING:
1/2 fresh lemon, unpeeled
1 clove garlic
1/2 cup salad oil
1/2 tsp. salt

Salad:
1/2 mild white or red onion,
    sliced and separated into rings
2 oranges, peeled and cut in half
1 head lettuce, sliced

Quarter and seed lemon half. Insert ⚓. With machine running, add lemon pieces and garlic one at a time through the feedtube. Continue processing and add salad oil and salt. Stop machine and scrape down sides. Replace pusher. Let machine run until lemon is finely chopped. Leave FRESH LEMON DRESSING in workbowl but remove blade. Insert ⌒ (2-3mm). Place onion in feedtube flat side down. Process onion with medium pressure on pusher. Insert medium (4mm) ⌒. Cut off ends of orange so you have a flat surface. Place one or two orange halves* in feedtube and process using medium pressure on pusher. Leave in workbowl. Use the same slicing disc or insert a thick(6-8mm) disc. Cut the head lettuce to fit the feedtube and process using a medium pressure. Empty workbowl as needed. Invert workbowl over a salad bowl and toss. Separate any onion rings. Top with heated Walnut Croutons.

*PROCESSING SINGLE ITEMS
TIP: The SLICING DISC in a food processor operates in a counter clockwise direction. To keep single items from falling over place them by the side of the feedtube that the blade will push the food towards.

WALNUT CROUTONS

1/2 Cup

1 Tbsp. butter
1/2 cup walnuts

Just before serving, melt butter in skillet and add nuts. Heat until walnuts are crisp and browned, about 8-10 minutes, or microwave on HIGH power for 3-5 minutes.

MAYONNAISE

1-1/4 Cups

1 large egg
1/2 tsp. salt
1 tsp. dry mustard
Dash of pepper
1 tsp. lemon juice
1 tsp. red wine vinegar
1 tsp. Dijon style mustard
Pinch of sugar
1 cup oil (preferably corn
    or olive oil or a mixture of the two)

Insert ⟁, add the egg and all remaining ingredients except the oil to the workbowl. Process for 8 seconds. With the machine running drizzle 1/4 cup of the oil through the feedtube in a thin steady stream.* If your pusher has a small hole in it, pour about 1/4 cup oil into the pusher and it will drizzle slowly into the workbowl.** The mayonnaise will thicken as the oil is added slowly. You may let the remaining oil drizzle through the pusher or add the remaining oil in a slow steady stream through the feedtube. Continue processing 30 seconds after all the oil has been added.*** Refrigerate the mayonnaise in an air tight jar. It can be stored in the refrigerator for 2-4 weeks.

*THICK MAYONNAISE
    TIP: The secret to thickening mayonnaise is to add oil slowly to egg at first while the machine is running.

**TINY HOLE IN PUSHER
    TIP: This hole will allow oil to drip slowly into the workbowl giving a nice thick mayonnaise. Use it for the melted butter when making a hollandaise sauce or any other liquid that should be added slowly.

***METAL BLADE, CLEANING
    TIP: To easily remove creamy, sticky dips, spreads or batters from the blade, first scrape most of the mixture from the workbowl. Put METAL BLADE and workbowl back on base, cover and lock machine. Pulse machine 2-3 times. The food clinging to the blade will spin off leaving a clean blade. Then remove the clean blade and scrape out any remaining mixture from the workbowl. Most blades have a knob or special notch to hold onto when the blade is soiled or slippery.

VARIATION: For a less seasoned mayonnaise, use 1 egg and 1 cup oil with 1 tsp. lemon juice, 1 tbsp. cider vinegar, 1/2 tsp. dry mustard, 1/4-1/2 tsp. salt, pinch of sugar and dash of red pepper. Prepare as directed under MAYONNAISE.

DONA'S COLESLAW DRESSING   1-1/4 Cups

1 to 1-1/4 cups MAYONNAISE
2 Tbsp. sugar
2-3 Tbsp. vinegar
1-1/2 tsp. salt
1-1/2 tsp. celery seed

Insert ⚙. Prepare MAYONNAISE for dressing if necessary. Add remaining ingredients and pulse-chop 3 times to blend. Use amount desired on coleslaw.

CREAMY GARLIC DRESSING   3-1/2 Cups

1 clove garlic
1-3 oz. pkg. cream cheese
2 cups sour cream
3 Tbsp. lemon juice
1/4 tsp. salt
Dash of cayenne pepper
1 small onion (1/2 cup chopped)
1/2-1 cup milk

Insert ⚙. With machine running, add garlic through the feed-tube. Process the garlic until finely minced. Stop machine, add cream cheese and sour cream. Pulse-chop 4-5 times or until creamy. Add lemon juice and seasonings. Cut onion in quarters, add to workbowl. Pulse chop 2-3 times. With machine running, add milk through the feedtube. Add enough milk until the dressing reaches desired consistency.

NOTE: Make LO-CAL CREAMY GARLIC DRESSING by substituting 2 cups (1/2%) cottage cheese, 1/4 cup water and 2 tablespoons sour cream for the 2 cups of sour cream. Process with METAL BLADE until smooth, about 30 seconds.

MAURICE SALAD DRESSING

1-1/2 Cups

1/2 cup MAYONNAISE
2 hard cooked egg yolks
1/2 cup salad oil
1 Tbsp. pickle juice
1 Tbsp. Worcestershire sauce
1/4 cup vinegar
1/4 small onion (2-3 Tbsp. chopped)
3 sweet gherkins (1/4 cup chopped)

Insert ⚒. Prepare MAYONNAISE according to directions in SALADS. Leave 1/2 cup in workbowl. Add remaining ingredients and pulse-chop 3-4 times, stopping machine to scrape down sides of bowl. Chill for 1 hour before serving.

NOTE: For quick hard cooked yolks, separate 2 fresh eggs. Put yolks in small dish, pierce the yolks with a fork. Cover dish with plastic wrap, microwave on HIGH for 1 minute until yolks are firm and cooked. Save egg whites to brush over bread dough or freeze for later use.

ROQUEFORT DRESSING

2-1/2 Cups

A nice light flavorful "Blue cheese" dressing. Package in a jar and give with a recipe card as a gift.
1/2 cup MAYONNAISE
1 clove garlic
1-3 oz. pkg. cream cheese
3 oz. Roquefort or blue cheese
1/2 cup light cream
1/4 tsp. Dijon mustard
1/2 tsp. Beau Monde seasoning

Insert ⚒. Prepare MAYONNAISE from SALADS if you have none on hand, reserve 1/2 cup in workbowl. With machine running, drop garlic through feedtube and process until finely minced. Add cream cheese and Roquefort cheese, each cut in four pieces. Pulse-chop 3-4 times, add remaining ingredients and process until well blended. Refrigerate unused portion. Will keep 3-4 weeks.

LO-CAL SOUR CREAM   1 Cup

1 cup cottage cheese
3 Tbsp. milk
1 Tbsp. lemon juice

Insert ⬥, add all ingredients and pulse 3-4 times. Continue processing 1 minute or until smooth and creamy. Use in place of sour cream. Eliminate even more calories by using lo-fat cottage cheese (1/2%) and lo-fat milk.

VARIATIONS: Use any combination or just one of the following with the LO-CAL SOUR CREAM: Add crisp bacon, onion wedge, fresh chives, garlic clove, cube of cheddar or parmesan cheese to workbowl and pulse-chop with METAL BLADE until desired consistency. Use LO-CAL SOUR CREAM TOPPINGS on salads, baked potatoes, or plain as a substitute for sour cream in any recipe.

SWEET WINE VINEGAR DRESSING   1-1/2 Cups

3/4 cup salad oil
1/4 cup wine vinegar
1/3 cup cider vinegar
1/2 cup sugar
4 tsp. salt
1 Tbsp. oregano
1 Tbsp. pepper

Insert ⬥, add the ingredients for the dressing. Process until well mixed (10 seconds). Add to GREEK SALAD, sprinkle with croutons, toss and serve.

CHEESE GARLIC CROUTONS

3-4 Cups

1 oz. parmesan cheese(1/4 cup grated)
1 clove garlic
1/2 cup butter or margarine
6 slices day old bread

Insert ⊸. With machine running, add cheese and garlic, processing until fine. Remove and set aside. Without rinsing bowl, tear bread in quarters and place in workbowl. Pulse 5-6 times to get chopped bread pieces. Melt butter in a skillet on medium-low heat. Stir in cheese and garlic, add bread and fry until golden brown. Use over a favorite tossed salad or as a casserole topping.

NOTE: Coarser textured breads like French or Italian are best for these croutons.

BREADS

| METAL BLADE | SHREDDING DISC | DOUGH BLADE | SLICING DISC | FRENCH-FRY DISC |

There is nothing that smells better than the aroma of bread baking in the oven. Fresh homemade bread is loved by all, but many people feel that it is either too hard to make or takes too much time. The ease of kneading dough in your food processor will enable you to win the hearts of your family by creating any of the following recipes in this chapter.

In the following recipes we have listed the ingredients appropriate for varying workbowl capacities. The flour capacity for your food processor will decide which amount you use. Food processors such as General Electric®, J.C. Penny®, Sears®, Toshiba®, and Hamilton Beach® do not come with a dough blade so the metal blade is inserted and the ingredients under 3 cups of flour will be used. Cuisinart®, Sunbeam®, Farberware®, KitchenAide®, and Robot Coupe® food processors come with a dough blade. Check your instruction booklet as to when you should use the dough blade.

When using 3 cups or less of flour the METAL BLADE should be used in all processors. The metal blade can "catch" the small amount of flour and knead it. The length of the dough blade is too short to catch the 3 cups of flour and cannot knead it properly. The DOUGH BLADE can knead 4 cups or more of flour. The following recipes say to "insert blade." Choose the metal blade or dough blade according to the workbowl capacity, food processor brand and the amount of flour being used. Using the dough blade for over 4 cups flour is less taxing on the machine. The dough blade was designed to better handle the larger amount of flour due to the short stubby design. Do not try to process more dough than your machine can handle. It is better to process in two separate batches, in order to accommodate your machine.

Remember—making bread in your food processor is "oh", so easy.

CONVERTING YEAST BREAD RECIPES

Perhaps you have been making bread for years. Perhaps you never have made bread before. In either case we want you to be able to convert your bread recipe or any bread recipe to use in the food processor. The following pointers should help you in converting any yeast bread recipe to the food processor. If you are a novice at bread baking be sure to read the notes and tips in this section to help you start enjoying home baked bread right away.

STEP 1—Always dissolve yeast in 1/4 cup warm liquid. The remaining liquid can be at room temperature or cold. The proportion of flour to liquid in most bread recipes is 1/3 cup liquid to 1 cup flour.

STEP 2—Measure flour into the workbowl reserving 1/2 cup. This 1/2 cup will be added later if needed. It is better to make dough a little sticky and then add more flour, than to make it too dry and then compensate by adding more liquid. If using a special flour like rye or whole wheat with bread flour, measure the total amount of the special flour into the workbowl. Reserve the 1/2 cup of flour out of the total white or bread flour quantity. Use bread flour for best results. We do not recommend using only whole grain flours without any bread flour. The resulting loaf of bread will be very heavy. It will also take a long time to rise properly.

STEP 3—Add dry ingredients such as salt, sugar, spices, etc. to flour in workbowl.

STEP 4—Add butter, shortening, honey or molasses to the workbowl with flour. It's not necessary to melt these ingredients when using the food processor. Pulse all ingredients together.

STEP 5—Combine *DISSOLVED* yeast with any other liquid ingredients like milk, eggs, oil, remaining water or potato water. These do *NOT* need to be warm.

STEP 6—Pour liquid mixture in a steady stream through the feedtube while the machine is running. Give the machine time to mix the liquid with the flour. Process about 10 seconds after a ball is formed.

STEP 7—Stop the machine. If dough is sticky add remaining flour and pulse twice. Process until the dough forms a ball and continue processing for 30 seconds. This is equivalent to 5 minutes of hand kneading.

STEP 8—Check the dough consistency. It should be smooth and elastic. Add more flour to develop smoothness if necessary. Process about another 10-30 seconds after ball forms.

STEP 9—To test if the dough is properly kneaded, remove the dough and pull it apart. If it breaks as you pull it should be kneaded more but if it stretches then the gluten in the flour is properly developed and the dough is well kneaded. The resulting dough will feel soft like the end of the ear lobe.

STEP 10—Bread dough usually takes about 2 minutes total processing time from adding the liquid to the final amount of processing time needed after the dough forms a ball. Once bread dough forms a ball it is processed between 60-90 seconds which is the equivalent of 10-15 minutes of hand kneading. Thus 30 seconds of processing time is equal to 5 minutes of hand kneading. As the machine is processing the dough, it is kneading it.

We have included many notes and tips in this section on breads in order to simplify the "secrets" of bread-making. We want you to realize that you don't need a lot of different recipes to make a great variety of breads. Once you learn the basics and realize how you can adjust bread baking to your schedule, then the food processor and you will have freshly baked bread on your table more often. The food processor can make bread better than any other appliance or better than if you made it by hand.

BREAD MAKING NOTES

The following is a list of some bread-making facts. These were compiled so one can better understand the process involved in bread-making. We hope these will help you.

WATER TEMPERATURE AND YEAST

NOTE: Water temperature should be between 105°-115°. A temperature higher than 130° is too hot and will kill the yeast. This means the dough won't rise.

NOTE: Water that is too cold (below 85°) doesn't allow the yeast to grow. This also means the bread won't rise.

NOTE: It is best to sprinkle yeast on water. The yeast will fall to the bottom. *DO NOT STIR.* After 10 minutes it will rise to the top of the water and burst like fireworks. Stir just before adding to flour. Sugar does help to activate yeast but it does not necessarily need to go in with the yeast.

NOTE: When doubling a recipe for bread the yeast does not need to be doubled because yeast activates itself. By doubling the yeast amount the bread will rise faster but it will also have a "yeasty" after taste.

NOTE: Salt contributes flavor. It also helps to control the action of the yeast. Too much slows down the growth of the yeast. For salt free diets, eliminate all the salt in the recipe and stay on your diet while taking advantage of bread-making in the food processor.

NOTE: The new fast-acting yeasts can be used in breads made in the food processor. To activate yeast use liquid at a higher temperature than normal. Water at 115°-120° is the best temperature. Sprinkle in yeast, stir and yeast will burst to the top like fireworks in about 10 minutes.

NOTE: Yeast consists of living plants, which feed upon sugar and flour as they multiply. They give off carbon dioxide gas which makes dough rise. Active dry yeast comes with an expiration date. Use yeast before this date is up. Yeast stays fresher in refrigerator or freezer.

TIME FOR BAKING YEAST BREADS

NOTE: Sometimes it is hard to find a block of time for "baking day". Just split the process between two days by letting the dough rise in a warm spot for the first rising. Shape dough into desired form (loaf, rolls, etc.), cover and refrigerate up to 24 hours for the second rising. When ready to bake take dough out of the refrigerator and let stand 15-30 minutes before baking.

KNEADING

NOTE: The end result of kneaded bread dough should feel soft like the end of your ear lobe.

NOTE: Processing a ball of dough for 60-90 seconds in the food processor is equivalent to 10-15 minutes of hand kneading.

RISING

NOTE: Rising the dough in an overly warm place (temperatures above 85°) will kill the yeast. It may rise on the first rising, but not for the second rising.

NOTE: Bread should rise twice; once in a large enough bowl (preferably glass or ceramic) so it has room to double in bulk and once after it has been reshaped into loaves, rolls, pizza, etc.

NOTE: Bread dough may be frozen up to 4 weeks. Let dough rise once in a warm place, punch down, shape, and wrap well in freezer wrap. When ready to use remove from freezer and let stand in warm place to rise to desired size.

NOTE: A damp cloth over the rising bread dough is used for moisture. Moisture helps the rising process. Plastic wrap may also be used to cover the dough during rising. It will retain the moisture created by the gas bubbles.

NOTE: Sugar contributes flavor. It also helps to manufacture gas bubbles. Gas bubbles make the dough rise. Sugar also helps in browning the crust during baking.

FLOUR

NOTE: Flour is the basic framework of bread. Add enough so that the dough does not stick to your hands. If it is added *AFTER* the dough has risen, it could give a coarser texture.

NOTE: Regardless of what other recipes say, using bread flour produces a better dough. Bread flour may be bought at the grocery store in bags marked bread flour. Sometimes it may be bought at certain bakeries. Check on a couple of bakeries in your neighborhood.

NOTE: Most supermarkets carry bread flour. If you can't find it you may use all-purpose flour. The difference in the flours is in the variety of wheat. Bread flour has a special blend of high-protein wheats to give a flour that is higher in gluten than most all-purpose flours. More gluten means the yeast bread can rise higher and bake into light, tender bread. Also use bread flour for a more flexible dough when making strudels.

SHAPING THE DOUGH

NOTE: Some recipes call for rolling out the bread dough with a rolling pin. This is done to remove all the bubbles that would otherwise make large holes in the baked bread.

NOTE: Let bread rest or relax for 10 minutes after punching down. It will roll out more easily after this resting period.

NOTE: Bread may be shaped into various forms. Besides making rectangular loaves, rolls, pizza or French loaves try braiding the dough, cutting large slashes through the top of the dough or make round loaves. These variations in shapes may be done with almost any bread recipe.

CRUSTS

NOTE: For a tender, brown crust brush the bread with melted shortening, butter or oil before baking.

NOTE: A crisp, shiny crust will result if you brush the bread with milk or egg diluted with water. An egg white, yolk, or the entire egg may be used.

NOTE: Spray or brush loaf with water before baking and twice during the first ten minutes of baking to achieve a crusty exterior. Wonderful technique for crusty FRENCH BREAD!!

NOTE: Liquids used in making bread are water, milk, potato water, and fruit juices. Pasteurized milk need not be scalded. Water gives bread a crisp crust. Bread made with milk has a velvety grain, a creamier white crumb, and a browner crust then that of a loaf made with water. Potato water and fruit juice give the bread more flavor and moisture.

CARE AND STORAGE AFTER BAKING

NOTE: To slice warm bread lay the bread on its side and slice with a bread knife or electric knife. Any other way and the bread will not slice properly.

NOTE: Let bread cool in pan 5-10 minutes or as recipe directs. Remove bread from pan immediately after cooling period to prevent a soggy bottom crust.

NOTE: Fat such as butter, margarine, lard, vegetable shortening, or salad oil makes the bread dough tender. It also improves the shelf life, flavor, and browning of the bread.

NOTE: Freshly baked bread may be frozen and is kept fresher by freezing than if stored at room temperature. Wrap cooled bread in freezer wrap and freeze up to six months before using. If baked bread isn't going to be frozen then store it in a plastic bag so the bread won't dry out.

ENGLISH MUFFIN BREAD

1-2 Loaves

	3 Cups	6 Cups
Bread flour	3 cups	6 cups
Water (105°-115°)	1/4 cup	1/2 cup
Yeast	1 pkg.	1 pkg.
Sugar	1-1/2 tsp.	1 Tbsp.
Salt	1 tsp.	2 tsp.
Baking soda	1/8 tsp.	1/4 tsp.
Milk	1 cup	2 cups
Cornmeal		
	1 loaf	2 loaves

Sprinkle yeast in warm water in a liquid measuring cup. *DO NOT STIR.* Let rest 10 minutes, when yeast is ready it will rise to the top of the water. Insert blade. Add flour, sugar, salt and baking soda; pulse 3-4 times to mix dry ingredients. Measure milk and set aside. While waiting for the yeast prepare 8-1/2x4-1/2 inch loaf pan(s) by greasing lightly and sprinkling with cornmeal. When yeast has surfaced, stir and add the milk to the yeast mixture. With machine running add the yeast mixture in a steady stream through the feedtube. Process 30 seconds after dough forms a ball. The dough will be stiff but very sticky. If using a double recipe, divide dough in half and shape each portion to form a loaf. Place dough in loaf pan(s); sprinkle top with additional cornmeal. Cover with damp towel or plastic wrap and let stand in warm place until almost doubled in bulk, 1 to 1-1/2 hours. Bake at 400° for 25 minutes, or until top of loaf is lightly browned and loaf sounds hollow when tapped with fingers. Remove from pan(s) at once and let cool on wire rack.

NOTE: This recipe only has one rising period before baking.

FRENCH BREAD

1-3 Loaves

	3 Cups	6 Cups	8 Cups
Bread flour	3 cups	6 cups	8 cups
Yeast	1 pkg.	1 pkg.	1 pkg.
Water (105°-115°)	1 cup	2 cups	2-2/3 cups
Sugar (optional)	1-1/2 tsp.	1 Tbsp.	4 tsp.
Salt	1 tsp.	2 tsp.	1 Tbsp.

Sprinkle yeast in warm water in a liquid measuring cup. *DO NOT STIR.* Let rest ten minutes, when yeast is ready it will rise to the top of the water. Insert blade in workbowl; add flour holding back 1/2 cup flour for each 3 cups in the recipe. Add sugar and salt, pulse 2-3 times to combine ingredients. When yeast has surfaced, stir. With machine running add yeast mixture in steady stream through the feed-tube. When the mixture forms a ball let dough process for about 30 seconds. Stop machine, if dough is sticky add remaining flour. Pulse 4-5 times to blend in flour. Process an additional 30 seconds. Dough should pull away from sides of workbowl and form a ball. This is when the dough is kneading. Stop the machine and check the consistency of the dough. It should feel soft like your ear lobe. If necessary, add 2 tablespoons of flour, pulse flour in and then continue processing another 10 seconds. Dough should look smooth and elastic.

Place dough in a large greased bowl, turn to grease top. Cover with plastic wrap or a damp towel. Let rise until doubled, about 2-3 hours. Punch down. Use the ball of dough or divide dough in half if using 6 cups of flour and thirds if using 8 cups of flour.

Shape into a French loaf by rolling each portion on a lightly floured surface to a 10x15 inch rectangle. Roll up jelly roll fashion* starting with the long edge. Pinch the edge of the roll to itself. Tuck in the ends to the seam or taper together. Place the shaped loaf seam side down on a greased baking sheet. Let rise until double, about 30 minutes. Bake in a 375° oven for 30 to 40 minutes.

*NOTE: The dough is rolled into a rectangle, then formed in a jelly roll to eliminate air bubbles and to insure an even interior texture.

FRENCH BREAD VARIATIONS   6 Recipes

After basic FRENCH BREAD dough has risen once try one of these variations. Use the amount of dough from 3 cups of flour which is equal to about 1-1/2 pounds of dough.

GARLIC BUBBLE LOAF   1 Loaf

1 to 1-1/2 pounds FRENCH BREAD dough
1/4 cup melted butter
1 egg
1/8 tsp. garlic powder
1 Tbsp. chopped parsley (3-4 sprigs)
1/4 tsp. salt

Insert ⌐Ꮶ, add butter, egg, garlic, parsley and salt. Pulse-chop 4-5 times. Remove ⌐Ꮶ. Cut or tear bread dough into walnut size pieces. Dip in mixture in workbowl and place each ball in one layer in a 9x5x3 inch loaf pan. It will look crowded. Let rise 20-30 minutes. Bake at 375° for 30 minutes.

CINNAMON BUBBLE LOAF   1 Loaf

1 to 1-1/2 pounds FRENCH BREAD dough
1/2 cup sugar
1-1/2 tsp. cinnamon
1/4 cup melted butter

Mix sugar and cinnamon together. Melt butter either in microwave on LOW for 30 seconds or on low heat in a saucepan. Cut or tear bread dough into walnut size pieces. Dip in butter, roll in sugar mixture. Place in one layer in a well greased 9x5x3 inch loaf pan. It will look crowded. Let rise 20-30 minutes. Bake at 375° for 30 minutes.

AUNTIE'S PEPPERONI BREAD   1 Loaf

1 to 1-1/2 pounds FRENCH BREAD dough
1 egg
1 tsp. water
1/4 pound pepperoni or hard salami(frozen)
6 oz. mozarella cheese (1-1/2 cups shredded)
4-6 green onions (1/2 cup sliced)

After dough has risen once, roll out on a lightly floured board
into a 13x9 inch rectangle. Beat egg and water together. Brush dough
with egg mixture, save any remaining for glazing crust. Insert thin
(1-2 mm) ⌒. Place frozen pepperoni* or hard salami in feedtube,
making sure the feedtube is packed. Process using a gentle pressure
on the pusher. Spread slices on dough. (Pepperoni or hard salami
may be pulse-chopped 6-8 times using the ⌒.Sprinkle chopped pepperoni or salami on dough. Remove metal blade and insert thin ⌒.)
Process green onions by "dancing" onion up and down on ⌒
through the feedtube.** Sprinkle sliced onions on pepperoni. Remove
slicing disc and insert ⊙. Process cheese*** using push-release
method***. Sprinkle cheese over meat and onions. Roll up tightly
starting with the long edge. Pinch the edge of the roll to itself to
form a seam. Tuck in ends to seal. Lay seam side down on a
greased baking sheet. Cover and let rise for 10-15 minutes. Brush
with remaining beaten egg. Bake in a 375° oven for 30-40 minutes.

*PEPPERONI, SLICED
*TIP: Pepperoni must be frozen for successful slicing because of the high
fat content. Remove casing, if desired, before freezing. If you can't slice
the pepperoni with a knife then the food processor can't either. Do not push
hard on the pusher when processing the pepperoni. The processor will be
noisy when slicing pepperoni. Use a thin slicing blade like 1-2mm for best
results.*

**SLICES—EVEN SLICES OF LONG SLENDER VEGETABLES OR "DANCING"
TIP: This tip applies especially to celery and green onions. Insert SLICING DISC. Lock cover in place. Hold onto UNTRIMMED tops and insert in feedtube. With the machine running move the vegetable up and down in the feedtube and stop slicing when the tops of the vegetable reach the top of the feedtube. DO NOT try to process your fingers.

***MOZARELLA CHEESE, SHREDDED
TIP: Place cheese in freezer for 20 minutes to insure good shredding results. Use this idea with any soft cheese like mozarella, Monterey jack or muenster.

***CHEESE, PUSH-RELEASE METHOD
TIP: Place piece of very cold cheese into the feedtube. Set pusher in feedtube and lock cover. Turn machine on, press moderately on the pusher. release pressure by pulling up on the pusher. Repeat pressing and releasing of pusher until last piece is processed.

BAKED FRENCH TOAST   4 Servings

1 loaf FRENCH BREAD (baked)
1/2 cup butter or margarine
2/3 cup brown sugar
1-2 tsp. cinnamon
1 cup milk
3 eggs
1/4 tsp. salt

Insert ⚒. Add butter, sugar and cinnamon, pulse-chop 6-8 times and then process until creamy. Spread butter mixture evenly in a 10 x 15 inch baking pan. Cut loaf of bread into 1 to 1-1/2 inch slices (8 slices will work best). Add milk, eggs, and salt to workbowl. Pulse-chop 3-4 times until blended. Pour mixture in deep dish and soak each bread slice until well saturated. Place bread slices on top of butter mixture. Bake at 350° for 25-35 minutes. Serve with sour cream and jam, or with maple syrup.

NOTE: One to two day old bread is best for this recipe.

PIZZA

A bread recipe using three cups of flour will yield one pizza. Follow the FRENCH BREAD recipe, but add 2 tablespoons of oil for each 3 cups of flour. After yeast has surfaced, add the oil to the yeast mixture before pouring into the flour. When finished kneading the dough should feel soft and satiny. Let rise 2-3 hours or until double in bulk. Punch down dough. Let dough rest for 10 minutes. This resting time makes it easier to roll or pat dough into a 10x15x1-1/2 inch baking sheet. Brush the top with oil and cover with plastic wrap. Let rise for 30-60 minutes.* While it rises prepare the sauce and process the different toppings that you wish. Make the simple PIZZA SAUCE listed or experiment with your own variations.

*NOTE: The longer the pizza dough rises in the the baking sheet the lighter and thicker it will be. The dough could rise as little as 30 minutes or as long as 2 hours. The different rising time will give varying textures. Professional pizza parlors use this long rising technique also. Experiment with different rising times to see how your family likes it.

PIZZA SAUCE

1 Cup

1-8 oz. can tomato sauce
1/4 tsp. garlic powder
1/2 tsp. salt.
1/2 tsp. oregano
1/2 tsp. basil
2 tsp. minced onion (optional)

Place all ingredients in a saucepan and simmer for 30 minutes. To complete PIZZA—Preheat oven to 425°. Remove plastic wrap from crust. Add sauce (1 cup per pizza), pepperoni, mushrooms, peppers, cooked crumbled sausage, or any other food toppings you desire *EXCEPT* for the mozzarella cheese. See INDEX for TIPS on processing various toppings. Bake 20-25 minutes at 425° or until bottom crust is golden brown. Remove pizza, sprinkle cheese on top of pizza. Return to oven, turn off oven and heat cheese for another 5 minutes. Pizza will be thick and yummy with the cheese just melted and delicious!

WHOLE WHEAT CINNAMON-RAISIN BREAD

1-2 Loaves

	3 Cups	6 Cups
Water (105°-115°)	3/4 cup	1-1/2 cups
Yeast	1 pkg.	1 pkg.
Bread flour	2 cups	4 cups
Whole wheat flour	1 cup	2 cups
Salt	1 tsp.	2 tsp.
Cinnamon	1 tsp.	2 tsp.
Brown sugar	3 Tbsp.	1/2 cup
Butter or margarine	3 Tbsp.	6 Tbsp.
Eggs	1 egg	2 eggs
Raisins	1/2 cup	1 cup
	1 loaf	2 loaves

Sprinkle yeast in warm water in a liquid measuring cup. *DO NOT STIR.* Let rest 10 minutes, when yeast is ready it will rise to the top of the water. Insert blade. Add flours, salt, cinnamon, sugar and butter; pulse-chop 6-8 times to mix ingredients. When yeast has surfaced, stir. Add egg(s) to the yeast mixture. With the machine running add yeast mixture in a steady stream through the feedtube Process for 30 seconds after dough forms a ball. Stop machine, if dough is sticky add 1-2 tablespoons flour. Pulse 4-5 times to blend in flour. Process dough an additional 30 seconds. Add raisins and pulse-chop 4-6 times just to combine raisins and dough. Place dough in a large greased bowl, turn to grease top. Cover with plastic wrap, let rise in a warm place until doubled in bulk, about 2-3 hours. Punch down dough, divide IF making a 6 cup recipe. Grease one or two 9x5x3 inch loaf pans. Roll out dough in a 9x12 inch rectangle to remove air bubbles. Roll up short side and tuck ends under. Place in pans. Cover with plastic wrap, let rise about 1-1/2 to 2 hours or until doubled in size. Bake at 375° for 30-35 minutes, until brown on top and bread sounds hollow when tapped lightly with fingers.

Cool 10 minutes in pan(s). Remove from pan and cool completely on wire rack. Frost if desired with 1 cup confectioners' sugar mixed with 1-2 tablespoons milk or lemon juice.

NOTE: Eliminate cinnamon and raisins for a plain WHOLE WHEAT BREAD variation.

CHEESE BREAD

1 Loaf

1 pkg. (1/4 oz.) active dry yeast
1/2 cup warm water (105°-115°)
1 oz. parmesan cheese (1/4 cup grated)
4 oz. cheddar cheese (1 cup shredded)
3-1/4 cups bread flour
2 Tbsp. butter or margarine
4 tsp. sugar
1 tsp. salt
1/2 cup milk
Butter, melted

Sprinkle yeast in warm water in a liquid measuring cup. *DO NOT STIR.* Let rest 10 minutes, when yeast is ready it will rise to the top of the water. Insert ⚒. Cut parmesan cheese in four small pieces. With machine running drop parmesan through feedtube, replace pusher. Process until it is finely grated. Leave cheese in workbowl. Cut cheddar cheese into 4-6 small pieces and put in workbowl. Pulse-chop 3-4 times. Add the flour, butter, sugar and salt to the workbowl. Pulse the flour mixture and cheeses together until thoroughly mixed, about 10 pulses. When the yeast has surfaced, stir. Add milk to the yeast mixture. With the machine running add the yeast mixture* in a steady stream through the feedtube. Continue processing for 30 seconds after the mixture has formed a ball.** This is when the food processor is kneading the dough. Place dough in a large greased bowl, cover with plastic wrap or a damp towel. Keep in a warm place; let dough rise until double in bulk, about two hours. Punch down and shape to fit into a 9x5x3 inch greased loaf pan. Brush with melted butter or margarine. Cover and allow dough to rise in pan until doubled in bulk, about 1-1/2 hours.

Bake in a 375° oven for 50-60 minutes or until bread sounds hollow when tapped and is golden brown. Cool 10 minutes in pan, then turn out onto a wire rack, cool.

NOTE: You may double this recipe for a larger capacity food processor. Use the beginning directions for processing the cheese. Then remove the METAL BLADE and insert the DOUGH BLADE, proceed as directed.

*BREADS, YEAST—ADDING LIQUIDS

TIP: When making bread first put flour and other dry ingredients in workbowl. Then add liquids through the feedtube as machine is running. The blade will not incorporate the ingredients properly if this sequence is not followed.

**OVERLOADING MACHINE

TIP: When making bread in the food processor the dough should clean the sides of the workbowl. If dough is too sticky then add flour 1 tablespoon at a time while machine is running. You may also turn machine off and add flour, then pulse flour in until a ball is formed. Continue to process 30-60 seconds.

**OVERLOADING MACHINE

TIP: When making bread the motor may slow down if too much dough is being processed for your size machine.

CRUSTY POTATO BREAD   1 Loaf

	3 Cups	6 Cups
Yeast	1 pkg.	1 pkg.
Water (105°-115°)	3/4 cup	1-1/4 cups
Flour	3 Tbsp.	3 Tbsp.
Salt	1-1/2 tsp.	3 tsp.
Caraway seeds	1/2 tsp.	1 tsp.
Mashed potato*	1/4 cup	1/2 cup
Bread flour	2-1/2 cups	4-1/2 cups
	6 Inch Loaf	9 Inch Loaf

Stir yeast and 3 tablespoons flour into warm water in a liquid measuring cup. Cover with plastic wrap and let rise for 30 minutes.** Insert blade in workbowl. Add bread flour less 1/2 cup, salt, caraway seeds, and potato. Pulse 4-5 times to blend ingredients. With machine running add yeast mixture in a steady stream through the feedtube. Process 30 seconds after it forms a ball. Stop machine, if dough is sticky add remaining flour. Pulse 4-5 times to blend in flour. Process dough an additional 30 seconds.*** Place dough in a large, lightly greased bowl; turn to grease top. Cover and let rise in a warm place until doubled, about 1-1/2 to 2 hours. Punch dough down, shape into a ball. Place in a well greased 6 or 9 inch ovenproof skillet or casserole and flatten to fit. Let rise until doubled, about 35 minutes. Brush loaf with water. With a knife make a 1/2 inch deep cut in the center of the loaf in the form of a cross. Bake in a 375° oven for 60-75 minutes or until loaf is golden brown and sounds hollow when tapped. Turn out onto a wire rack to cool. Crustiness is best when served the same day, but bread is great sliced and made into sandwiches.

NOTE: This size loaf is great for appetizer recipes that are hollowed out and have a dip served in them. Use the center of the bread for dippers.

***NOTE:** No leftover mashed potatoes? Microwave a small (3-1/2 inch) potato on HIGH until soft, or boil a potato in a saucepan until fork tender. Peel, insert SHREDDING DISC, add potato to feedtube and shred into workbowl before proceeding with flour mixture. You may also freeze mashed potatoes to use when you bake this bread.

****NOTE:** The wonderful crusty exterior of this bread is due to proofing the yeast and flour together for an extended time.

***BREADS, YEAST—BLADE RISING

TIP: Over processing the dough or overloading the machine may cause the blade to rise in workbowl. If overloading is the problem, stop the machine, remove half of the dough and process it in 2 batches instead of one.

FRESH FRUIT SOUR CREAM COFFEECAKE

9-Inch Coffeecake

2-1/2 cups all-purpose flour
1 tsp. baking powder
1/2 tsp. baking soda
2/3 cup walnut pieces
1/2 pound fresh fruit
   about 1 cup sliced or chopped
2 Tbsp. sugar

1/2 tsp. cinnamon
1 cup butter or margarine
1-1/4 cups sugar
1 tsp. vanilla
2 eggs
1 cup sour cream (8 oz.)

Insert ⚙, add flour, baking powder and baking soda. Pulse for 3 seconds to combine. Remove and set aside on wax paper. Add walnuts,* fresh fruit, 2 tablespoons sugar and cinnamon, pulse chop 3-4 times until walnuts are medium fine and fruit is chopped. Remove and set aside in a bowl. Do not wash workbowl. Put butter, cut in 16 pieces, into workbowl and pulse-chop 3-4 times to soften butter. Add eggs, sugar and vanilla, pulse 3-4 times. Process continuously until fluffy, about 1 minute. Add sour cream, pulse 3 times. Scrape down sides of workbowl. Add flour mixture and pulse-chop 2-4 times or just until blended.**

Spread 1/3 of the batter into a greased and floured 9 inch tubepan. The layer will be about 1/2 inch thick. Sprinkle with half the fruit mixture. Add 1/3 more batter, remaining fruit mixture and cover with remaining batter. Mix together 1 tablespoon sugar and 1/4 teaspoon cinnamon, sprinkle on top. Bake at 350° for 55-65 minutes. Remove when crumbs just cling to toothpick. Cool ten minutes, then turn out on wire rack to complete cooling. Cool with top side on rack so bottom does not stick to rack.

NOTE: Fruits like rhubarb, sour cherries, plums, peeled peaches or apples are good choices for this recipe. Frozen fruit may be substituted for fresh. Measure out 1-1/4 cups loose frozen fruit, pulse-chop frozen fruit 2-3 times then add the nuts and proceed with recipe.

*NOTE: For chunky nut lovers, first pulse-chop fruit, sugar and cinnamon 2-3 times, THEN add nuts and pulse-chop 2 more times.

**NOTE: A small (4 cup) processor workbowl will be quite full. Scrape down sides and pulse once more. If flour is not incorporated stir by hand so you don't overprocess batter that is at the bottom of the workbowl.

SWEET BREAD DOUGH   12-30 Buns or 1-3 Loaves

	3 Cups	4 Cups	6 Cups	8 Cups
Bread flour	2-1/2 to 3 cups	3-1/2 to 4 cups	5-1/2 to 6 cups	7-1/2 to 8 cups
Water (105°-115°)	1/4 cup	1/4 cup	1/4 cup	1/4 cup
Yeast	1 pkg.	1 pkg.	1 pkg.	1 pkg.
Sugar	2 Tbsp.	3 Tbsp.	4 Tbsp.	6 Tbsp.
Salt	1/2 tsp.	3/4 tsp.	1 tsp.	1-1/2 tsp.
Milk	1/2 cup	3/4 cup	1 cup	1-2/3 cups
Egg	1 egg	1 egg	2 eggs	2 eggs
Butter	1/4 cup	6 Tbsp.	1/2 cup	12 Tbsp.
	12 buns/ 1 loaf	15 buns/ 1 loaf	24 buns/ 2 loaves	30 buns/ 3 loaves

Sprinkle yeast in warm water in a measuring cup. *DO NOT STIR*. Let rest 10 minutes, when yeast is ready it will rise to the top of the water. Insert blade in workbowl. Add flour, salt, sugar, and butter. Pulse 6-10 times or until butter is mixed into the flour. When yeast has surfaced, stir and add egg(s) and milk. With machine running add yeast mixture in a steady stream through the feedtube. If dough is too sticky and slows machine down, add more flour. Process for another 30 seconds or until smooth and elastic.* (If your machine seems strained, follow this procedure. Leave dough in food processor and let rest 15 minutes. Pulse 3-4 times and let machine run for 30 seconds to knead or until dough is smooth and elastic. It should not be sticky. If dough is still sticky add more flour. Process for another 30 seconds.) Place in a large, lightly greased bowl, cover, and let rise in a warm place until doubled in bulk, about 2 hours.**

Pinch off balls of dough about 1-1/2 to 2 inches in diameter and place on a greased baking sheet, allowing at least 3 inches between the balls. Let rise until puffy, about 10 minutes, in a warm place. Flatten each ball of dough with fingers to about 3/8 inch thickness. Let rise again until puffy, about 10 minutes, then flatten *CENTERS* of rounds, leaving edges slightly higher to hold in the filling. Beat

1 egg and brush rounds with egg, spoon 2-3 tablespoons of the filling mixture into center of each round. Bake in 375° oven for 15-20 minutes or until filling is set and crust is golden brown. Serve hot; or cool and wrap well in foil or plastic wrap and freeze. Remove from freezer a half hour before serving; slip into a 375° oven until heated through, about 5 minutes. May heat in microwave oven for 1 minute on MEDIUM-HIGH power for 2 rolls.

NOTE: Dough may be shaped into number of loaves listed under ingredients instead of rolls.

*PROCESSING TIME FOR YEAST BREADS
TIP: When processing sweet breads process about 30 seconds. When processing typical bread dough process about 60 seconds.

**BREAD DOUGH RISING SLOWLY
TIP: The dough may be rising in a location that has too cool a temperature. The best temperature for good rising is between 75-80°. If the dough is very rich with fat, sugar, or eggs it will take longer to rise.

CREAM CHEESE FILLING   2 Cups

1/4 cup sugar
Zest of one lemon (2 tsp. grated)
1-8 oz.pkg. cream cheese
2 eggs
1 Tbsp. lemon juice
1 tsp. vanilla
1/2 cup sour cream

Insert⟨⟩ , add sugar to workbowl. Peel lemon with vegetable peeler. With machine running drop lemon peel through feedtube and let process until very fine, about 1-2 minutes. Add cream cheese and pulse chop 6-7 times. Add eggs, lemon juice and vanilla and pulse chop 3-4 times. Add sour cream and pulse chop 2-3 times or until smooth. Fills 20-24 buns. Putting jelly or jam on top of the cheese mixture after it is cooked is a real treat!

NOTE: Increase or decrease CREAM CHEESE FILLING recipe depending on the quantity of dough prepared.

VARIATIONS: Add PIZZA SAUCE and cheese to unfilled dough and serve as PIZZA BUNS for an afternoon snack or noontime meal. Add jam or thick cranberry sauce to unfilled dough for JAM/FRUIT BUNS.

CRACKED WHEAT BREAD

1-2 Loaves

	3 Cups	6 Cups
Water for soaking	1/3 cup	3/4 cup
Bulgar wheat	1/3 cup	3/4 cup
Yeast	1 pkg.	1 pkg.
Warm water(105°-115°)	1/4 cup	1/4 cup
Whole wheat flour	1/2 cup	1 cup
Bread flour	2 to 2-1/2 cups	4-1/2 to 5 cups
Salt	1/2 tsp.	1 tsp.
Honey	3 Tbsp.	1/3 cup
Butter or margarine	1-1/2 Tbsp.	3 Tbsp.
Apple juice	3/4 cup	1-1/2 cups
	1 loaf	2 loaves

Combine first quantity of water with bulgar wheat. Place in microwave and cook on HIGH power until water has been absorbed (4-5 minutes). If using the range top, place in a small saucepan over medium heat. Heat water and bulgar to boiling point. Reduce heat and cook until water has been absorbed, about 2-3 minutes. Set aside to cool.

Sprinkle yeast in 1/4 cup warm water in a liquid measuring cup. *DO NOT STIR*. Let rest ten minutes, when yeast is ready it will rise to the top of the water. Insert blade, add wheat and bread flour holding back 1/2 cup bread flour. Add cooled bulgar wheat to flour in workbowl and pulse twice. Add salt, honey and butter* to workbowl and pulse 4-5 times. When yeast has surfaced, stir. Add the apple juice to the yeast mixture. With machine running add yeast mixture in steady stream through the feedtube. Process for 30 seconds after it forms a ball. Stop machine; if dough is sticky, add remaining flour. Pulse 4-5 times to blend in flour. Process dough an additional 30-40 seconds. The dough should be smooth except for the grains of bulgar wheat that are noticeable.

130

Shape dough into a ball and place in a large and generously oiled glass or ceramic bowl. Turn once to coat entire surface of dough. Cover with a damp towel or plastic wrap and let rise in a warm place until doubled in bulk, about 2-3 hours.** Punch down dough, divide if making a double recipe. Grease one or two 8-1/2x4-1/2 inch loaf pans. Shape dough and place in pan(s). Cover with a damp towel or plastic wrap, let rise about 2 hours or until double in size. Bake at 400° 30-35 minutes or until brown on top and bread sounds hollow when tapped lightly with fingers. Cool 10 minutes in pans. Remove from pan(s) and cool completely on wire rack. Wrap tightly in plastic wrap. Freeze if necessary.

*WARMING INGREDIENTS FOR YEAST BREADS
TIP: No need to melt butter or margarine, or heat honey or molasses when using the food processor. The food processor will incorporate these ingredients well enough to eliminate these steps.

**BREAD DOUGH RISING SLOWLY
TIP: The dough may be rising in a location that has too cool a temperature. The best temperature for good rising is between 75-80°. If the dough is very rich with fat, sugar, or eggs it will take longer to rise. Whole grain flours make heavier doughs and these take longer to rise.

NOTE: Bulgar wheat can be purchased in health food stores and the foreign food section of the supermarket. It comes in different grain sizes from 0-5. A coarser grain (#4-5) is best in this recipe.

RYE BREAD

1 Loaf

1 pkg. (1/4 oz.) active dry yeast
3/4 cup warm water (105° - 115°)
Zest* of half a large orange
2 Tbsp. brown sugar
2 cups bread flour
1 cup medium rye flour
1 tsp. salt
1/2 tsp. fennel seed
2 Tbsp. butter
2 Tbsp. dark molasses
1 egg

Sprinkle yeast in warm water in liquid measuring cup. *DO NOT STIR.* Let rest 10 minutes, when yeast is ready it will rise to the top of the water. Insert ⬚. With machine running add orange zest and process 30 seconds. Stop machine, scrape sides of workbowl and add brown sugar, pulse 3-4 times. Continue processing about one minute until orange zest is fine.** Add both flours less 1/2 cup bread flour, salt and fennel. Pulse 3-4 times. Add butter, molasses*** and egg, pulse 5-6 times. When yeast has surfaced, stir. With machine running add yeast mixture in a steady stream through the feedtube. The dough should leave the sides of the workbowl forming a ball, process for 30 seconds. Stop machine, if dough is sticky add remaining flour. Pulse 4-5 times to blend in flour. Process dough an additional 30 seconds. The dough should be smooth and elastic. Place in a greased 2 quart bowl and turn to grease top of dough. Cover with plastic wrap or a damp towel. Let rise in a warm place until doubled in size, about 2-3 hours.

Punch down and shape in a loaf. Place in either an 8 or 9 inch loaf pan and let rise again until dough reaches top of pan, about 2-3 hours. Bake at 375° for 30-40 minutes or until loaf is brown and sounds hollow when tapped.

*NOTE: Zest of an orange is the orange peel. Use either a zester or a vegetable peeler to remove thin pieces of skin.

**CITRUS PEEL, GRATED LEMON, ORANGE, LIME
TIP: Any citrus fruit skin may be processed in the food processor to give you grated rind. Peel a thin layer from the entire fruit with a vegetable peeler. Insert METAL BLADE in clean dry workbowl for best results. With machine running drop peelings through feedtube. Process 2-3 minutes. Scrape bowl down if necessary. If peel is not fine enough add some of the sugar called for in the recipe. The metal blade can grate the peel more easily when there is a larger quantity of food in the workbowl. Use immediately or freeze.

**NOTE: You may double this recipe for a larger capacity food processor. Use the directions for processing the zest and brown sugar. Then remove the METAL BLADE, insert the DOUGH BLADE and proceed as directed. This dough will strain the motor if you do not use the DOUGH BLADE with a double recipe.

***WARMING INGREDIENTS FOR YEAST BREADS
TIP: No need to melt butter or margarine, or heat honey or molasses when using the food processor. The food processor will incorporate these ingredients well enough to eliminate these steps.

CROISSANTS

	3 Cups	6 Cups
Bread flour	3 cups	5 cups
Yeast	1 pkg.	1 pkg.
Water(105°-115°)	1/4 cup	1/2 cup
Sugar	1 Tbsp.	2 Tbsp.
Salt	1/2 tsp.	1 tsp.
Shortening	1 Tbsp.	2 Tbsp.
Milk	1/2 cup	1 cup
Egg	1 egg	2 eggs
Butter (softened)*	1/2 cup	1 cup
	12 rolls	24 rolls

Sprinkle yeast in warm water in a liquid measuring cup. *DO NOT STIR.* Let rest 10 minutes; when yeast is ready it will rise to the top of the water. Insert blade. Add flour (less 1/2 cup), sugar, salt, and shortening. Pulse-chop 5-6 times to combine ingredients. When yeast has surfaced, stir. Add milk and eggs to yeast mixture. With machine running add the yeast mixture in a steady stream through the feed-tube. This will take about 30-45 seconds. The dough will be sticky and soft. Add remaining 1/2 cup flour and process until dough pulls away from side of bowl and forms a ball, about 30-40 seconds more. This dough will be very soft, but should also be smooth and elastic. If it is still not forming a ball add 1-2 tablespoons of flour and pro-cess 10 seconds more. Place ball in a large greased bowl, turn to grease top. Cover with plastic wrap, let rise in a warm place until double in bulk, about 1-2 hours. Punch dough down. Cover; chill 1 hour or overnight.

Punch dough down again. Roll out dough on lightly floured board into a rectangle 18 x 12 inches; spread with 1/3 of the butter. Fold rectangle into thirds (6x12 inches), making 3 layers . Turn dough so folded sides will be the new long sides, roll out evenly to a 12x18 inch rectangle. Repeat butter layer, folding, and rolling twice more. Divide dough in half if using a double recipe; chill 1 hour. Shape 1 section at a time. Roll into a rectangle 18x12 inches about 3/8 inch thick. Cut lengthwise in half, then crosswise into 3 sections. Cut each square into 2 triangles. Roll up each triangle beginning at long side.

Place rolls with point underneath on an ungreased baking sheet. Curve to form crescent. Cover and let rise in a warm place for 1 hour or until double in bulk. Chill for 15 minutes while oven preheats to 425°. This chilling makes the butter solid again and produces lighter, flakier croissants.

Use a technique called double panning to keep the rolls from burning. Place another baking sheet of same size or slightly larger under croissant baking sheet.** Place croissants in preheated oven. Bake for 15 minutes, reduce heat to 375° and bake 10-15 minutes longer until golden brown. Serve hot or freeze for later use.

NOTE: These are really fun to make. If you can't prepare these all in one day, divide the process into two days. The satisfaction and savings of making croissants is worth the time. The croissants will freeze well.

*BUTTER, SOFTENING
TIP: No need to worry about letting butter get soft again. Use the METAL BLADE. Cut cold butter in 4-6 equal pieces and add to workbowl. Pulse-chop 4-5 times, stop machine and scrape down sides of workbowl. Continue processing until butter is light, soft and fluffy.

NOTE: Beat one egg and 1 teaspoon of water together. Brush on croissants before baking for a shiny glaze. Freeze any remaining glaze to use the next time you bake bread.

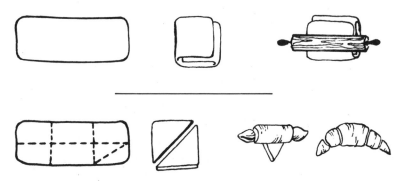

CROISSANT VARIATIONS   3 Recipes

HAM AND CHEESE:

Split baked croissant in half, add slices of ham and cheese and heat in microwave on LOW power until cheese is melted.

DESSERT:

Split baked croissant in half. Fill pastry bag or tube with STRAWBERRY BUTTER or BUCHE DE NOEL FROSTING. (See GIFTS WITH LOVE). Use star tip and pipe into split croissant for an elegant dessert. Dust with confectioners' sugar.

CINNAMON:

Just before rolling dough in croissant shape; sprinkle with cinnamon and sugar, then roll up. Proceed with rising and baking as directed.

BANANA BRAN BREAD   1 Loaf

1-1/2 cups all-purpose flour
2 tsp. baking powder
1/2 tsp. baking soda
1/2 tsp. salt
3 Tbsp. butter or margarine
1/2 cup sugar
1/4 cup water
1 egg
2-3 ripe bananas (1 cup mashed)
1/2 cup nut pieces, optional
1 cup ready-to-eat bran cereal

Insert ⚒, add dry ingredients. Process for 3 seconds and set aside on wax paper. Add butter, sugar, water, and egg to workbowl. Process 10-15 seconds until ingredients are well creamed. Scrape down sides of workbowl once during processing. Add bananas and pulse-chop 2-3 times. Add 1/2 cup loose nuts at this time if you wish a nut bread.* Place dry ingredients and bran in workbowl; pulse-chop 4 times, just until ingredients are blended. Put batter in a greased 9x5x3 inch loaf pan and bake in a preheated 350° for 45 to 50 minutes. Let cool 10 minutes, remove from pan and cool on a wire rack.

*NOTE: For chunky nut lovers; place dry ingredients and bran in workbowl first, before adding nuts, pulse-chop 2 times. Scrape down sides of workbowl, add nuts and pulse-chop 2 more times. DO NOT OVER PROCESS.

ZUCCHINI BREAD

1-2 Loaves

Flour, all-purpose	1-1/2 cup	3 cups
Baking soda	1/2 tsp.	1 tsp.
Baking powder	1/8 tsp.	1/4 tsp.
Cinnamon	1 tsp.	2 tsp.
Salt	1/8 tsp.	1/4 tsp.
Zucchini, unpeeled	1 small(1 cup)	1 medium(2 cups)
Eggs	2 eggs	3 eggs
Vegetable oil	1/2 cup	1 cup
Sugar	3/4 cup	1-1/2 cups
Brown sugar, packed	1/4 cup	1/2 cup
Vanilla	1 tsp.	2 tsp.
	1 loaf	2 loaves

Insert⚜, add dry ingredients and pulse-chop 2-4 times. Set aside on wax paper. Preheat oven to 350°. Insert ⊙ and shred zucchini, using medium pressure on pusher. Remove zucchini, measure, and set aside (amount of zucchini may be a little more or less and it won't affect the results.) With ⚜ in workbowl, add eggs and pulse 4 times, add oil and pulse twice. Add both sugars and vanilla; pulse twice, add dry ingredients and pulse twice. Scrape down sides of bowl. Add zucchini, pulse 2-3 times or just until flour disappears* and zucchini is coarsely chopped into the mixture. Place mixture** into a greased 9x5x3 inch loaf pan(s). Bake 40-50 minutes or until toothpick comes out with a few crumbs.*** Let cool 10 minutes, then turn out onto a wire rack to cool.

*MIXING QUICK BREADS
TIP: When doing quick breads in the food processor just pulse until flour disappears into the batter. Remember working with a food processor means seconds.

**METAL BLADE, CLEANING
TIP: To easily remove creamy, sticky dips, spreads or batters from the blade, first scrape most of the mixture from the workbowl. Put METAL BLADE and workbowl back on base, cover and lock machine. Pulse machine 2-3 times. The food clinging to the blade will spin off leaving a clean blade. Then remove the clean blade and scrape out any remaining mixture from the workbowl. Most blades have a knob or special notch to hold onto when the blade is soiled or slippery.

***NOTE:** When baking quick breads and cakes remember that they continue to cook 10 minutes after they are removed from the oven. Therefore, remove quick breads and cakes from the oven when there are still crumbs (not raw dough) on toothpick. The quick bread or cake will be very moist and delicious.

PUFFY PANCAKES

2-4 Servings

This recipe makes two large pancakes also known as German pancakes. This recipe is very impressive for a brunch or lovely breakfast and yet very easy.

2 Tbsp. butter or margarine
2/3 cup flour
1/4 tsp. baking powder
1/2 tsp. salt
4 eggs
1 Tbsp. sugar
2/3 cup milk

Preheat oven to 425°. Divide butter between two 9 inch pie pans; place in preheating oven to melt butter. Check after 3-5 minutes, don't let butter burn. Insert ⬥, add flour, baking powder and salt, pulse-chop 3 times. Add eggs, sugar and milk, pulse-chop just *TWICE. DO NOT OVERPROCESS.* The batter will be lumpy. Tilt baking dishes to coat with butter. Divide batter between two pans. Bake 15 minutes or until golden brown. Pancakes may collapse slightly when removed from oven. Serve with powdered sugar, fresh sweetened fruit, honey butter or syrup.

*NOTE: These pancakes are unlike regular pancakes, don't overprocess or they will not puff. Remember, 1 pulse is equal to 1 second.

SYRUP FOR WAFFLES AND PANCAKES

1-1/2 Cups

BROWN SUGAR MAPLE SYRUP:
1 cup dark brown sugar
1/2 cup warm water
1/4 tsp. maple flavoring

Insert 🔪. Add all ingredients to workbowl. Pulse 3-4 times. Process 1 minute. DO NOT COOK. Store in refrigerator.

BUTTERY MAPLE SYRUP:
2 Tbsp. butter
1/2 cup brown sugar
1 cup light corn syrup
1/2 cup water
1/4 tsp. maple flavoring

Insert 🔪. Pulse-chop sugar, butter and corn syrup together until blended. With machine running pour water and flavoring through feedtube. Process until combined. Heat through and serve.

NOTE: One of these variations can save the morning if you run out of syrup as long as you keep a bottle of maple flavoring on hand.

PRETZELS

20 Pretzels

This recipe is fun to make with children and it is very fast because there isn't any rising time.

Prepare the FRENCH BREAD dough as directed under 3 Cups of flour. Do not let the dough rise. After the dough is kneaded in the processor, divide it into 20 even portions. Roll each into a ball, then into a long rod. Twist into a pretzel or figure eight shape. Lay twisted pretzels on greased baking sheets. Brush with beaten egg, sprinkle with coarse salt. Bake at 425° for 12-15 minutes.

NOTES

DESSERTS

| METAL BLADE | SHREDDING DISC | DOUGH BLADE | SLICING DISC | FRENCH-FRY DISC |

Desserts are a pleasure to create in the food processor. Time consuming operations are accomplished in just seconds. It performs the operations of a kitchen mixer, blender and more. Easily cream cookie dough, chop nuts, whip cream or blend pie crusts with just the metal blade. Shave chocolate or shred nuts for garnish with the shredding disc. Top off a fruit dessert with lovely slices of fruit using the food processor or slice all the apples for a pie in just two minutes. You will find that many desserts can be prepared without washing the workbowl until after the preparation is completed.

Several of the tips that pertain to many dessert preparations are listed here. Make any dessert in the food processor and you'll soon see how indispensable this machine can be.

METAL BLADE, CLEANING

TIP: To easily remove creamy, sticky dips, spreads or batters from the blade, first scrape most of the mixture from the workbowl. Put METAL BLADE and workbowl back on base, cover and lock machine. Pulse machine 2-3 times. The food clinging to the blade will spin off leaving a clean blade. Then remove the clean blade and scrape out any remaining mixture from the workbowl. Most blades have a knob or special notch to hold onto when the blade is soiled or slippery.

OVERPROCESSED CAKES, COOKIES, QUICK BREAD

TIP: Flour mixtures are the last ingredients added to creamed mixtures in cakes, cookies, and quick breads. Overprocessing can occur once flour is added to the creamed mixture. Three to five pulses is all that is needed to mix flour into a creamed mixture. More than that will over process and you'll have "tough" baked products.

SIFTING INGREDIENTS

TIP: Pulsing all dry ingredients together in the workbowl, using the metal blade, combines them evenly just as sifting does.

WORKBOWL, HOLDING METAL BLADE WITH

TIP: Some processors have openings in the bottom of the METAL BLADE. Insert the index or middle finger through the outside center of the workbowl into this opening while the METAL BLADE is in the workbowl. Hold tightly with the finger and place thumb around bottom outer side of workbowl. Fan out the rest of the fingers over the bottom of the workbowl. Then remove contents of workbowl while holding onto the blade.

CHOCOLATE ZUCCHINI CAKE   1-9x13 Inch Cake

2-1/2 cups flour
1 tsp. baking soda
1/2 tsp. baking powder
1/4 cup cocoa
1/2 tsp. cinnamon
1/2 tsp. cloves
2 medium zucchini, unpeeled (2 cups shredded)
2 eggs
1-3/4 cups sugar
1/2 cup butter or margarine
1/2 cup oil
1/2 cup sour milk
1 tsp. vanilla
1/2 cup nut pieces, optional
1/4 cup chocolate chips

Insert ⚒, place the flour, baking soda, baking powder, cocoa, and spices in the workbowl; process for 2 seconds. Remove from workbowl and set aside on wax paper. Insert the ⊙ and cut zucchini to fit feedtube. Process using medium pressure on pusher. Measure and set aside.* Do not wash workbowl.

Insert ⚒, add eggs and sugar to the workbowl; process for 1 minute or until the mixture is thick and light colored. Add margarine and oil; process 1 minute or until the mixture is fluffy, stopping the machine once to scrape down the sides of the workbowl. Add milk and vanilla, pulse once. Add dry ingredients, pulse 2 times. Add zucchini and pulse 2 times. Do not over process. Nuts may be added at this point and pulse-chopped twice.** Spread batter into a greased and floured 9x13 inch pan. Sprinkle with chocolate chips. Bake at 325° for 40-45 minutes. No frosting is necessary. This cake freezes well.

*NOTE: Extra zucchini can be saved for use in salad or frozen for use in another recipe. During summer months shred extra zucchini and package in 2 cup quantities. Freeze—no blanching is necessary. Defrost, drain off extra liquid and use in ZUCCHINI QUICHE. Salting the zucchini for the ZUCCHINI QUICHE is not necessary if this method is used. You can also use the thawed zucchini without draining the liquid, in any cake or bread recipe as the liquid from the zucchini is part of those recipes.

**NUTS, CHOPPED DURING MIXING
TIP: Recipes in this book calling for nuts have the time needed for chopping as part of the recipe. If you omit the nuts, then pulse twice more since the pulsing for nuts was eliminated.

PEANUT BUTTER TORTE

10-12 Servings

3 oz. square milk chocolate
1/3 cup dry roasted peanuts
1/2 cup butter or margarine
1 cup flour
2/3 cup dry roasted peanuts
1-8 oz. pkg. cream cheese
1/3 cup peanut butter
1 cup confectioners' sugar
2 cups non-dairy whipped topping
  reserve half for last layer
1 pkg. (3-3/4 oz.) instant chocolate pudding
1 pkg. (3-3/4 oz.) instant vanilla pudding
2-3/4 cups milk

Insert (⊚). Place chocolate* in the feedtube and with very little pressure on the pusher, process the chocolate. Remove and reserve for garnish. Insert ⟲ and pulse chop 1/3 cup nuts 3-4 times. Set aside for garnish. With the ⟲ in the workbowl, add the butter or margarine. Cream by pulsing on and off. Add the flour, pulse twice. Add 2/3 cup nuts and pulse 3-4 times or until soft and mixture begins to form a ball. Put nut mixture in the bottom of a 9 inch springform pan. Bake 20 minutes at 350°. Cool.

Without washing workbowl or blade put the cream cheese and peanut butter in the workbowl. Process by pulsing until blended. Add the confectioners' sugar and process until creamy. Add half the whipped topping and pulse 3 times. Spread on top of the cooled base in the springform pan. Using the same workbowl and blade, add the pudding mixes.** With the machine running add the milk through the feedtube; process until the pudding thickens, 1-2 minutes. Spread on cream cheese layer in pan. Spread reserved whipped topping over the pudding layer. Sprinkle with reserved chocolate and 1/3 cup nuts. Refrigerate overnight. If the torte is cut too soon it will not be firm.

*CHOCOLATE SHAVINGS
TIP: Insert SHREDDING DISC. Put chocolate in the feedtube and with very little pressure on the pusher, process the chocolate. Do not process chocolate into a warm workbowl or it will melt the shaved chocolate.

**LEAKY WORKBOWL
TIP: By adding the dry ingredients first and then adding the liquid ingredients you keep the mixture from seeping out of the workbowl through the center workbowl opening.

PUMPKIN CAKE RING   12-16 Servings

LEMON GLAZE:
1/4 of a lemon*, zested
1 cup confectioners' sugar
1 tsp. lemon juice
1-1/2 Tbsp. cream or milk

PUMPKIN CAKE:
1 (18-1/2 oz.) pkg. yellow cake mix
2 tsp. cinnamon
1/2 tsp. ginger
1/2 tsp. nutmeg
2 eggs
1 cup pumpkin
Water as directed less 1/3 cup
Oil as directed in cake mix
1 cup nut pieces

Insert ⚙. With machine running drop lemon zest through feedtube and process until fine. If large pieces remain, add confectioners' sugar and continue processing. The processor will remove any lumps from the confectioners' sugar and finely grate the peel at the same time. Remove to small mixing bowl, add lemon juice and milk. Do not wash out workbowl. Add cake mix and spices to workbowl, pulse 3-5 times to combine. Add eggs, pumpkin, water and nut pieces, pulse-chop 4-5 times or just until ingredients are blended. Pour into a greased and floured 10 inch tube pan or a bundt pan. Bake at 350° for 40-45 minutes. Cool 10 minutes, remove from pan. Poke holes in cake and drizzle glaze slowly over cake. Cool before serving.

*NOTE: Zest of a lemon is the outside skin. Use either a zester or a vegetable peeler to remove thin pieces of skin.

GLAZED RUM CAKE

12-16 Servings

RUM CAKE:
1 cup walnut or pecan pieces
1 pkg. (18-1/2 oz) yellow cake mix
1 pkg. (3-3/4 oz.) instant vanilla pudding mix
4 eggs
1/2 cup cold water
1/2 cup oil
1/2 cup dark rum (80 proof)

BUTTER RUM GLAZE:
1/2 cup butter
1/4 cup water
1 cup sugar
1/2 cup dark rum (80 proof)

Preheat oven to 325°. Grease and flour a 10 inch tube pan or 12 cup bundt pan. Insert ⏚ in workbowl; add nuts, pulse chop 3-4 times or until nuts are coarsely chopped. Sprinkle nuts in the bottom of the cake pan. Place dry ingredients in the workbowl; add eggs, water, oil and rum. Pulse 2 times, scrape down sides of workbowl. Pulse twice more.* Pour batter over nuts in pan and bake 1 hour or until toothpick comes out with crumbs. Cool 10 minutes and invert on serving plate. With a skewer poke holes in the top of the cake so the glaze will be absorbed.

Prepare the glaze by melting butter in saucepan. Stir in water and sugar. Bring to boil and boil 5 minutes, stirring constantly. Remove from heat and stir in rum. (The glaze may also be prepared in the microwave. Melt butter in a 4 cup glass measure on HIGH for 45 seconds. Add water and sugar, bring to a boil using HIGH power. Stir, continue to boil 2-3 minutes longer being careful that glaze does not boil over. Stir in rum.) Drizzle and spread glaze evenly over top and sides of cake. Allow cake to absorb glaze and repeat process until all the glaze is gone.

*CAKE MIX

TIP: *Cake mixes require the METAL BLADE. Place the mix in the workbowl first, then add the liquid ingredients, eggs, water, or oil. Process 2 seconds, scrape down sides of the bowl, process 3 seconds more. Processing in this order prevents the batter from rising up the center shaft and onto the base causing a real mess and an unhappy food processor owner. Overprocessing will make a dry cake. Honest, 5 seconds is enough.*

*METAL BLADE, CLEANING

TIP: *To easily remove creamy, sticky dips, spreads or batters from the blade, first scrape most of the mixture from the workbowl. Put METAL BLADE and workbowl back on base, cover and lock machine. Pulse machine 2-3 times. The food clinging to the blade will spin off leaving a clean blade. Then remove the clean blade and scrape out any remaining mixture from the workbowl. Most blades have a knob or special notch to hold onto when the blade is soiled or slippery.*

SURPRISE BARS   4 Dozen Bars

2 cups flour
2 tsp. baking soda
1 tsp. salt
1/2 tsp. nutmeg
2 tsp. cinnamon
1-1/4 cup nuts (optional)
1 pound carrots (4 cups shredded)
2 cups sugar
4 eggs
1-1/2 cups vegetable oil
1 cup raisins

Insert ⚒. Add flour, baking soda, salt and spices to the workbowl and process for 2 seconds. Add nuts and pulse chop two times to coarsely chop nuts. Remove ingredients to waxpaper. Insert ⊙ and shred carrots, using firm pressure on pusher. Remove from workbowl. No need to wash the workbowl. Using the ⚒; process the eggs and sugar together until they are thick and lemon colored, about 1 minute. With the machine running, pour the oil through the feedtube and process for one minute more or until the mixture is fluffy. Add carrots and process 3 seconds. Add dry ingredients with nuts. Combine by pulse-chopping 2-3 times or until the flour just disappears. Pour the batter into a greased and floured 10-1/2x15-1/2x1 inch jelly roll pan. Bake at 350° for 30-40 minutes. Frost when cool with CREAM CHEESE FROSTING.

CREAM CHEESE FROSTING

1-1/2 Cups

1/4 cup butter
4 oz. cream cheese (1/2 of an 8 oz. pkg.)
2 cups confectioners' sugar
1 tsp. vanilla

Rinse workbowl while bars bake and prepare the frosting. Insert the 🔪 and cream all the ingredients together until fluffy, about 40-60 seconds.* Spread on cooled bars. This frosting recipe can be doubled to frost a standard 8-9 inch layer cake like MOM'S BANANA CAKE.

*METAL BLADE, CLEANING
TIP: To easily remove creamy, sticky dips, spreads or batters from the blade, first scrape most of the mixture from the workbowl. Put METAL BLADE and workbowl back on base, cover and lock machine. Pulse machine 2-3 times. The food clinging to the blade will spin off leaving a clean blade. Then remove the clean blade and scrape out any remaining mixture from the workbowl. Most blades have a knob or special notch to hold onto when the blade is soiled or slippery.

RUM FROSTING

1-1/2 to 2 Cups Frosting

1/4 cup butter
2-1/2 cups confectioners' sugar
1-1/2 tsp. rum extract
2 Tbsp. milk

Insert 🔪 , add butter and soften by pulsing. Scrape down sides of bowl if necessary. Add sugar, process until smooth and creamy. Add rum, pulse 2-3 times. Add milk, process until smooth. Use more milk if you want a creamier consistency. Frost EGGNOG COOKIES or a favorite spice cake.

HOLIDAY NUT COOKIES

32 Cookies

2 eggs, separated
1/2 cup sugar
1 cup butter or margarine
1 tsp. vanilla
2 cups flour
1 tsp. baking powder
1 cup pecan pieces

Insert ⌾. Add egg yolks and sugar. Pulse-chop 2-3 times, then process 30 seconds. Add butter or margarine, pulse-chop 4-5 times and continue processing 30 seconds. Add vanilla, pulse once. Add flour and baking powder, pulse once. Add nuts, pulse-chop 2-4 times. Remove dough and chill until firm enough to roll into balls about the size of a walnut. Beat egg whites and roll each ball in whites. Place on greased baking sheet. Press small pieces of candied cherry, candied fruit or a nut half on top of each. Bake in a 400° oven 10-15 minutes.

NOTE: This dough may be refrigerated several days. After the cookies are baked and cooled they may be frozen 1-3 months.

EGGNOG COOKIES

4 Dozen Cookies

1 egg
3/4 cup sugar
1 cup butter
2 tsps. vanilla extract
2 tsps. rum extract
1/4 tsp. salt
2 tsps. nutmeg
2 cups flour

Insert ⌾, add egg and sugar. Pulse 2-3 times. Add butter cut in 10-12 pieces, pulse 3-4 times. Continue processing for one minute. Add extracts, pulse once. Add salt, nutmeg and flour, scrape down sides of workbowl. Pulse 3-4 times. Chill mixture until it is firm enough to shape into balls. Use one tablespoon dough for each cookie. Place on an ungreased baking sheet and bake in a 350° oven 12-15 minutes. Cool and frost with RUM FROSTING if desired.

DEVIL'S FOOD WHIRLIGIG CAKE   2-9 Inch Layers

2 cups sifted cake flour*
1 tsp. salt
1/2 tsp. baking powder
1-1/2 tsp. baking soda
3 oz. unsweetened chocolate
2 cups sugar
1/2 cup shortening
3 eggs
1 tsp. vanilla
1-1/4 cups sour milk or buttermilk**

Insert ⚙, add flour, salt, baking powder and baking soda. Pulse 3-4 times and set aside. Break chocolate squares in half and place in workbowl. Pulse-chop coarsely 6-10 times. Add sugar and process 1 minute, or until the chocolate is as fine as the sugar.*** Add shortening and pulse-chop 4-6 times, continue to process for 1 minute. Add eggs and vanilla, pulse-chop 3-4 times, continue to process 40 seconds or until fluffy. Add sour milk, pulse 30 seconds. Add flour mixture. Pulse 2 times, scrape down sides of workbowl. Pulse 2 more times being careful not to overprocess. Pour into two 9 inch layer pans which have been greased and floured. Bake at 350° for 35-40 minutes. The cake will continue to cook 10 minute after it is out of the oven so crumbs should cling to a toothpick. Cool for 10 minutes in cake pans. Remove from pans and cool on wire racks. Frost with EASY CHOCOLATE PUDDING FROSTING.

*NOTE: 1-3/4 cup all-purpose flour equals 2 cups cake flour.

**NOTE: To make sour milk add 1 teaspoon vinegar to 1 cup whole milk.

***NOTE: Processed chocolate appears as very fine specks in the batter. The chocolate will melt when baked.

PROCESSING FRESH PUMPKIN:

Don't throw out your Halloween Jack-O-lantern. Use it in PUM-PKIN COOKIES, PUMPKIN ROULADE, or in pumpkin cakes or bread. The small pumpkins have more flavor than the larger ones.

Prepare Jack-o-lantern by removing the face and bottom of the Jack-o-lantern and any black spots or wax from the candle. Scrape away any seeds or spots. Cut the pumpkin into 6-8 large pieces.

MICROWAVE—Place pieces in an ovenproof covered casserole with 1/4 cup water. Microwave for 10-20 minutes on HIGH power or until tender.

RANGE TOP—Place pieces in a large saucepan, add 1/4 cup water. Cook over low heat for one hour or until pumpkin is soft.

OVEN—Cook trimmed half in oven at 325° for 1 hour. Put cut side down in baking pan. Cover with foil using two pieces if necessary.

Pumpkin makes its own water so very little water is necessary for cooking. Drain off water after cooking, let cool. Peel skin off pumpkin with a knife or scoop out pulp if baked as a shell.

Insert 🔪. Put pumpkin pulp in workbowl. Fill the workbowl no more than half full. Pulse-chop 4-5 times, continue processing 30 seconds or until pumpkin is smooth. Repeat if necessary. Use this pumpkin for the following pumpkin recipes or freeze in one cup quantities to use at a later time. Pumpkin freezes very well, even up to a year.

PUMPKIN ROULADE CAKE

10-12 Servings

3/4 cup flour
1 tsp. baking powder
2 tsp. cinnamon
1 tsp. ginger
1/2 tsp. nutmeg
1/2 tsp. salt
1 cup nut pieces (1 cup chopped)
Zest of 1/2 lemon*
1 cup sugar
3 eggs
2/3 cup cooked pumpkin

FILLING:
1-8 oz. pkg. cream cheese
4 Tbsp. butter
1 cup confectioners' sugar
1/2 tsp. vanilla

Grease a 15x10x1 inch jelly roll pan. Line with wax paper, grease and flour the wax paper. Preheat oven to 375°. Insert ⚒, add flour, baking powder and seasonings, pulse two seconds. Set aside. Add nuts to workbowl, pulse-chop 7-10 times until finely chopped.** Remove from workbowl. Set aside. Prepare FILLING now to eliminate washing workbowl. Leave ⚒ in workbowl, and cut cheese and butter into 6-8 equal pieces; put in workbowl. Pulse-chop 4-6 times and then process until creamy. Add the confectioners' sugar and vanilla, process until smooth; about 30 seconds. Scrape mixture cleanly from workbowl and blade, set it aside. Do NOT wash workbowl. This order of processing eliminates washing the workbowl.

Insert ⚒. Add lemon zest and sugar, process 1 minute or until lemon is finely grated. Add eggs, process for 15 seconds. Add pumpkin and pulse-chop 4-5 times until pumpkin is combined with egg mixture. Scrape down sides of workbowl. Add flour mixture to workbowl and pulse-chop 2-3 times or until flour mixture just disappears. *DO NOT OVERPROCESS.* Spread mixture in prepared pan and top with chopped nuts. Bake for 15 minutes. While cake bakes sprinkle a clean dish towel with confectioners' sugar. Turn hot cake out onto prepared towel. Carefully remove wax paper. Roll cake and towel together starting with the narrow end. It is very important to do this while the cake is very hot as the cake is more flexible then. Let the cake cool in the towel, about 1 hour. When the cake is cool, unroll carefully. Spread the filling over the cake and reroll the cake, without the towel, very carefully and as tightly as possible. Gently transfer to serving platter, seam side down and chill for 2-3 hours. May wrap in aluminum foil and chill overnight or freeze.

*NOTE: Zest of a lemon is the outside skin. Use either a zester or a vegetable peeler to remove thin pieces of skin.

**FINELY CHOPPED NUTS
TIP: Processing more than one cup of nuts at a time gives a very fine chop. If a chunky texture is desired chop one cup or less.

**EVENLY CHOPPED NUTS
TIP: Nuts may also be processed with the shredding disc. Insert SHRED-DING DISC, add nuts to feedtube and process. This is a good way to process a large quantity of nuts and there is no worry of overprocessing.

EASY CHOCOLATE PUDDING FROSTING   2-3 Cups

1/2 cup unsweetened cocoa
1/4 cup cornstarch
1-1/2 cups sugar
2 cups milk

Insert ⚙, add dry ingredients and pulse-chop 2-3 times. With machine running add milk through feedtube. Pour mixture in a 2 quart glass mixing bowl. Place in microwave on HIGH power for 2 minutes, stir. Microwave 2 minutes more and stir again. Microwave on MEDIUM-HIGH power 2 minutes or until thick. Let rest 10 minutes for after-cooking. Cool and frost cake. If a microwave is not available, cook frosting over medium heat until thick like pudding.

CHEESE FILLED CHOCOLATE CAKE

1-8 oz. pkg. cream cheese
1/3 cup sugar
1 egg
1/4 tsp. vanilla
Batter for 9x13 inch chocolate cake
1 cup chocolate chips (6 oz.)

Insert ⚓. Cut cream cheese in eight pieces, add to workbowl with sugar, egg and vanilla. Pulse-chop 6-8 times. Continue processing 30-40 seconds or until smooth and creamy.* Scrape mixture into a mixing bowl. Do *NOT* wash workbowl. Prepare a chocolate cake mix or DEVIL'S FOOD WHIRLIGIG CAKE in the processor. Pour 1/3 of the cake batter into a greased and floured 9x13 inch cake pan. Drop spoonfuls of filling mixture over batter. Cover with another 1/3 of the batter. Sprinkle chips over batter and cover with remaining batter. Bake as directed in cake recipe used. Frost if desired with EASY CHOCOLATE PUDDING FROSTING.

*CREAM CHEESE, SOFTENING
TIP: Cream cheese does not need to be at room temperature when using a food processor. In fact, the cream cheese may break down into a liquid if too soft and over processed. Remember the colder the cream cheese the longer it will take to process. The friction of the blade against the cream cheese does the softening.

PUMPKIN COOKIES

4 Dozen Cookies

2 cups flour
4 tsp. baking powder
1 tsp. salt
2-1/2 tsp. cinnamon
1/2 tsp. nutmeg
1/4 tsp. ginger
2 eggs
1 cup sugar
1/2 cup shortening
1 cup cooked pumpkin
1 cup nut pieces, optional (1 cup chopped)
1 cup raisins

Insert ⚙. Add flour, baking powder, salt, and spices to workbowl, process for 2 seconds to combine. Set aside. Add eggs and process for 30 seconds. Add sugar, pulse 3-4 times and process an additional minute. Add shortening, pulse 4-5 times, then process 20 seconds more until creamy. Add pumpkin, pulse 4-5 times. Add flour mixture and pulse twice. Add nuts if desired and pulse twice.* Add raisins and pulse once. Do not over process.** Stir in by hand any raisins not blended in. Drop by teaspoonsful onto a greased baking sheet. Bake at 350° for 15 minutes.

*NUTS, CHOPPED DURING MIXING
TIP: Recipes calling for chopped nuts in this book have the time needed for chopping as part of the recipe. If you omit the nuts, then pulse twice more since the pulsing for nuts was eliminated.

NOTE: These cookies freeze very well.

**OVERPROCESSED CAKES, COOKIES, QUICK BREAD
TIP: Flour mixtures are the last ingredients added to creamed mixtures in cakes, cookies, and quick breads. Overprocessing can occur once flour is added to the creamed mixture. Three to five pulses is all that is needed to mix flour into a creamed mixture. More than that will over process and you'll have "tough" baked products.

MOM'S BANANA CAKE

2-9 Inch Layers

2 cups cake flour*
1 tsp. baking powder
1 tsp. baking soda
1 tsp. salt
1 Tbsp. vinegar
1 Tbsp. water
4 eggs, separated
1-1/4 cups sugar
1/2 cup shortening
2 bananas (1 cup mashed)
2 tsp. vanilla
1/4 cup sour milk or buttermilk**

Insert ⬩, add flour, baking powder, baking soda, and salt. Pulse 3-4 times to mix dry ingredients. Remove from workbowl and set aside.*** Pre-measure all ingredients because egg whites will break down if they aren't used quickly. Wipe workbowl and blade with a paper towel.

Insert ⬩. Add egg whites to workbowl. Process 8 seconds. Mix together water and vinegar. With machine running, slowly add vinegar mixture through feedtube. Process 2 minutes or until they hold their shape. Set aside in mixing bowl.

Without washing out workbowl, insert ⬩, add egg *YOLKS* to workbowl. Pulse 6-7 times. Add sugar and process for 1 minute. Add shortening; pulse 6-8 times, process 45 seconds longer. Add bananas, process 4-6 times. Add 1/3 of flour mixture to workbowl and pulse once. Add vanilla to milk. Add 1/2 milk mixture to workbowl and pulse once. Add 1/2 of remaining flour mixture and pulse once. Add rest of milk, pulse once. Add rest of flour, pulse twice or until flour disappears. *DO NOT OVER PROCESS*. Add egg whites to workbowl. Pulse twice. *DO NOT OVER PROCESS*.

Pour into 2 greased and floured 9 inch round cake pans. Bake 35 minutes at 325°, or until toothpick comes out with crumbs. The cakes continue to cook for ten minutes after removal from the oven. That is why the crumbs will still cling to the toothpick. Cool cake 10 minutes before inverting on cooling racks. Cool completely before frosting with CREAM CHEESE FROSTING or BUCHE DE NOEL FROSTING without adding the chocolate.

*NOTE: 1-3/4 cup all-purpose flour equals 2 cups cake flour.

**NOTE: To prepare sour milk add 1/4 teaspoon vinegar to 1/4 cup milk.

***SIFTING INGREDIENTS
   TIP: Pulsing all dry ingredients together in the workbowl, using the metal blade, combines them evenly just as sifting does.

MONTA'S WALNUT CRUST CHEESECAKE

8-10 Servings

WALNUT CRUST:
1-1/2 cups walnuts (1-1/2 cups
 finely chopped)
2 Tbsp. suger
2 Tbsp. butter

CHEESECAKE
3-8 oz. pkgs. cream cheese
3/4 cup sugar
3 eggs
2 Tbsp. milk*
2 Tbsp. flour
1 tsp. vanilla

Insert ⟨blade⟩, add nuts and pulse-chop 10-12 times. Add sugar and butter, pulse-chop 3-4 times until mixture is well blended. Pat into 9 inch springform pan and bake at 400° for 6 minutes. Cut each cream cheese in 8 pieces, add one package at a time to workbowl. Pulse-chop 10-12 times, add another cream cheese, pulse-chop 6-8 times and add remaining cream cheese. Pulse-chop 6-8 times then add eggs and process until creamy. Add 3/4 cup sugar, milk, flour and vanilla; pulse-chop 3-4 times or until well blended. Pour onto warm crust and bake at 400° for 10 minutes. Reduce temperature to 250° and bake 35-45 minutes or until center is firm. Cool, before removing outside band. Chill 4-5 hours before cutting and serving.

*NOTE: Use 1 tablespoon lemon juice in place of 1 tablespoon of milk for a LEMON CHEESECAKE.

Use the following TIP to prepare a GRAHAM CRACKER CRUST instead of the WALNUT CRUST.

TIP: Insert METAL BLADE. Break 14 graham crackers squares into the workbowl. Pulse-chop 6-8 times. Add 1/4 cup butter cut in several pieces and 1/4 cup sugar. Pulse-chop 6-8 times more or until crumbs are finely chopped and well combined with butter and sugar. Wasn't that simple? No more beating with a rolling pin. Bake as directed in WALNUT CRUST recipe.

ALMOND MOIST

16 Squares

1/2 cup nut pieces
1/4 cup brown sugar, packed
1/2 cup butter
1 cup sugar
Dash of salt
1 tsp. almond flavoring
2 eggs
1 cup flour

Insert ⌐, add nuts and brown sugar. Pulse-chop 3-4 times or just until nuts are coarsely chopped, set aside. Cut butter into 6 pieces. Pulse-chop 3-4 times, scrape down sides of workbowl. Add 1 cup sugar and process 15 seconds until creamy. Add salt, almond flavoring, and eggs. Pulse-chop 5-6 times until well combined. Add flour, pulse 2-3 times just until flour disappears. Spread in an ungreased 8 inch square baking pan. Sprinkle evenly with reserved nuts and brown sugar. Bake at 325° for 30 minutes. Cut when cool.

SOUR CREAM TOPPED
CHEESECAKE

1 Cup Topping

1 cup sour cream
3 Tbsp. sugar
1/2 tsp. vanilla

Insert ⌐, add sour cream, sugar and vanilla. Pulse-chop 3-4 times until combined. Process 10 seconds longer. Spread mixture over top of just baked CHEESECAKE, bake at 325° for an additional 10 minutes.

APPLE BETTY

6 Servings

This is a very easy and quick recipe with the help of the processor. It's just as good as an apple pie and no crust to roll.

Filling:
6-8 large tart apples (6 cups sliced)
1/4 cup orange juice

STREUSEL TOPPING:
1 cup sugar
3/4 cup flour
1/2 tsp. cinnamon
1/4 tsp. nutmeg
Dash salt
1/2 cup butter, FROZEN

Peel, quarter, and core apples.* Insert medium to thick (4-8mm) ⌒. Place apple quarters upright in feedtube. Process using firm pressure on the pusher. Mound apples in a greased 9 inch pie plate; sprinkle with orange juice. Do *NOT* wash workbowl.

Insert ⬷, add sugar, flour, spices and salt. Pulse 2-3 times to blend ingredients. Cut butter** in six pieces. Add to workbowl. Pulse-chop 5-6 times or until mixture is crumbly. Sprinkle over apples.*** Bake at 375° for 45 minutes or until apples are tender and topping is crisp. Serve with whipped cream, warm cream or ice cream.

*SLICING, EVEN
TIP: Always cut the ends of fruit, vegetables, meat, etc. flat for a more even cut. Lay the food flat side down on the SLICING DISC. Use the palm of hand with an even pressure on pusher to guide the food through the feedtube. Always stop the machine to refill the feedtube. Pack the feedtube evenly and as fully as possible.

**BUTTER CRUMB TOPPINGS
TIP: Butter or margarine must be frozen in order to achieve a nice crumb mixture.

***STREUSEL TOPPING
TIP: This streusel topping recipe can be used for any fruit filling. You may substitute 1/2 cup packed brown sugar for 1 cup granulated.

BROWNIES

20 Brownies

2 oz. unsweetened chocolate
1 cup sugar
1/3 cup butter or margarine
2 eggs
1/4 tsp. salt
1 tsp. vanilla
1/2 tsp. baking powder
2/3 cup sifted flour
1/2 cup walnuts(or pecans)

Insert ⬱, break unsweetened chocolate in half, and add to workbowl. Pulse-chop the chocolate coarsely 6-10 times. Add sugar and process for 1 minute or until the chocolate is as fine as the sugar. Add the butter and pulse-chop 2-3 times then process mixture for 1 minute, or until well creamed. Add eggs, salt and vanilla, pulse-chop 6-7 times; then process 30 to 40 seconds more. Add flour, baking powder and pulse-chop twice. Scrape down sides of bowl. Add nuts and pulse-chop 2-4 times, being careful not to over process. Pour batter into an 8x8 inch greased and floured baking pan. Bake 25-30 minutes at 350°. Do not over bake; when testing for doneness crumbs should appear on toothpick. The brownies will continue to cook 10 minute after they are out of the oven so crumbs should cling to toothpick.

NOTE: Processed chocolate appears as very fine specks in the batter. The chocolate will melt when baked.

ALMOND WHIPPED CREAM

2 Cups Topping

1 cup whipping cream
1/4 tsp. almond extract
2 Tbsp. confectioners' sugar

Insert ⬱. With machine running pour whipping cream in a steady stream through the feedtube. Process one minute, with machine running add extract and sugar. Do not over process or whipped cream will turn into butter. Use ALMOND WHIPPED CREAM as a dessert topping for APPLE BETTY or for a cake frosting to be used just before serving.

161

BASIC PASTRY DOUGH

2-9 Inch Single Pie Shells

1-1/2 cups all-purpose flour or pastry flour
1/2 cup butter, margarine, lard or shortening-FROZEN
1/2 tsp. salt (omit if using salted butter or
   margarine)
1/4 cup ice water

Insert ⬳, add flour, salt and *FROZEN* fat,* which has been cut into several pieces. Process 8-10 seconds or until mixture has consistency of coarse meal. With machine running, pour ice water** through feedtube in a steady stream. *STOP* processing just before pastry begins to form a ball. *DO NOT* let pastry form into a ball.*** This timing is so important! Use the pulse button on the machine so you can stop immediately.

Scrape the dough onto a sheet of plastic wrap. Pull up each corner of plastic wrap to the center and use your hands around the plastic wrap to press the dough into a ball. Use pastry immediately or wrap in plastic wrap and refrigerate up to 3 days, or freeze for later use. Divide dough in half and roll each half out separately onto a lightly floured pastry cloth.

NOTE: Process the pastry mixture just until it looks like popcorn in the workbowl.

VARIATIONS: Use this rich, BASIC PASTRY DOUGH for pies, tarts, and quiches. For PIE CRUST VARIATIONS alter the basic recipe by adding two tablespoons of sugar for a SWEET CRUST PASTRY. Add one egg yolk with the flour and reduce the ice water by one tablespoon for a tender, EASY TO HANDLE PASTRY but less flaky pie crust.

NOTE: To bake an unfilled pie shell, first prick the sides and bottom of the shell with a fork. Pricking allows the steam to escape and prevents bubbling. Place wax paper in the shaped pie crust. Add a layer of dry beans to weight the shell. You may also use a smaller empty pie pan inside the shell to prevent shrinking. Bake the shell at 450° for 10-12 minutes. Remove the empty pan or beans by lifting the wax paper when the crust has cooked two-thirds of the baking time. Remember not to stretch the crust as you lay it in the pan. This will also prevent shrinkage.

*GOOEY PIE CRUST
TIP: Fat must be frozen to insure that it will cut into the flour correctly. Room temperature fat will become too warm in the processor and make a gooey pie crust.

**TENDER PIE CRUST
TIP: Use ice water so the crust is cool and ready to roll out immediately after being processed. Crust kept cool is more tender and flaky.

***TOUGH PIE CRUST
TIP: Processing the pastry into a ball will overprocess the flour resulting in a tough crust. Any pie crust that is overhandled by rolling and rerolling will also become tough.

***OVERPROCESSED PIE CRUST
TIP: RASPBERRY FOLDOVERS are a great recipe to make if you happen to over process the pie crust by letting it ball together.

RASPBERRY FOLDOVERS   32 Cookies

1-3 oz. pkg. cream cheese
1 Tbsp. milk
1 recipe PASTRY DOUGH
Raspberry jam

Insert ⟨blade⟩. Add cream cheese and milk. Pulse 5-6 times, scraping down sides of workbowl when necessary. Process mixture until smooth. Break pie crust into 6-8 pieces, add to workbowl. Pulse 4-5 times. Divide dough in half; roll each half in a 10 inch square about 1/8 inch thick. Cut each square into 16 (2-1/2 inch) squares. Place 1/2 teaspoon jam in center of each. Dampen two opposite corners with water and pinch firmly together over center of jam. Place on a greased baking sheet and bake at 400° for 10-12 minutes. Remove immediately to cooling rack. Cool, sift confectioners' sugar over top if desired.*

*SIFTING CONFECTIONERS' SUGAR
TIP: Use METAL BLADE in a clean, dry workbowl and add confectioners' sugar. Pulse-chop 4-6 times until lumps disappear. Now you can throw the flour sifter away!

163

CHEESECAKE BARS

16 Squares

1 cup flour
1/3 cup brown sugar
1/2 cup walnuts
1/3 cup butter (FROZEN)
1-8 oz. pkg. cream cheese
1/4 cup sugar
1 egg
2 Tbsp. milk
1 Tbsp. lemon juice
1/2 tsp. vanilla

Insert ⌐⌐, add flour and brown sugar. Pulse-chop 3-4 times. Add nuts and butter, cut into 4 pieces. Pulse-chop 6-7 times or until mixture is crumbly. Reserve 1 cup of crumb mixture for topping. Press remainder into an 8 inch square pan. Bake at 350° for 10-15 minutes or until lightly browned. Leave ⌐⌐ in workbowl. Cut cream cheese into 6-8 pieces; add to workbowl, and pulse-chop 5-6 times. Add 1/4 cup sugar, egg, milk, lemon juice and vanilla. Pulse-chop 4-5 times, stop machine and scrape down sides of workbowl. Pulse-chop 3-4 times more or until mixture is smooth and creamy. Pour over warm baked crust. Sprinkle with reserved crumb mixture. Bake at 350° for 25 minutes. Cool and cut into 2 inch squares.

FAVORITE CHOCOLATE CHIP COOKIES

4-6 Dozen

2-1/4 cups flour
1 tsp. baking soda
1/2 cup shortening
1/2 cup butter or margarine
3/4 cup firmly packed brown sugar
3/4 cup granulated sugar
1 tsp. salt
2 eggs
1 tsp. vanilla
1 cup nut pieces, optional
2 cups chocolate chips (12 oz. pkg.)

Insert ⚒ in workbowl. Add flour and baking soda, pulse 2 times. Set flour mixture aside on wax paper. Cut butter into 4-6 pieces. With ⚒ in place; add butter, shortening and both sugars to workbowl. Process for about 1 minute until creamy. Add salt, eggs and vanilla, process by pulsing 4-5 times. Scrape down the sides of workbowl and add the flour mixture. Pulse two times, add nuts and pulse once. Add the chocolate chips* and pulse twice more. Drop a teaspoonful at a time onto a greased cookie sheet. Bake at 375° for 8-10 minutes.

*CHOCOLATE CHIPS, ADDING TO COOKIE DOUGH
TIP: Chocolate chips should be poured onto the dough and not around the shaft of the metal blade. If the chips fall to the bottom of the workbowl, the metal blade will chop them. If the metal blade is covered with dough and the chips rest on the dough, they will blend into the dough in 1-2 pulses, without being cut-up.

FUDGE NUT BARS

1 cup nut pieces (1 cup chopped)
2-1/2 cups flour
1 tsp. soda
1 tsp. salt
1 cup butter or margarine
2 cups brown sugar
2 eggs
2 tsp. vanilla
3 cups oats, regular or quick cooking
1-12 oz. pkg. chocolate chips (2 cups)
1-14 oz. can sweetened condensed milk
2 Tbsp. butter
1/2 tsp. salt

Insert ⚓, add nuts. Pulse-chop 5-6 times or until coarsely chopped. Put nuts in medium glass mixing bowl or large saucepan. Place flour, soda, and 1 teaspoon salt in workbowl. Pulse for 2 seconds, set aside on wax paper. Cut butter or margarine into 8 pieces, add to workbowl. Pulse-chop 6-8 times or until creamy. Add sugar, eggs, and vanilla. Process 10-15 seconds until fluffy. Scrape sides of workbowl if necessary. Add flour mixture and oats, pulse-chop 2-3 times or just until combined.

Combine chocolate chips with nuts in mixing bowl or saucepan. Put glass bowl in microwave and use MEDIUM power for 5 minutes or until chocolate is melted. If using saucepan, melt on range top using LOW heat. Add milk, 2 tablespoons butter, and 1/2 teaspoon salt to melted chocolate nut mixture, stir well. Spread 2/3 of oat mixture evenly in a 10x15x1-1/2 inch baking pan. Cover with chocolate nut mixture, dot with spoonfuls of remaining oatmeal mixture. Bake at 350° for 25-35 minutes. Cool, cut into bars.

LEMON PIE BARS

3/4 cup butter or margarine, refrigerated or frozen
1/2 cup confectioners' sugar
1-1/2 cups flour
1 lemon, peeled and juiced*
Reserved lemon juice (3 Tbsp.)
3 eggs
1-1/2 cups sugar
3 Tbsp. flour
Confectioners' sugar for garnish

Cut butter into four even pieces. Insert ⌐⎨⌐, add butter, confectioners' sugar and 1-1/2 cups flour. Pulse-chop 4-6 times until butter is finely cut into flour. It should be the consistency of coarse crumbs. Pat this mixture into a 13x9x2 inch baking pan. Bake at 350° for 20 minutes. Insert ⌐⎨⌐. With machine running, add lemon peel through the feedtube. Process until finely chopped, 1-2 minutes. Add eggs, remaining flour, sugar and three tablespoons of lemon juice from the reserved juice. Process 20 seconds or until well blended. Pour this mixture over the hot crust and bake 20-25 minutes longer. Cut while warm into bars. When cool, sprinkle top with about 2 tablespoons confectioners' sugar.

*NOTE: Roll the lemon on the counter top to soften and release the juices. Use a vegetable peeler to remove thin slices of lemon peel for the flavoring. Do not cut into the white membrane as this is the bitter part. Then cut the lemon in half and juice, reserving the juice.

PUFF SHELLS

Try this elegant food in your food processor and find out how easy it is to make. You will love the great reviews you will get from so little effort.

1 cup water
5 Tbsp. butter
1 Tbsp. sugar
Pinch of salt
1 cup flour
4 large eggs

Combine water, butter, sugar, and salt in a saucepan. Using medium heat; bring to a boil, stirring occasionally. Remove the pan from the heat and add flour all at once. Beat with a wooden spoon until the flour is absorbed. Return the pan to medium heat and beat the mixture for 2 minutes with a wooden spoon. Remove from heat and let stand for 5 minutes. Insert 🔩, add dough to workbowl and pulse-chop 7-10 times. Add eggs and pulse-chop 4-5 times; process 1 minute, stopping the machine once to scrape down sides of bowl. The dough should be thick and shiny, and it should hold its shape when lifted with a spoon.

At this point the dough may be refrigerated for 1-2 days or used immediately. Make small puff shells for appetizers, medium puff shells for cream puffs and eclairs, or large puff shells for ice cream filled puffs. Size will depend on usage of puff shells. Drop dough in mounds (about 1/2 the size desired for cooked puffs) onto lightly greased baking sheet.

Bake in preheated oven 425° for 10 minutes. Reduce heat to 375° and bake an additional 20-25 minutes or until puffed and browned. (Small puff shells may take less baking time. Check oven after 15 minutes at 375°). Remove from oven and after 10 minutes, gently poke holes with fork on sides of puff shells to let steam escape. Let puffs cool before cutting in half and filling. Makes about 40 small puffs (1-1/2 inches), about 20 medium sized puffs (2 inches), or about 12 large puffs (3 inches). For APPETIZER PUFFS fill with egg salad mixture, shrimp salad mixture, tuna salad, or minced ham.

ICE CREAM

This is a great recipe to use with very ripe fruits or just to enjoy the fresh summer fruits. Packaged frozen fruit may also be used. Peel, pit or seed fruit as desired. Insert (4-8mm)⊝ . Fill feedtube with prepared fruit pieces. Slice using a medium pressure on the pusher. Freeze two cups sliced fruit, whole berries or fruit chunks in a single layer on a cookie sheet. Insert ⟨blade⟩ , add 2 cups frozen fruit and pulse-chop 6-8 times. Add 2-3 tablespoons sugar and pulse-chop until fruit is finely chopped about 6-8 times. With machine running, add 1/2 cup whipping cream through feedtube and process until smooth and creamy. Serve immediately or keep in freezer up to 3 hours. If frozen longer, reprocess and serve. Use strawberries, peaches, raspberries, plums, bananas, etc. May double amounts for larger capacity food processors.

SHERBET

This is a good recipe for using left over fruits from a picnic or party; etc. Use your imagination and try any fruit combination you enjoy—bananas and strawberries, watermelon and raspberries, peaches and apricots. Let your imagination and your fruit basket guide you.

2 cups frozen fruit (watermelon or peaches)
1/2 cup berries (raspberries)
2-3 Tbsp. whipping cream
2 Tbsp. orange or almond based liqueur

Seed or peel fruit if desired and freeze in 1 inch chunks on a cookie sheet. Insert METAL BLADE, add half the frozen fruit and pulse-chop 6-8 times. With machine running add remaining fruit cubes and the berries through the feedtube. Replace pusher. When fruit is finely chopped, remove pusher. Add the cream and liqueur through the feedtube while machine is running. The texture should be smooth. May double quantity processed with a larger capacity food processor. Serve immediately or store in freezer up to three hours. If frozen over three hours, reprocess and serve.

NOTES

GIFTS WITH LOVE

| METAL | SHREDDING | DOUGH | SLICING | FRENCH-FRY |
| BLADE | DISC | BLADE | DISC | DISC |

FRESH STRAWBERRY JAM   4-6 Jars

3 cups strawberries, crushed (2 quarts whole berries)
6 cups sugar
Dash of salt
1 cup cold water
1 (1-3/4 oz.) pkg. powdered pectin

Insert ⟨🔪⟩. Add strawberries to the workbowl, fill workbowl no
more than half full. Pulse-chop 6-8 times until berries are coarsely
chopped. Repeat with any remaining strawberries. Place strawberries in a large mixing bowl. Stir in sugar. Let stand at room
temperature for 1/2 hour. Put water and pectin in a medium
saucepan, stir and bring to a boil; boil one minute. Pour pectin mixture over strawberries and stir well. Let sit for four hours. Place in
sterilized jars and freeze. Store jam in a freezer set at 20° or less
if storing longer than one month or keep in refrigerator up to 3
weeks.

NOTE: Jars may be cleaned and sterilized in a dishwasher. Run jars through
complete dishwasher cycle, remove jars and fill immediately while jam and
jars are hot IF using canning lids or sealing with melted paraffin. Since the
jam is cool in the above recipe and it will be frozen, it is not necessary to
fill the jars when they are hot.

NOTE: Make jam during peak growing season and give as gifts all year long.

FREEZER RASPBERRY JAM   6-8 Jars

Tastes just like raspberry jam! A great way to use up green
tomatoes at the end of harvest time.

10 medium size green tomatoes (5 cups chopped)
3 cups sugar
1-6 oz. pkg. raspberry gelatin

Insert ⟨🔪⟩. Core tomatoes. Cut tomatoes in fourths and place in
workbowl. For best results do 3-5 tomatoes at a time. Pulse-chop
6-7 times or until finely cut. Repeat with remaining tomatoes.
Measure, place in an 8 quart kettle. Add the sugar to the tomatoes,
bring mixture to a boil. Boil for 10 minutes, stirring constantly.
Remove from heat. Add the gelatin mix and stir until dissolved. Let
cool and place in sterilized jars. When completely cool, freeze.

PLUM RASPBERRY JAM

6 Pints

A rosy red jam which is fun to make and delightful to give and receive. Fresh berries can be used if you have them or use the frozen packages along with Santa Rosa plums. A Christmas sampler of jam and a loaf of homemade CRACKED WHEAT BREAD, ENGLISH MUFFIN BREAD, or FRENCH BREAD is innovative and less time consuming than the standard cookie tray.

2-1/2 to 3 pounds Santa Rosa plums
1-10 oz. pkg. frozen raspberries in syrup(thawed)
 or 3 cups fresh raspberries
10 cups sugar
2/3 cup lemon juice
1-6 oz. bottle liquid pectin

Insert ⤳. Cut plums in half, pit and place in workbowl. Fill workbowl no more than half full. Pulse-chop 8-10 times or until finely chopped. Repeat if necessary. You should have about 4 cups chopped plums. Place chopped plums and raspberries in an 8 quart kettle. Add sugar and lemon juice, stir until blended.

Use high heat; bring mixture to a rolling boil, stirring constantly and boil 1 minute. Remove from heat; stir in pectin at once. Skim off foam and discard. Ladle jam into hot sterilized jars to within 1/2 inch of top. Cover immediately with a thin layer of hot paraffin (about 1/8 inch thick). Make sure paraffin touches all sides of glass.

RHUBARB SPREAD

This jelly can be lo-cal for your friends who are weight watching. Substitute artificial sweetener for the small amount of sugar.

1-20 oz. pkg. frozen rhubarb
  or 6-8 stalks fresh rhubarb
1/2 cup water
1/2 cup sugar or artificial sweetener to equal 1/2 cup
  sugar
1 Tbsp. lemon juice
1 env. unflavored gelatin

Insert medium or thick $\ominus$; pack fresh rhubarb in feedtube. Process rhubarb using medium pressure on pusher. Stop machine, repeat procedure until all rhubarb is sliced. Combine fresh or frozen sliced rhubarb with 1/4 cup water, sugar or sweetener, and lemon juice in a saucepan. Cook over moderate heat for 20 minutes or until rhubarb is cooked. Sprinkle gelatin over remaining 1/4 cup water to soften. Let stand 5 minutes. Add to cooked rhubarb mixture, stirring until gelatin is dissolved. Insert ⚒, add rhubarb mixture. Pulse-chop 6-8 times, continue processing about 30 seconds. Mixture will be consistency of jelly. Keep refrigerated or frozen.

NOTE: Also use this RHUBARB DESSERT as a baby food by reducing the amount of sugar to 1/4 cup.

STRAWBERRY BUTTER

3-4 Cups

A nice gift would be a loaf of homemade FRENCH BREAD or CROISSANTS and a pretty jar filled with the strawberry butter. It will win the love of anyone's tummy!

1/2 cup butter
1 cup fresh strawberries
3/4 cup confectioners' sugar
1 tsp. vanilla
1-8 oz. pkg. cream cheese

Insert ⌄. Add butter, pulse-chop 4-5 times. Stop and scrape down sides of bowl. Process 30 seconds or until smooth and creamy. Add sugar, pulse 5-6 times then process until creamy. Add vanilla and strawberries, run machine 30-60 seconds or until mixture is creamy. Mixture looks grainy until completely blended. Cut cream cheese in 6 pieces and add to workbowl.* Process until smooth. Refrigerate up to one week or freeze. Serve with homemade bread or croissants for a real treat.

NOTE: Substitute any fruit for strawberries. Use a sweet liqueur instead of vanilla for flavoring.

*CREAM CHEESE, SOFTENING
TIP: Cream cheese does not need to be at room temperature when using a food processor. In fact, the cream cheese may break down into a liquid if too soft before processing. Cut cold cream cheese into 6-8 even pieces and using METAL BLADE pulse-chop 6-8 times until creamy. Scrape down the sides of the workbowl and pulse-chop until cheese is soft and fluffy. Remember the colder the cream cheese the longer it will take to process. The friction of the blade against the cream cheese does the softening.

BUCHE DE NOEL

1 Cake

This is a delightful French jelly roll which is served as a Christmas cake. Eliminate the decorative Christmas topping for a mouthwatering dessert any other time of the year.

Cake:
1/2 cup cake flour
1/4 cup cocoa
1 tsp. baking powder
1/4 tsp. salt
4 eggs
3/4 cup sugar
1 tsp. vanilla

Grease sides and bottom of a 15x10x1 inch jelly roll pan or cookie sheet. Line with wax paper, grease and flour the wax paper well. Preheat oven to 375°. Insert ⟨blade⟩, add cake flour, cocoa, baking powder, and salt. Pulse 3-4 times, remove flour mixture and set aside. Without cleaning out bowl, add eggs, pulse 3-4 times and continue processing 10 seconds. Add sugar and process 20 seconds. Add vanilla, pulse once. Add flour mixture, pulse 2 times. Do not over process. Pour into prepared pan and bake for 10-12 minutes. While cake bakes dust a clean dish towel with confectioners' sugar. When cake is baked turn it onto the towel immediately. Carefully remove wax paper. Tightly roll cake and towel together starting at the narrow end. Let it sit until cool, about 1 hour. Prepare frosting while cake cools.

BUCHE DE NOEL FROSTING   4 Cups Frosting

1 egg
4 cups confectioners' sugar
1 cup butter
1 tsp. vanilla
3 oz. unsweetened chocolate

Insert ⬛, add egg and sugar, pulse twice. Add butter and vanilla, pulse 4-5 times, stopping to scrape down sides of workbowl. Continue processing until smooth and creamy. Set aside 1/3 cup of the white frosting. Break the chocolate into several pieces, add to the remaining mixture in workbowl and pulse-chop 6-7 times, then continue processing until chocolate blends in smoothly, 1-2 minutes.* Unroll cake, remove towel and spread a thin layer of chocolate frosting on cake. Roll up cake tightly, place seam side down on serving plate. Frost ends with reserved white frosting. Frost top and sides of cake with remaining chocolate frosting. This cake should look like a log. Use a fork to make bark-like lines in the frosting. Decorate with mint leaf candy and red cherries on top to look like sprigs of holly.

*NOTE: If the chocolate is not well blended by 2 minutes, let the frosting sit while the chocolate softens and then proceed. It would be best if you melted the chocolate the next time you prepare the recipe if this happens.

NOTE: If necessary add a little hot water to soften the frosting before spreading.

CRISP PICKLE SLICES

8 Pints

Share the bounty of your garden with these fresh tasting bread and butter pickles. A delightful treat any time of year.

4 quarts unpeeled cucumbers
6 medium white onions or 12 small
1/3 cup medium-coarse salt
3 cloves garlic
2 green peppers
5 cups sugar
1-1/2 tsp. tumeric
1-1/2 tsp. celery seed
2 Tbsp. mustard seed
3 cups vinegar

Purchase or pick cucumbers that will fit the feedtube.* Wash cucumbers well. Insert thin** (1-3 mm)⌒. Trim top and bottom off the cucumbers. Fit cucumber tightly in feedtube. Applying light pressure on the pusher, process all the cucumbers, emptying workbowl when it fills to the top. Put onions in feedtube, process using light pressure on the pusher. Place cucumbers and onions in a large container, sprinkle with salt. Cover with several trays of ice cubes. Mix thoroughly and let stand 3 hours. Prepare pickling liquid while cucumbers soak. Wipe out workbowl and processor cover with a paper towel. Insert⚒. With machine running, add garlic through feedtube. Replace pusher. Process garlic about 30 seconds or until finely minced. Cut green peppers into 8 pieces. Pulse-chop 3-4 times, being careful not to overprocess.*** Remove peppers and garlic to large kettle. Drain soaked cucumbers thoroughly. Combine with green pepper, garlic, sugar, spices, and vinegar. Heat just until liquid starts to boil. Have prepared hot sterilized jars ready. Add hot cucumber mixture to jars, wipe rims and seal. Let jars cool. Press center of each lid. If lid stays down when pressed, jar is sealed.

NOTE: Store any unsealed jars in refrigerator and use within 6 weeks.

*FOOD PROCESSOR EYE
 TIP: When you want whole slices of fruits or vegetables select ones that will fit the feedtube of the food processor.

**SLICES, THIN

TIP: Not all machines have thin slicing discs or you may not have this disc for the processor. To produce thinner slices pack the feedtube very tightly and apply a light pressure on the pusher. The slices should be thinner. It is the next best technique to owning a 1-2 mm slicing disc.

***GREEN PEPPERS, CHOPPED

TIP: The FRENCH FRY DISC will also cube green peppers evenly. Slice the top and bottom off the green pepper and then cut it into fourths. Stand up in the feedtube so the round side of the pepper is across the width of the feedtube. The feedtube must be tightly packed. In a large feedtube it takes 2 green peppers to pack the feedtube. Process using a quick firm pressure on the pusher.

HERB BUTTER   1/2 Cup

2-3 garlic cloves
1 green onion top or 10 chive stems (2 tsp. chopped)
3 sprigs parsley (2 tsp. chopped)
1/2 cup butter
1 tsp. salt
1 tsp. rosemary

Insert ⚙. With machine running drop garlic through feedtube and process until finely minced. Scrape down sides of workbowl if necessary. Add onion or chives and parsley, pulse-chop 4-6 times or until coarsely chopped. Cut butter into 6 pieces. Add butter, salt, and rosemary to workbowl. Pulse-chop until butter is soft and ingredients are well blended. Use soft butter spread on sliced FRENCH BREAD or CRUSTY POTATO BREAD. This recipe will butter both sides of one 9x5 inch loaf. Wrap bread with aluminum foil, leaving the top uncovered. This produces a crusty top. Bake in 400° oven for 15-20 minutes. If desired, store HERB BUTTER in crock in refrigerator or freezer for later use.

NOTE: Serve this soft spread with hot rolls. Make CRACKED WHEAT BREAD into dinner rolls and give with this HERB BUTTER for a yummy, good present.

ZESTY BLUE CHEESE BALL
1 Ball

1/2 cup nut pieces (1/3 cup chopped)
8-10 parsley sprigs (2-3 Tbsp. chopped)
2 oz. cheddar cheese (1/2 cup shredded)
1-3 oz. pkg. roquefort or blue cheese
1-8 oz. pkg. cream cheese
1/4 cup milk
1 small wedge of onion
1 tsp. Worcestershire sauce
1/4 tsp. garlic salt

Insert ⚙, add nuts and pulse-chop 4-6 times or until nuts are finely chopped. Set aside on wax paper. Add parsley sprigs and pulse-chop 4-6 times until finely chopped, remove and combine with nuts. Insert ⊚ and shred cheddar cheese using push-release method.* Leave cheese in workbowl. Insert ⚙, being careful that it is resting on the bottom of the workbowl. Add rest of cheeses, milk, onion, Worcestershire sauce, and garlic salt. Pulse-chop until ingredients are well combined and onion is chopped. Coat mixture with parsley and nuts, and roll in a ball using wax paper to aid in shaping. Chill, serve with crackers.

*CHEESE, PUSH-RELEASE METHOD
TIP: Place piece of very cold cheese into the feedtube. Set pusher in feedtube and lock cover. Turn machine on, press moderately on the pusher, release pressure by pulling up on the pusher. Repeat pressing and releasing of pusher until last piece is processed.

VARIATIONS
1 Ball

The above recipe gives the basic method for making a cheese ball. Only your imagination is the limit now. Try any of these CHEESE BALL VARIATIONS. Just the METAL BLADE and the SHREDDING DISC do all the work of chopping, creaming, whipping and shredding. Now let's have some fun in the kitchen. Vary the outside coating with almonds, walnuts, pecans, peanuts, dried chipped beef, bread crumbs, parsley or even paprika. Eight ounces of cream cheese plus 1 cup of shredded cheese with seasonings is the basis for all cheese balls. Adding mayonnaise or milk will make the ball softer. Also the longer the cheese ball is at room temperature the more pliable it becomes.

Strong flavored cheeses like cheddar or blue cheese give tasty results. Try using one of the cold pack cheeses with wine or bacon flavor to create your own "signature" cheese ball. Wrap a cheese ball in plastic wrap, then in a colorful nylon netting and tie with a bow for gift giving. Make several ahead and freeze them.

CHEDDAR NUT BALL

1 Ball

2/3 cup nut pieces (1/2 cup chopped)
4 oz. cheddar cheese (1 cup shredded)
1-8 oz. pkg.cream cheese
1 green onion (1 Tbsp. chopped)
2 tablespoons mayonnaise or milk
1/4 tsp. garlic salt
1/4 wedge of green pepper

Insert ⬛, add nuts and pulse-chop 4-6 times, set aside on plastic wrap. Insert ⬛. Shred cheddar cheese using push-release method,* leave in workbowl. Insert ⬛ being careful that it is resting on the bottom of the workbowl. Add all ingredients except green pepper. Pulse-chop until well combined, then add pepper and pulse-chop 3-4 times or until pepper is coarsely chopped. Coat with nuts and chill. Serve with crackers.

*CHEESE, PUSH-RELEASE METHOD
TIP: Place piece of very cold cheese into the feedtube. Set pusher in feed-tube and lock cover. Turn machine on, press moderately on the pusher, release pressure by pulling up on the pusher. Repeat pressing and releasing of pusher until last piece is processed.

NOTE: These cheese balls freeze wonderfully. You can make 2 balls from one recipe if you wish.

NOTE: When unexpected guests arrive these cheese balls are quick snacks. Remove cheese ball from freezer. Leave wrapped and defrost in microwave on LOW power for 2 minutes or HIGH power for 10 seconds on and 10 seconds off; repeat 4 times.

NOTE: Make your own cheese pack gifts for the holiday with one or several of these recipes. Be sure to include the recipe, giving food processor direc-tions of course! Maybe they haven't found out how easy cooking with a food processor can be!!

FRUIT ROLLUPS

10 cups peeled, sliced fruit
1 cup sugar

Wash, peel and pit fruit. Insert medium (3-4 mm) ⌒. Pack fruit in feedtube and process using medium pressure on the pusher. Stop machine, fill feedtube again, process and continue this procedure until workbowl is full or you have 10 cups of sliced fruit. Place fruit and sugar in a large kettle, bring to a boil, stirring until sugar is dissolved. Remove from heat and let cool while preparing drying pans. Cover three 10x15x1 inch jellyroll pans with plastic wrap. Let plastic wrap extend up sides and ends of pans. Insert ⚒. Fill workbowl half full with warm mixture. Process until smooth and pour into another container. Repeat until all fruit is pureed. Cool to lukewarm. Measure by cupfuls onto the prepared trays using equal amounts of puree on each tray. Set trays of fruit in 150° oven, leaving door ajar. Fruit is dry when puree can be peeled off plastic easily. The oven door is left ajar to keep the humidity lower and speed the drying process. This may take 12-24 hours. For storing, roll up fruit in plastic wrap. Keep at room temperature for 1 month or store in refrigerator for up to 4 months. Wrap well and freeze for up to a year. Tear or cut into strips to eat.

NOTE: Any fresh fruit in season is a good choice or combine two fruits like peaches and apricots, plums and pears, or apples and strawberries. Each 10 inch roll may be cut in thirds and then stored. This is also a nice size for gift giving.

WONDERFUL FUDGE SAUCE   3-1/2 - 4 Cups

3 oz. unsweetened chocolate
1-1/2 cups sugar
1/4 tsp. salt
1/8 tsp. cream of tartar
1 cup evaporated milk
3/4 cup butter - no substitution
1 tsp. vanilla

Insert ⚒. Break chocolate squares in quarters and add to workbowl. Pulse-chop 6-8 times to break up chocolate. Add sugar and process for 1-2 minutes or until chocolate is as fine as the sugar. Add salt and cream of tartar to the chocolate — sugar mixture. Heat milk and butter in a four cup glass measure in microwave on HIGH for 2 minutes or heat using large saucepan over low heat until butter is partially melted. With machine running pour warm mixture and vanilla through feedtube and process for 1 more minute.

Pour fudge sauce from workbowl into the measuring cup or saucepan. Microwave on MEDIUM-LOW for 3-5 minutes or cook in a saucepan using low heat until sugar is dissolved and sauce is thoroughly warmed. Cool slightly and serve. Store extra sauce in small glass jars in refrigerator. Warm in microwave or in pan of water before serving. May store at room temperature for 3-4 days.

NOTE: Give a package of medium-size PUFF SHELLS (see DESSERTS) and WONDERFUL FUDGE SAUCE for an 'Instant Dessert Kit.' Just tell the recipient to add ice cream to the puff shells and top with warm sauce. Prepare PUFF SHELLS ahead and freeze. Make a sampler of fudge sauce and several jams or jellies. It's a delicious treat any way you package it.

NOTES

FEED BABY RIGHT

| METAL | SHREDDING | DOUGH | SLICING | FRENCH-FRY |
| BLADE | DISC | BLADE | DISC | DISC |

186

FEED BABY RIGHT

Please don't pass this chapter by if you don't happen to have a baby in the house. There are excellent recipes that you can adapt to family use. Also the recipes in this chapter would be great for someone on a bland diet, low sugar or fat or a low salt diet. Check the PINEAPPLE-BANANA SHERBET for a naturally sweetened dessert or try TROPICAL FRUIT DRINK for a tasty beverage. Healthful eating is important for everyone, not just babies.

We feel this chapter is a very important one. If you are not the parent of a baby, please share this chapter with a friend or relative that has a newborn. A freezer package sampler of several of the recipes and this cookbook would be a nice gift as a "welcome" baby present. If the new baby's parents live faraway send this cookbook with a note about FEED BABY RIGHT. The foods a baby is fed from the time she/he is born are a determining factor in their growth and disposition. A child well fed is calm, alert, has good motor development and is a very happy child. Poor nutrition causes deficiencies that often are not detected until later in life.

A child who does not know "junk" foods or sweet foods does not cry for these foods. Do not introduce "empty" calorie foods to baby nor feel that putting these foods in a baby's mouth will make him happy. "Empty" calorie foods only bring problems later in life. Do you wonder why as adults we eat so much when we are upset or down? Is there a relationship there from the times we cried as babies? What do you do when you hear a baby cry—walk into the kitchen? Parents should never feel love is measured by the amount of sugar we feed a baby or child. Remember, babies are not born knowing sugar. Making your own baby food does take time. In this chapter the recipes have little or no sugar. Sugar and sugar products were purposely left out or decreased, as were artificial colors, salt, and preservatives your baby doesn't need. Too much sugar may be a reason that baby is crying. The increased blood sugar level causes a type of hyperactivity in the child.

You are in control of your baby's diet. Don't introduce him/her to foods that are not going to help the child grow. It may take a little effort on your part in preparing baby foods at home, but in the long run you will be well rewarded with a very healthy and happy child. Remember, what you feed your baby today builds his body for the rest of his/her life. Give your baby a good start with good sound nutrition.

Some commercially prepared baby foods do contain preservatives, starch, and/or sugar additives like corn syrup, tapioca and extra fructose, besides that which is naturally occurring. Commercial baby foods are available as a convenience. Use it as such, don't depend on it. If some of the recipes in this chapter do not sound "yummy" to you, don't let the baby know it. When feeding your baby have a big SMILE on your face, especially when feeding a food you're not fond of. The baby doesn't know about food likes and dislikes. They pick these up from the expressions on your face. Body language says a lot to children.

Also remember that giving children foods between meals like toast, cookies, crackers keeps him/her from eating at mealtime. It isn't the meal you made that he/she doesn't like, it's all the food he/she ate before the meal that has filled up his/her tummy. Remember, babies have small tummies. Make snacks more nutritional with fresh fruits and vegetables, then if a child, doesn't want to eat dinner it's okay because he/she has had good snacks. Remember, foods with no nutritional value predicate a whiny child.

As baby grows older, don't think he/she has out grown his need for nutritional food. Carbonated beverages, sweet fruit punches and drinks, candy and potato chips are still not good for him. Real fruit juices (apple, orange, grapefruit, or pineapple) should be what he/she drinks—or water, which is a great thirst quencher. For snacks, process in the food processor carrot sticks, celery, cucumber slices or apples (sprinkle with lemon juice so they don't turn brown), or any fresh fruit. Make a dip with cottage cheese processed to sour cream consistency or plain yogurt mixed with fruit juice to go with the fresh fruits and vegetables. When these foods are available to a child, he will eat them. Don't feel because non-nutritional foods are available in the grocery store that you must buy them. You and your food processor together can prepare some great meals and snacks.

The processing of the baby food meals in this chapter takes only minutes with the food processor. When cooking for the rest of your family add some "extra" for the baby. These meals or any leftover foods may be processed quickly and served immediately or frozen for baby's meal at a later date. This is also a very economical way to feed baby since prepared baby food can get expensive. Process several kinds of food together like meat, vegetables, and fruits. Even if there are only little bits of each of these foods left over, they can make very tasty combinations and a complete meal. Babies who eat foods prepared in your own kitchen will have a much improved palate over those children who eat commercially prepared food. You also eliminate the "weaning" period a baby goes through when switching from commercially prepared baby foods to the introduction of "table foods."

A food processor makes feeding your family and baby an easy and fun task. Along with the help of a microwave oven, you'll be done much faster than making a trip to the grocery store. With the extra "free time" your food processor gives you, take a nice walk with your baby. For those of you who have questioned the safety of microwaves, the answer is they are perfectly safe to use. In fact, it is the best way to cook fresh fruits and vegetables because it preserves the vitamins and minerals since you cook with little or no water. Also, when using a microwave the dish you heat baby's food in is the same dish you use to serve baby his/her meal.

The following recipes in this chapter were selected for you to use as a guideline. Feel free to make substitutions or additions (as long as it is not too sweet) and enjoy preparing your baby's meals!!

A schedule a doctor might follow for introducing new foods to babies is.

4-1/2 — 5-1/2 months	Cereal and/or fruits
5-1/2 — 6-1/2 months	Vegetables
6-1/2 — 7-1/2 months	Meat and meat combinations
7 months	Onion in foods
8 months	Egg yolk (cooked)

Introduce one new food at a time to baby to see if there are any food reactions. New foods are introduced 2-4 weeks apart to allow enough time for any food reactions to become apparent.

NOTE: Babies under 1 year of age need 24-32 ounces of milk per day. Do not over satisfy baby with solid foods.

NOTE: Nursing babies do not need food introduced until the baby is about 6 months old. A nursing mother must make sure SHE is eating very well during baby's first six months.

STORING LEFTOVER BABY FOOD

In all of the following recipes the procedure for the storage of leftover baby food is the same. Place leftover baby food in ice cube trays, insert divider, cover with aluminum foil or plastic wrap and freeze. One cup of homemade baby food will yield about 6 food cubes. No extra ice cube trays? Cover any flat dish or baking sheet that will fit in the freezer with wax paper. Make small mounds of food on the dish, cover and freeze.

When frozen solid, remove food cubes or mounds from tray or dish, store in freezer-proof plastic bags or containers. Label and store in freezer. If properly wrapped and stored these food cubes will last several months. Depending on the appetite and size of the baby, two food cubes should be enough for one serving.

SERVING HOMEMADE FOOD CUBES

To serve frozen food cubes, remove desired amount from freezer container. There are several options listed for heating the food cubes.

MICROWAVE OVEN—Place food cubes in a small ovenproof dish. Cover. Microwave 1-2 minutes on LOW power, stirring after 1 minute.

BABY WARMING DISH (ELECTRIC)—Place food cubes in warming dish. After 5-10 minutes break up food cubes with a spoon. Continue heating until just warm. Do not let food sit in dish heating for several hours because dish is just the right temperature for bacteria to grow.

DOUBLE BOILER—Place food cubes in the top of a double boiler or in heat resistant custard cups in a pan of hot water. Let simmer until just warm.

EGG POACHER—Set food cubes in egg poacher with hot water underneath. Let simmer until just warm.

DEFROSTING—Just leave food cubes at room temperature for about 1 hour before meal time. Leave out no longer than one hour because food spoilage could occur. There is nothing wrong with baby eating cold food or drinking cold milk.

NOTE: Food spoilage occurs most often in the temperature range of 70° to 140°. This spoilage occurs if food is left for a long period of time in this temperature range. Usually we serve food cold from the refrigerator, which keeps food about 40°. Hot foods from the oven may be over 140°. For example a beef roast at 140° internal temperature is rare and 160° is medium. Food may be served at this temperature range of 70° to 140° but just should not be kept at this temperature range for a long time period.

BABY FOOD FOR TRAVELING

Place homemade frozen food cubes in a small plastic container. If carrying a bottle, place the cubes in a bag with baby's milk. The food cubes will keep the milk cold and when the food cubes thaw out they are ready to serve. This works best for short trips. For longer traveling time, place a frozen commercial ice pack with the food cubes. It is better to keep the cubes chilled than to be concerned about improper storage.

NOTE: Many commercial baby foods contain fillers such as tapioca and cereal. They may also contain sugar and salt. The only advantage of commercial baby food is convenience. Freezing homemade baby food in food cubes as described before is just as convenient and less expensive. It also lets the baby share in the family diet and the baby always knows the taste of "real" food versus processed baby food. The bonus for you is the baby develops a broad range of tastes. It is so fast and easy to make baby food in the food processor that sometimes you may feel it was too easy!

NOTE: When buying foods in the grocery store always check list of ingredients on package. The ingredient listed first is present in that food in the largest quantity.

MEATS

BASIC MEAT RECIPE

2 Cups or 12 Food Cubes

When making plain meat dinners, follow this basic meat recipe.

1-1/2 cups cooked, cubed meat (chicken, beef, lamb, liver, pork, etc.)
1 cup liquid (formula, evaporated milk,milk,gravy, or vegetable water)

Insert ⌐, place meat in workbowl, pulse chop 4-6 times. With machine running add liquid through the feedtube.* Continue processing until smooth and creamy, about 1 minute.

*ADDING LIQUID
TIP: Remove the pusher when adding liquids through the feedtube as the machine is running.

NOTE: Bacon, hot dogs, and bologna contain nitrites and salt in high concentration. Eliminate or at least limit these foods in your child's diet. There are many food alternatives.

NOTE: The younger the baby the finer the meat mixture should be. More liquid may be necessary in the food mixture for a younger baby. After 7 months the food can be thicker. Baby depends on his tongue and gums to get the food down. Sucking his/her thumb helps to force the food down, too. As the baby gets older, leave the food more chunky. Serve immediately or freeze as previously directed.

NOTE: When baby is around 8 months old process food more coarsely. If food is processed too fine for too long, the baby may reject coarser textures in food later on.

CHICKEN BROTH
2-3 Cups or 18 Food Cubes

Use this recipe any time CHICKEN BROTH is needed for preparation of baby food.

2-3 cups water
Bones from 1 chicken

When cooking chicken for the family, debone the chicken before cooking it. Use the bones, chicken backs, and wings or any combinations of these with the water. Bring to a boil; skim the surface foam, and simmer for 45 minutes. The bones make the best chicken broth. The meat of the chicken does not make a good broth. Freeze any left over broth in ice cube trays for future use when a recipe calls for chicken broth. You may season the broth for the family and add homemade noodles for a delicious chicken soup. If you decide to make the soup and noodles, any remaining can be processed for the baby. It makes a wonderful cream-like soup without using cream.

BEEF BROTH
4-6 Cups

4-6 cups cold water or enough to cover bones
Meaty beef bones

Place meaty bones in a sauce pot, brown slightly to give more flavor. Add enough cold water or vegetable water to cover bones. Bring water to a boil. Skim the surface foam and discard. Simmer, partially covered, on low heat for at least two hours. Remove bones and meat from broth. Remove meat from bones. Process meat with METAL BLADE. If necessary, add some beef broth through the feedtube while the machine is running. Use the processed meat in BASIC MEAT DINNER or freeze as previously directed. Use broth in any recipe calling for BEEF BROTH. Freeze any remaining broth in food cubes.

BASIC COMPLETE
MEAT DINNER

3 Cups or 18 Food Cubes

1 cup cooked, cubed meat
1/4 cup cooked vegetable
1/2 cup cooked rice, pasta, potato, or baby cereal
1 cup liquid (formula, evaporated milk, milk, gravy, or vegetable water)

Insert ⟨⬥⟩, add meat, vegetable, and rice, pasta, potato or baby cereal. Pulse-chop 6-8 times. With machine running add liquid through feedtube and process until smooth and creamy, about 1 minute. More liquid may be used if too thick. Leave a coarser texture for baby over 8 months. Serve immediately or freeze as previously directed.

BABY PATE

2 Cups or 12 Food Cubes

1 pound chicken livers
1/2 cup CHICKEN BROTH, unseasoned

Put livers and broth in a saucepan, bring to a boil, reduce heat and simmer about 8 minutes. Insert ⟨⬥⟩ in workbowl, add liver and broth. Pulse-chop 4-6 times. Continue running food processor 30-60 seconds or until desired consistency. Add more liquid if desired. Serve immediately or freeze as previously directed.

NOTE: If baby is over 7 months add a small slice of onion to the liver and broth while it is cooking. Remove before pulse-chopping the liver. This gives the broth a little added flavor. As the child gets older the onion can be pulse-chopped with the liver.

COMPLETE LIVER DINNER

2-1/2 Cups or 15 Food Cubes

1 cup cubed cooked liver
1/2 cup cooked potatoes
1/2 cup BEEF BROTH
1/2 cup formula or evaporated milk

Insert ⤶, add cooked liver and potatoes. Pulse-chop 6-8 times. With machine running add liquid, process until smooth. More or less liquid may be used depending on desired consistency. Serve immediately or freeze as previously directed.

NOTE: Use a fresh potato rather than instant potatoes in baby food. The instant potatoes have preservatives and chemicals that are not present in the fresh potato. Also, cook potatoes with skins on to retain vitamins. Peel skin from the potato after it is cooked. As baby gets older, the skin can be left on the potato. The food processor will chop the skin fine. Just make sure to wash the skin well before cooking.

LIVER AND ONION DINNER

3 Cups or 18 Food Cubes

1 onion
3 small carrots
1/2 cup water
1 pound calves liver

Steam together onion, carrots, and water until fork tender. Add liver and cook an additional 7 minutes. Insert ⤶ in workbowl. Add vegetables and cup up liver. Pulse-chop 6-7 times. With machine running add liquid (taken from cooked vegetables and liver) through feed-tube. Process to desired consistency. Serve immediately or freeze as previously directed.

WHITE SAUCE

1 Tbsp. butter
1 Tbsp. flour
3/4 cup milk

Melt butter in saucepan and stir in flour, using a wire whisk. Add milk gradually to butter-flour mixture, stirring constantly. Keep stirring until mixture thickens. Simmer 2-3 minutes. Sauce will keep up to 4 days refrigerated. You can use this white sauce with any pureed leftovers. Use this WHITE SAUCE as directed for other recipes in this chapter.

To prepare white sauce in microwave, place butter in a 4-8 cup glass measuring cup. Melt butter 30 seconds on MEDIUM-HIGH power. Stir in flour. Gradually stir in milk. Microwave 45 seconds on MEDIUM-HIGH POWER, stir. Microwave another 30-45 seconds or until thickened.*

*SAUCES, CREAM
TIP: If cream sauce gets lumpy, process in the food processor with the METAL BLADE until smooth.

NOTE: You may use rice, potato, baby cereal, or pasta noodles as a substitute for WHITE SAUCE.

NOTE: We suggest using butter instead of margarine because butter is a natural cream and margarine is filled with unnecessary chemicals.

CHICKEN DINNER   3 Cups or 18 Food Cubes

1 cup cooked, cubed chicken
1/4 cup cooked carrots
1/2 cup cooked rice
1/2 cup chicken broth
1/2 cup formula or evaporated milk

Insert ⟨⬥⟩, add chicken, carrots, and cooked rice. Pulse-chop 6-8 times. With machine running add liquid and process until smooth and creamy. More liquid may be used if too thick. Serve immediately or freeze as previously directed.

NOTE: In these recipes the rice or potatoes could be substituted with macaroni, spaghetti or any cooked pasta noodle. Save the water from the pasta and add to other baby food dishes when liquid is needed. That water contains many of the vitamins lost in the cooking.

NOTE: The water left from the cooked vegetables should be used in the food that is being processed. That water contains many of the vitamins lost in the cooking.

CHICKEN SUPREME   3 Cups or 18 Food Cubes

1 cup cooked chicken (skin removed)
1 cup cooked asparagus
1/2 cup WHITE SAUCE (see recipe in this chapter)
1/4 cup formula or evaporated milk

Insert ⟨⬥⟩, add cubed chicken to workbowl and pulse-chop 3-4 times. Add asparagus and white sauce, process until smooth. With machine running add milk or formula if necessary. Serve immediately or freeze as previously directed.

TURKEY WITH STUFFING   2 Cups or 12 Food Cubes

1 cup cooked, cubed turkey
1/4 cup leftover stuffing
1/4 cup vegetables (yams, squash, etc.)
1/4 cup gravy
1/4-1 cup formula or milk

Insert ⬕ in workbowl, add turkey. Pulse-chop 3 times. Add stuffing and vegetables, pulse-chop 2-3 times. With machine running add desired amount of liquid and process until smooth. Serve immediately or freeze as previously directed.

NOTE: To eliminate the step of heating baby food, try to give baby the same food you eat at dinner. Take a little of all the foods the family is eating and process while warm, such as the turkey dinner above.

NOTE: Heat only the amount of food needed. The more often food is heated the less vitamins the food retains. Heat destroys vitamins.

NOTE: Thawed food can be kept refrigerated and covered for 1-2 days.

MEAT STEW   4-5 Cups or 24 Food Cubes

4 potatoes
5 carrots
1-1/2 pounds stew meat cut in 1 inch cubes
1/3 cup flour
4 Tbsp. oil
3 cups liquid (BEEF BROTH, vegetable
    water, or formula)

Insert ◯ in workbowl, add potatoes to feedtube. Process potatoes using medium pressure on the pusher. Leave in workbowl. Place carrots in feedtube making sure they are packed. Process using firm pressure on pusher. Place flour in paper bag, add meat and shake to coat meat with flour. Heat oil in a skillet. Add coated meat and brown. Add liquid and cover. Cook for 1-1/2 hours. Add potatoes and carrots. Cook an additional 30 minutes.

Insert ⚙ in workbowl. Fill workbowl half full of meat and vegetables. Pulse-chop 5-6 times. With machine running add liquid through feedtube until desired consistency. Processing should take about 30 seconds. Repeat with any remaining meat, vegetables and liquid. Serve immediately or freeze as previously directed.

NOTE: Sprinkle potatoes with lemon juice to keep them from turning brown.

NOTE: Prepare MEAT STEW as a main dish for the entire family, but do not puree. Add to the beef broth a bay leaf, salt, and garlic if desired.

CHOPPED MEAT-HAMBURGER   3-6 Food Cubes

Chopped or ground meat can be used instead of the meat called for in any meat recipe. Use either beef or pork.

1/2 to 3/4 pound chuck roast or pork pieces,
   cold or partially frozen*

Insert ⚙. Cut meat into 1-1/2 inch cubes and remove gristle.** Use some of the fat or the meat will be very dry. Pulse-chop 10 times or until desired consistency. Cook in frying pan until lightly browned, breaking up meat as you cook it. If meat gets too browned it will not make a smooth puree. Meat may also be microwaved. Cook on MEDIUM power 30-60 seconds. If using pork make sure pork is thoroughly cooked. Drain off fat. Return to workbowl with ⚙ in place. Pulse-chop 5-6 times. With machine running add milk, formula, or broth and process until smooth. Add 1/2 cup cooked vegetables to make an entire meal.

NOTE: More tender, expensive cuts of meats contain more fat and less protein than less tender, less expensive cuts of meat. For example: T-bone steak versus round steak. Less tender cuts of meat such as chuck roast, round steak, hamburger, etc. are not only more economical but much better for baby to eat.

*CHOPPING MEAT
   TIP: When meat is partially frozen it chops better. To partially freeze meat, place in freezer for 30-60 minutes.

**GRISTLE IN CHOPPED MEAT
   TIP: The gristle in meat will not chop when processing meat in the food processor. Remove the gristle before chopping. If the gristle is to be removed after chopping it can easily be picked out of the chopped meat.

FISH

Fish is a great food to give baby after 10 months. Babies like fish and it is a very nutritious food. Fish is also easy to process to a smooth consistency. Be sure to remove all bones before processing.

BROILED FISH   1 Cup or 6 Food Cubes

2-3 oz. fish (cod, sole, flounder, etc.)
1/2 tsp. lemon juice
Extra liquid (milk, vegetable water or formula)

Brush fish with a little oil and lemon juice. Place on broiler rack and broil 3-4 inches from heat source for about 7 minutes. Check thoroughly for bones. Insert ⚒ in workbowl. Add fish, pulse-chop 3-4 times. Add fish liquid from broiler pan. Use up to 1/4 cup liquid for each cup of cooked fish. Continue processing until smooth. Serve immediately or freeze as previously directed.

NOTE: Prepare BROILED FISH as a main dish for the entire family, but do not puree. Add seasonings as desired.

BAKED FISH STEW

2 Cups or 12 Food Cubes

2-3 oz. fish (cod, sole,
    flounder, etc.)
1/2 small carrot (cooked)
1/2 stalk celery (cooked)
1 small potato (cooked)
1/4 cup vegetable water
1/2 tsp. lemon juice
1/2 tsp. butter
Chopped parsley (optional)

Place fish in casserole dish with cooked vegetables. Add vegetable water, lemon juice, butter and parsley. Bake at 350° for 15-20 minutes. Fish can also be microwaved on HIGH for 2-3 minutes or until cooked. Insert 🔪 in workbowl, add cooked vegetables. Pulse-chop 2-3 times. Continue processing 10 seconds. Stop machine, scrape down sides of workbowl and add fish and liquid from casserole dish, pulse-chop 2-3 times. Use more liquid if desired. Process until desired consistency. Serve immediately or freeze as previously directed.

NOTE: Prepare BAKED FISH STEW as a main dish for the entire family, but do not puree. Add seasonings if desired. Increase the quantity as necessary.

PROTEIN ALTERNATES

We do not think of giving babies peanut butter because it is so thick, yet it is an excellent source of protein. The best, of course, is homemade peanut butter made with raw or roasted peanuts that you shell yourself. When you do buy peanuts in cans or jars do not buy those that have been preserved with BHT. Watch labels for sugar and salt content, too. Use peanut butter as a protein alternate after baby is 9 months of age.

PEANUT BUTTER

3/4 Cup

1 cup raw or roasted nuts,
  use walnuts, almonds, or any other nut, too
3 Tbsp. milk or formula

Insert ⚒ in workbowl, add nuts. Pulse-chop 4-6 time. Add milk, continue processing 1-2 minutes. Nuts will form a ball and then spread out. Makes 3/4 cup. Put some peanut butter on a spoon and let baby lick the spoon. Combine with other foods as suggested in the following recipe.

BANANA AND PEANUT BUTTER

1/2 Cup

Insert ⚒ in workbowl, add 1/4 cup home-processed peanut butter, and 1/2 banana, pulse until smooth and creamy. If too thick add a little milk or formula. Use for BANANA AND PEANUT BUTTER SANDWICHES.

MEAL-IN-ONE EGG

1/2 Cup

1 egg
1-2 food cubes of any fruit,
  vegetable, meat, or fish puree
  or 1/4 cup shredded cheese
  or 1/4 cup cooked cereal
  or 1/4 cup rice (cooked)
1 tsp. wheat germ
1 tsp. milk or formula

Insert ⚒ in workbowl; add egg, desired fruit, vegetable, or meat cubes, cheese or starch. Pulse-chop until smooth. Soften wheat germ with milk, add to puree. Pulse-chop 2-3 times. Pour into two custard cups and place in pan filled with 3/4 inch of hot water. Bake 30 minutes at 350° or until knife inserted in center comes out clean. May be cooked in microwave on MEDIUM power 2-3 minutes or until knife inserted in center comes out clean. Store covered in refrigerator 2-3 days.

SOUPS

Soups are an easy way of introducing meat, vegetable and pasta to baby.

CHICKEN SOUP   2 Cups or 12 Food Cubes

1/4 cup cooked chicken
1/4 cup cooked carrots
2 tsp. uncooked quick-cooking wheat
  cereal or baby cereal
1 tsp. butter
1/4 cup CHICKEN BROTH (warm)
1 cup milk or formula (warm)

Insert ⚙ in workbowl. Add cooked chicken, cooked carrots, butter, and cereal. Pulse-chop 5-6 times. With machine running add warmed broth and formula.* Pour into a saucepan and cook for 5 minutes stirring constantly. This may also be heated in a microwave on MEDIUM power for 2 minutes. Serve immediately or freeze as previously described.

NOTE: Broth and milk are added warm to prevent the fat from congealing in the soup.

NOTE: Prepare CHICKEN SOUP for the entire family as directed using milk instead of formula; adding onion, garlic, bay leaf and salt if desired.

NOTE: CREAMY CHICKEN SOUP may also be made with chicken broth and pasta noodles. Pulse-chop until fine. See directions under CHICKEN BROTH.

*LIQUIDS, ADDING TO MIXTURES
TIP: Insert the METAL BLADE. It is better to add liquids to solid food in the workbowl, than to add food to liquids in the workbowl. If the liquid is added to the food it forms a thicker mixture. This will usually prevent any leakage through the shaft that the blade rests on. This also allows larger quantities to be processed as the leakage is eliminated.

TOMATO SOUP   1-1/2 Cups

2 medium tomatoes (very ripe)
1/2 stalk celery (1/4 cup)
1 small slice onion (optional)
2 Tbsp. water
2 Tbsp. butter
1-1/2 Tbsp. flour
1 cup formula or milk

Insert ⊙ in workbowl. Remove stem end of each tomato. Lay tomato stem end down in feedtube, shred using light pressure. The skin of the tomato will remain on top of the shredding disc. Press tomato pulp from workbowl through a sieve to strain seeds out.* Insert ⊙ again, place onion and celery in feedtube, trying to pack feedtube if possible. Process using firm pressure on pusher. In a covered saucepan cook processed vegetables with water for 15 minutes or in a microwave 3-5 minutes on HIGH. Prepare a white sauce by melting butter in a saucepan and adding flour to the butter. Stir with a whisk. Slowly add milk, heat and stir until mixture thickens. (This white sauce may also be made in a microwave. Place butter in a 4-8 cup glass measuring cup. Melt butter 30 seconds on MEDIUM-HIGH power. Stir in flour. Gradually stir in milk. Microwave 45 seconds on MEDIUM-HIGH POWER, stir. Microwave another 30-45 seconds or until thickened.)** Insert ⚬, add cream sauce and cooked vegetables to workbowl. Process 30 seconds or until smooth.

*NOTE: During tomato harvest freeze additional tomato pulp for later use for fresh summer taste all year.

**CREAM SAUCE, LUMPY
   TIP: If cream sauce gets lumpy, process in the food processor with the METAL BLADE until smooth.

NOTE: Prepare TOMATO SOUP for the entire family as directed using milk instead of formula; adding salt and garlic, if desired.

CREAMY AVOCADO SOUP 1-1/2 Cups or 9 Food Cubes

1/2 large ripe avocado
1 cup formula, evaporated milk, or milk

Insert ⬧ in workbowl, add avocado and pulse chop 4-6 times. Scrape down side of workbowl if necessary. With machine running add milk through feedtube. Add more or less milk for desired consistency. Heat soup to serving temperature or use warm milk to avoid heating soup once it is made. Avocados are a very good source of vitamin A and honest, this soup is really good. Try it and remember, don't make faces while feeding it to baby. Smile, smile, smile!

NOTE: An avocado must be very soft in order to be ripe. A hard avocado is not ripe. Eating a hard avocado is like eating a green banana.

NOTE: Salt is an acquired taste. Babies usually do not discriminate between salted and unsalted food. Salt is not necessary in the soup recipes or in any of the recipes in this chapter. Do not give babies commercially prepared soup as there is a lot of salt in them, not to speak of the sugar and preservatives.

NOTE: If soup is too thin add wheat germ, powdered milk, or baby cereal to thicken it. Wheat germ is a good laxative so use it in small amounts.

NOTE: Prepare CREAMY AVOCADO SOUP for a family meal using milk and adding seasonings, if desired.

VEGETABLE SOUP
2-3 Cups or 12-18 Food Cubes

1 medium carrot
1 small potato
1/2 cup green beans
1 cup CHICKEN BROTH (see recipe in this chapter)
1-1/2 Tbsp. cereal

Place all ingredients (except cereal) in saucepan with CHICKEN BROTH. Cook on low heat until fork tender. If using a microwave cook 5-6 minutes on HIGH or until fork tender. Insert ⚖ in workbowl, add cooked vegetables. Pulse-chop 3-5 times. With machine running add broth through the feedtube. Stop machine when ingredients are smooth. Add baby cereal to thicken soup if necessary, process an additional 20 seconds. Serve immediately or freeze as previously described.

VEGETABLES

The best way to cook vegetables is in a microwave oven. This is the easiest, uses less water (for some vegetables no water at all) and the vegetables maintain more of their vitamins. Vegetables are placed in a covered, microwave casserole with about 1/8-1/4 cup water, depending on amount and type of vegetables being cooked. The vegetables are microwaved on HIGH for 3-6 minutes; depending on amount and type of vegetable. Remember to allow 5 minutes standing time after vegetables have been cooked. This further cooks the vegetables.

If a microwave is not available, cook vegetables on range top in a covered saucepan with minimum amount of water, about 1/4 cup. Place vegetable and water in saucepan, cover, and cook on high until water boils and steam comes out from under the lid. Without picking up the lid, lower the heat to simmer and continue cooking an additional 5 minutes. If the lid is lifted continuously during the cooking time, the water disappears, and the food may burn because there is not any water. If more water is used the vitamins in the vegetables are lost to the water. Always save any water remaining and use to process baby foods.

NOTE: Use fresh vegetables whenever possible. They should be washed quickly (don't soak in water or they will lose their vitamins). If fresh vegetables are not available use frozen but do not use canned as they may contain a great deal of salt, sugar, and preservatives.

The following are some suggested combinations of vegetables to process.

Green beans and peas
Sweet potatoes and squash
Carrots and peas
Carrots and apples
Potatoes and carrots
Potatoes and green beans
Potatoes and spinach

Swiss chard and carrots
Beet tops and carrots
Parsnips and carrots
Parsnips and squash
Squash and turnips
Red and green cabbage

BASIC VEGETABLE RECIPE   1 Cup or 6 Food Cubes

1 cup cooked vegetables
1/4-1/2 cup liquid (CHICKEN BROTH, formula, milk, evaporated milk, vegetable water)

Insert⤵, add vegetables and pulse-chop 2-3 times. With machine running add the liquid through the feedtube. Process until desired consistency. Serve immediately or freeze as previously directed. (If vegetable becomes too runny thicken with baby cereal, wheat germ, or add bread and process with the vegetables.)

NOTE: Always save the water from the cooked vegetables to process with the baby food.

BROCCOLI   1 Cup or 6 Food Cubes

1/4 pound fresh broccoli
1/3 cup liquid (broth, vegetable water, formula, evaporated milk)

Leaves should be cooked with broccoli stems and flowers as they contain the highest amounts of nutrients. Wash broccoli and remove lower edge of stalk.* Cook according to directions at the beginning of this section. Insert⤵, add cooked, cut-up broccoli stems, flowers, and leaves. Pulse-chop 3-4 times. With machine running add liquid through the feedtube, process 20 seconds, stop machine and scrape down sides of workbowl. Continue processing an additional 20 seconds. Serve immediately or freeze as previously directed.

NOTE: Broccoli can cause stomach gas. Introduce it to baby after 8 months of age. For older baby cooked broccoli flowers are a good finger food because they are soft.

*NOTE: Peel broccoli stalk if necessary.

BEETS

1 Cup or 6 Food Cubes

3 small fresh beets (cooked)
1/2 cup orange juice

Trim ends, peel, and slice or shred uncooked beets in the processor. Cook beets according to general directions under the VEGETABLE heading in this chapter. Save beet tops for another meal. Insert ⬩, add beets and pulse-chop 4-5 times. With machine running add liquid through the feedtube. Process 20 seconds. Stop machine and scrape down sides of workbowl. Process another 20 seconds or until smooth. Serve immediately or freeze as previously directed.

BEET TOPS

3-4 Food Cubes

3 beet tops

Pulse-chop cooked beet tops with the ⬩. Add desired liquid if necessary as machine is running. Serve immediately or freeze as previously directed.

209

BEETS WITH PINEAPPLE   1 Cup or 6 Food Cubes

3 small cooked beets
1/2 cup fresh pineapple pieces

Insert ⚙ in workbowl, add beets and pineapple. Process until smooth. With machine running add pineapple juice or water through the feedtube if necessary. Serve immediately or freeze as previously directed.

NOTE: Bowel movements change in color with the introduction of different foods and different colors of vegetables. Don't let that alarm you. In the case of beets the bowel movement will be reddish in color.

CABBAGE   1 Cup or 6 Food Cubes

1/4 pound cabbage

Cook cabbage according to general directions under the VEGETABLE heading in this chapter. Insert ⚙, add cabbage and any liquid left from cooking the cabbage. Pulse-chop 3-4 times. Continue processing until smooth. Add 1 tablespoon lemon juice if desired. Serve immediately or freeze as previously directed.

CABBAGE AND CARROTS   3 Cups or 18 Food Cubes

1/2 pound cooked cabbage
1/2 pound cooked carrots
1/4 cup liquid (broth, formula, milk,
    evaporated milk or vegetable water)

Insert ⚙, add cooked carrots and cabbage. Pulse-chop 3-4 times, add liquid through the feedtube while machine is running. Scrape down sides of workbowl if necessary. Process until smooth, about 1 minute. Serve immediately or freeze as previously directed.

CARROTS   1-1/2 Cups or 9 Food Cubes

1/2 pound carrots (cooked)
1/2 cup liquid (formula, vegetable water)

Follow general cooking directions under the VEGETABLE heading in this chapter. Insert⌐, add carrots. Pulse-chop 3 times. With machine running add liquid through feedtube. Process until smooth. Serve immediately or freeze as previously directed.

CARROTS AND CELERY   2 Cups or 12 Food Cubes

2 medium carrots (cooked)
3 large stalks celery (cooked)
1/2 cup liquid (CHICKEN BROTH, formula,
    evaporated milk or vegetable water)

Follow general cooking directions under the VEGETABLE heading in this chapter. Save vegetable water for either this dish or for future use. Insert ⌐, add vegetables. Pulse-chop 3-4 times. With machine running add liquid through the feedtube and continue processing until smooth. Serve immediately or freeze as previously directed.

VARIATIONS: Use either CARROTS AND PARSNIPS or CARROTS AND APPLES/ OR APPLESAUCE for a flavorful combination. Use similar amounts to above recipe and prepare as directed.

GREEN BEANS

1-1/2 Cups or 9 Food Cubes

1/2 pound fresh green beans
1/2 cup liquid (CHICKEN BROTH, formula,
  evaporated milk, or vegetable water)
1/2 tsp. butter (optional)

Wash beans and leave whole for cooking so they will not lose any vitamins. Cook either in microwave or on range top as directed under the VEGETABLE heading in this chapter. Cook until fork tender. Insert ⚙ in workbowl, add green beans. Pulse-chop 3-4 times. With machine running add liquid and butter through the feedtube Process until smooth. Serve immediately or freeze as previously directed.

PEAS

2 Cups or 12 Food Cubes

2 cups peas
1/2 cup liquid (CHICKEN BROTH, evaporated milk, formula or vegetable water)

Cook peas as directed under the VEGETABLE heading in this chapter. Insert ⚙ and place cooked peas in workbowl. Pulse-chop 3-4 times. With machine running add liquid through the feedtube and process until smooth. Serve immediately or freeze as previously directed.

NOTE: Soft cooked peas are a great finger food as baby gets older and feeds him/herself.

SPINACH   1/2 Cup or 3 Food Cubes

1/4 pound fresh spinach (2 cups lightly packed)
1/2 tsp. lemon juice
1/2 tsp. butter

Wash spinach leaves thoroughly in cold water being very careful to remove all sand and dirt. The water that is retained in the leaves is enough liquid for cooking. Cook either in a covered saucepan, on low heat about 10-12 minutes or in a microwave on HIGH for 3-5 minutes. Let stand 5 minutes after microwaving. Do not drain water. Insert ⟿, add spinach to workbowl and pulse-chop 3-4 times. Add butter and lemon juice and continue running until smooth. When baby is eating egg yolk, add cooked yolk to spinach in workbowl and process together. Serve immediately or freeze as previously directed.

CREAMED SPINACH   3/4 Cup

1/4 cup WHITE SAUCE
2 cups lightly packed fresh spinach
   or about 1/4 pound

Prepare WHITE SAUCE as directed under MEAT heading in this chapter. Cook spinach as directed under SPINACH. Insert ⟿, add cooked spinach and cooked white sauce. Pulse-chop until smooth. Remember, if white sauce gets lumpy it will smooth out when processed with the metal blade.

NOTE: Many greens, such as spinach and kale, contain oxalic acid which combine with calcium and prevent it from reaching the blood. It is wise to add 1 teaspoon or more of powdered milk to each serving whenever you prepare leafy vegetables for baby. Chocolate also contains oxalic acid and when eaten together with milk prevents the calcium from reaching the blood. Chocolate milk should not be used as a regular beverage.

NOTE: Serve CREAMED SPINACH as a family dish, increasing recipe as desired.

POTATOES

1/2-3/4 Cup

The potato is a very versatile vegetable and can be mixed with many different types of food, meats, and other vegetables.

1 potato

Microwave whole potato with skin (to retain vitamins) for 4-5 minutes depending on size of potato or cook whole in a saucepan until fork tender. Peel after it is cooked. Insert ⬡, place potato in feedtube. Process potato using light pressure on pusher. Remove shredding disc and insert ⬡ being careful that blade rests on the bottom of the workbowl with no food underneath it. Add about 2-3 tablespoons warm milk and butter. Pulse-chop once or twice. Do not overprocess or potato will get too starchy and become like glue. If that happens just add more warm milk and stir in by hand.*

*MASHED POTATOES
TIP: If potatoes become too gluey when processed with the metal blade, add more milk and stir by hand until potatoes are nice and creamy. For 1 medium potato you may need as much as 1/2 cup milk depending on desired consistency.

ACORN OR BUTTERNUT SQUASH

2 Cups or 9-12 Food Cubes

Winter squash are acorn, butternut, pumpkin, etc. They are sweet tasting, easy to cook and make wonderful baby food. Both winter and summer squash freeze very well.

1 small squash

Steam, bake, or microwave the desired squash until fork tender. Peel squash. Insert ⬡, add squash and process until smooth. Avoid adding any sugars or salt. Mix this vegetable with other baby foods or baby cereal.

NOTE: This recipe is also good for pumpkin. When buying a pumpkin to eat always buy the very small ones. These are also good for baking. See JACK-O-LANTERN under DESSERTS.

ZUCCHINI

3/4 Cup or 4 Food Cubes

There are different types of squash. One type is summer squash such as zucchini and yellow squash. These are blander, less starchy, and have more tender skins than winter squash. Use small zucchini. If a friend gives you a large zucchini it is over grown and is too tough for this recipe. Use the over grown zucchini for other recipes in this book, like the ZUCCHINI BREAD.

1 small zucchini (unpeeled)
4 Tbsp. water
1/2 tsp. butter (optional)

Scrub zucchini, do not peel. Insert ⌢, pack zucchini in feedtube, process using medium pressure.

STEAM—Place sliced zucchini in small saucepan. Add water, cover and cook on low heat 10 minutes or until fork tender. If there is a lot of water in the pan, drain; save and freeze water for processing other baby foods. Remember this water is rich in vitamins.
BAKE—Place zucchini and water in small baking dish. Wrap dish tightly with aluminum foil and bake 30 minutes at 350°. You may bake it in milk instead of water.
MICROWAVE—Place zucchini in a covered casserole and microwave for 5 minutes on HIGH power or until tender.

Insert ⫗ in workbowl, add cooked zucchini and pulse-chop 2-3 times. Add butter if desired. Continue processing until smooth. Freeze any remaining squash.

CORN

3/4 Cup or 5 Food Cubes

The cob of the corn is a good thing for baby to suck on, especially when teething. Introduce corn to a 9 month old baby or older.

1 ear corn

Cook corn in microwave with husks on for 4 minutes per ear of corn on HIGH power. Remove husk and cut kernels off cob. Insert ⫗ in workbowl, pulse-chop corn 3-4 times. With machine running add 1/4-1/2 cup vegetable water, milk, or formula through the feedtube. Process until smooth. Serve immediately or freeze as previously directed.

VEGETABLE SOUFFLE

1-1/2 Cups

2 eggs, separated
1 Tbsp. each of vinegar and water
1/2 cup WHITE SAUCE
1/2 cup cooked vegetable (carrots,
squash, peas, sweet potatoes, etc.)

Insert ⬯ in workbowl, add egg whites.* Process 8 seconds. With machine running add vinegar and water mixture through the feedtube. Continue processing 1-2 minutes or until egg whites are stiff. Remove from workbowl and set aside. Without washing out workbowl add cooked vegetable, white sauce, and egg yolks. Pulse 3-4 times. Continue processing until smooth, about 20 seconds. Add egg whites and pulse 1-2 times, do not overprocess. Bake 40 minutes at 350° in a greased casserole or individual dishes. This may be kept 1-2 days. The texture will change a little the longer it is refrigerated but baby won't mind.

*NOTE: If any egg yolk mixes into the egg white then the white will NOT whip. If whites sit for more than 10 minutes after they are whipped they will lose their firmness and have to be redone.

*NOTE: Have vegetables and white sauce cooked before processing egg whites for the souffle. Egg whites break down within 5-10 minutes.

NOTE: Double VEGETABLE SOUFFLE recipe to serve as a family dish.

VEGETABLE CUSTARD   1 Cup

1/4 cup baby rice cereal
1/4 cup formula or milk
1/2 cup cooked vegetable
1 egg

Mix together cereal and liquid. Insert ⬭ in workbowl, add vegetable and process 3-4 times. Add egg and continue processing until smooth about 10 seconds. Add cereal mixture and pulse 2-3 times. Pour into custard cups and place into pan of hot water that comes up to level of mixture. Bake 30 minutes at 350° or until knife inserted in the center comes out clean. Store covered in refrigerator 2-3 days.

FRUITS

Any of the following suggestions may be combined together for a fruit meal or sauce.

Applesauce and bananas
Applesauce and pears
Applesauce and apricots
Applesauce and peaches
Bananas and tapioca
Pineapple (fresh) and
banana

Peaches and tapioca
Prunes and tapioca
Peaches and pears
Bananas and pears
Apricots and pears
Melon and peaches
Bananas and kiwi

FRUIT WITH TAPIOCA   2-1/2 Cups or 16 Food Cubes

1 cup tapioca pudding
1 cup cooked fruit (peaches, pears, etc)

Prepare pudding as directed on package, but substitute apple juice for sugar and use 2 tablespoons less milk. Omit the salt. Insert ⬭ in workbowl, add fruit and pulse-chop 4 times or until well chopped. Add tapioca and pulse-chop 3 times. Serve immediately or freeze as previously directed.

APPLESAUCE

1/2 Cup or 3 Food Cubes

This recipe can be used with any fresh fruit to make it into a sauce.

1 medium fresh apple
1/4 cup pineapple juice or orange juice

Quarter and core apple. If necessary, remove skin. Cook in saucepan with pineapple juice until soft. May place apple and juice in small covered casserole and cook in microwave on HIGH power for 2 minutes. Insert ⚒, add apple and juice, pulse-chop 3 times or until smooth. *DO NOT ADD SUGAR.*

NOTE: Leave the skin on the apple to produce a thicker applesauce and retain more vitamins. Process about 10 seconds longer when skin is left on. See APPLESAUCE, FRESH in TIPS for more suggestions.

COTTAGE CHEESE WITH FRUIT

1-1/2 Cups or 9 Food Cubes

1/2 cup cottage cheese
1/2 cup applesauce
   or 1 pear or banana
4 Tbsp. fruit juice (apple, orange, pineapple)

Insert ⚒ in workbowl, add cottage cheese. Pulse-chop 4 times. Add fruit and fruit juice and pulse-chop 4 times or until desired consistency. Serve immediately or freeze as previously described.

AVOCADO AND BANANA   2 Cups or 12 Food Cubes

1 very ripe avocado
1 very ripe banana
1 tsp. lemon juice
1/2 cup plain yogurt
1/2 cup cottage cheese

Insert ⟨⟩ in workbowl, add cut up avocado, banana, and lemon juice. Pulse-chop 3-4 times. Stop machine and scrape down sides of workbowl, add cottage cheese and yogurt. Pulse until desired consistency. This mixture will be thick. Serve immediately and freeze remaining mixture as previously directed.

NOTE: You can omit the yogurt and cottage cheese and just process the avocado and banana with the lemon juice. Try it, baby will like it as long as you don't make faces.

STRAWBERRY YOGURT   1 Cup or 6 Food Cubes

1/2 cup fresh strawberries
1 Tbsp. apple juice
1/2 cup plain yogurt
1 tsp. vanilla

Insert ⟨⟩, process strawberries until fine. Add apple juice, yogurt and vanilla. Pulse until smooth. These are also delicious frozen and eaten as STRAWBERRY YOGURT POPSICLES.

NOTE: This recipe can be made with any fruit such as blueberries, apple, kiwi, pineapple, peaches, pears, bananas, etc.

YAMS AND APPLES PUREE   2 Cups or 12 Food Cubes

1 sweet potato, cooked
1 apple, cooked
1/2 cup liquid (fruit or vegetable water)

Cook sweet potato and apple with skins on to retain most of the vitamins. Peel after they are cooked. Insert ⏣, add cooked, peeled and cored apple and peeled sweet potato to workbowl. Pulse 4 times. With machine running add liquid through the feedtube. Process until smooth. Serve immediately or freeze as previously directed.

PINEAPPLE AND BANANAS   3 Cups or 18 Food Cubes

2 cups fresh pineapple chunks
1 ripe banana

Insert ⏣. Add pineapple and bananas, pulse-chop 6-7 times. Continue running machine until mixture is well blended. Mixture turns frothy and light. This is a great dessert for the entire family.

VARIATION: Freeze the pineapple chunks on a baking sheet. Insert METAL BLADE. Add frozen pineapple chunks, pulse-chop 10-12 times or until finely chopped. Add pieces of banana and process until it forms a sherbet for PINEAPPLE-BANANA SHERBET. Three-four servings.

TROPICAL FRUIT DRINK   1-3/4 Cups

1/3 cup orange juice concentrate
1/4 cup powdered milk
1 ripe banana
3/4 cup water

Insert ⬱ in workbowl, add orange juice concentrate, powdered milk, and banana. Pulse-chop 4-5 times. With machine running add water through the feedtube.* Process until smooth about 30 seconds. Great drink for the entire family, too. This drink may be frozen for TROPICAL FRUIT POPSICLES.

*BEVERAGES, PROCESSING
TIP: When making drinks in a food processor, place solid food items in first. With machine running add liquid through the feedtube. This thicker mixture will usually prevent liquids from seeping out of the workbowl.
TIP: Process no more liquid than to the top of the metal blade when making juice concentrates or other liquids which have no solids added to them.

FRUIT DRINK   2 Cups

1/2 banana
4 ripe strawberries
1 cooked egg yolk
1 cup apple juice (unsweetened)

Insert ⬱, add banana, strawberries, and egg yolk to workbowl, pulse-chop 6-8 times. With machine running add apple juice through the feedtube. Process until smooth. This is a good nutritional drink for baby or entire family and it may also be frozen for FRUIT POPSICLES.

YOGURT POPSICLES   4 Cups or 24 Food Cubes

2 cups plain yogurt
1-6 oz. can frozen orange juice concentrate
1 tsp. vanilla

Insert ⬭, add yogurt, juice and vanilla. Pulse-chop 6-8 times. Freeze in popsicle containers or small paper cups with sticks in the middle. When ready to serve remove paper around cup. May also use the cup as a holder while eating.

NOTE: If you own reusable plastic popsicle sets, keep one in the freezer filled with water. When a child falls and gets hurt and you need ice, you have an ice cube available with a handle on it. The child can hold it on his/her bruise.

BREADS

The following recipes will help fill your baby's need for carbohydrates. Try making some of these recipes before running out to the store for commercially prepared bread products.

BANANA BREAD STICKS   4 Dozen Sticks

1 loaf bread

Prepare BANANA BRAN BREAD. See INDEX. Omit the nuts. Cut the bread into thin sticks. Place sticks on a cookie sheet. Bake for 1 hour at 150°. Sticks will become crunchy when cooled. These sticks could be made with any quick bread recipe such as ZUCCHINI BREAD or carrot bread. Be sure to omit nuts and raisins until baby is old enough to chew these easily.

PASTINA

1 Cup

2 cups water
1 tsp. butter
1/2 cup pastina

In a saucepan boil water. To this add pastina, cook 5-7 minutes. Drain some of the water, to the rest add a little butter and serve. Also use in any of the recipes in place of cereal, rice, or potato. The noodles can also be cooked in CHICKEN BROTH or tomato juice. Do not drain off these liquids but serve with the pastina.

NOTE: Pastina is a small star shaped Italian noodle. It usually can be found in the pasta section of the grocery store in a 16 ounce bag or box. It can also be found in any Italian grocery store.

NOTE: If it is necessary to make this pasta finer, insert METAL BLADE in workbowl, add cooked pastina and liquid. Pulse-chop 1-3 times depending on consistency desired. Babies and children love this noodle and so will you.

BREAD CEREAL

1 Serving

1 slice bread, toasted (preferably homemade bread)
1/4-1/2 cup warm milk (formula or evaporated milk)

Insert ⌘ in workbowl. Break up toast, add to workbowl, pulse-chop 2-3 times. Add warm milk and pulse chop 4-5 times or until you reach desired consistency. Add a little butter. Serve warm.

GRAHAM CRACKERS

2 to 2-1/2 Dozen

1 cup whole wheat flour
1 cup unbleached flour
1 tsp. baking powder
2-4 Tbsp. sugar (optional)
1/4 cup butter (FROZEN)
1/2 cup milk

Insert ⚒ in workbowl, add flours, baking powder, and sugar. Cut butter into 4 pieces, add to workbowl. Pulse-chop 4-5 times or until mixture is the consistency of cornmeal. With machine running add milk through feedtube. Stop machine just as dough begins to form a ball. *DO NOT* let dough form into a ball which would mean you have overprocessed the dough. Roll dough out 1/4 inch thick onto a floured surface, preferably a pastry cloth. Cut into 3 inch squares and place on ungreased cookie sheet. Prick each square with a fork and brush with some milk. Bake at 400° for 15-18 minutes. Serve plain or try the following graham cracker recipe.

GRAHAM CRACKERS AND BANANAS   1 Cup

4 graham cracker squares
1 banana (ripe)
1/4 cup milk

Insert 🔪 in workbowl, break up graham crackers and add to workbowl. Pulse-chop 3-4 times. Add banana and milk; pulse-chop until smooth. A great dessert and snack for baby and rest of family.

NOTE: A banana is ripe when it is yellow with brown specks on it. If you use a banana that is too green there isn't a lot of flavor. Besides the potassium that is found in bananas is not present until fully ripe.

BREAD PANCAKES   1/2 Cup or 2 Pancakes

1 slice wheat bread
2 egg yolks *
2 Tbsp. formula or milk
1/4 tsp. maple extract or vanilla

Insert 🔪 in workbowl, add bread. Pulse-chop 3-4 times. Add remaining ingredients, pulse until smooth. Cook the same way as you would pancakes. Serve with fresh fruit or a little powdered sugar rather than syrup.

*NOTE: For a child over 1 year you may use 1 whole egg instead of the 2 egg yolks. Double the recipe and freeze remaining cooked pancakes. Heat either in toaster or in microwave oven on LOW power for 30 seconds. Heat just to remove frost. Do not overheat or the pancakes will become too hard. Then they will become a cookie.

*NOTE: Freeze egg whites and use for meringues or brush on homemade bread.

PEANUT BUTTER PANCAKES

6-8 Servings

1/2 cup peanuts
2 Tbsp. brown sugar (optional)
2 eggs
3/4 cup milk
1/2 tsp. vanilla
1/4 cup nonfat dry milk powder
2 tsp. baking powder
1 cup whole wheat flour

Insert ⚒ in workbowl, add whole peanuts. Pulse-chop 5-6 times. Continue running machine until peanut butter is made, about 2 minutes. Add sugar, eggs, milk, and vanilla; pulse-chop 3-4 times. Add dry ingredients and pulse twice. Stop machine to scrape down sides of workbowl. Pulse once more. Do not over process. Cook on lightly greased griddle. Serve warm or cool. Wrap each of the pancakes individually and freeze. Heat to take out the frost and serve cold as a finger food snack.

NOTE: When serving pancakes or waffles to baby make sure they are homemade and not the commercially frozen type. Commercially prepared products are filled with additives, lots of sugar and salt. Place homemade waffles, pancakes or French toast in workbowl, process with milk using the METAL BLADE. A couple of pulses and baby can eat what the rest of the family is eating. Top with fresh fruit. NO SYRUP FOR BABY.

DESSERTS

The following recipes are so called "desserts". Desserts should not be part of baby's diet but if you must these are some nutritious recipes to make.

VANILLA CUSTARD PUDDING   2-1/2 Cups

3 egg yolks
1/2 tsp. vanilla
2 cups hot formula, evaporated milk, or milk

Insert ⟨ ⟩ in workbowl, add eggs and process 1 minute. With machine running add hot milk and vanilla through the feedtube; process until blended, about 10 seconds. Place mixture in saucepan and cook over LOW heat stirring constantly. Cook until thick or mixture coats a spoon. Serve warm or cold. Remember babies don't mind cold food.

PEACH PUDDING   3 Cups

3 peach halves or 1 cup
   sliced fresh fruit, cooked
2 cups milk or formula
3-1/2 Tbsp. arrowroot or cornstarch

Insert ⟨ ⟩ in workbowl, add peach halves (or any fresh cooked fruit). Pulse-chop 3-4 times, add sugar and cornstarch. With machine running add milk through feedtube. Process until smooth, pour mixture into a saucepan and cook over medium heat until thickened. May place in 8 cup glass measuring cup or large casserole and microwave on MEDIUM-HIGH 3-5 minutes, stopping to stir after every 30-40 seconds. Let cool. This pudding can be frozen for PEACH PUDDING POPSICLES.

COTTAGE CHEESE CUSTARD

1/2 cup cottage cheese
2 tsp. sugar or fruit juice, optional
1 egg
3/4 cup hot milk
Nutmeg (optional)

Insert ⚫ in workbowl, add cottage cheese, sugar or juice and egg. Pulse-chop 5-6 times. With machine running add hot milk through feedtube. Process until smooth, about 10 seconds. Butter 3 custard cups. Pour cottage cheese mixture into custard cups. Sprinkle with nutmeg and set cups in pan containing 1-1/2 inches of hot water. Bake 40 minutes at 350° or until knife inserted in center comes out clean. Cool before serving.

NOTE: These could bake in an electric frying pan that is filled with hot water. Add custard cups; cover with lid, leaving vent open and bake at 180° for 40-50 minutes or until knife inserted in center comes out clean. Cool before serving.

VARIATION: Add any fruit, vegetable, fish, or meat food cube to this recipe. The food cube would be processed with the egg before adding milk.

ORANGE PUDDING   2 Cups

2 egg yolks
2 tsp. sugar or fruit juice
4 tsp. cornstarch
Juice of 2 oranges, freshly squeezed
2 egg whites, processed until fluffy
2 tsp. lemon juice

Insert ⟨blade⟩, add egg yolks, fruit juice or sugar, and process 10 seconds. Add cornstarch and pulse twice. With machine running add orange juice through the feedtube. Process until smooth, about 20 seconds. Transfer mixture to saucepan and cook on low heat until thick (about 5 minutes) being careful not to burn contents. Cool.

Wash out workbowl, cover, and blade; dry well. When orange pudding mixture has cooled process egg whites. Add egg whites* to workbowl and process for 1 minute. With machine running add lemon juice and process another minute or until fluffy and whites hold their peak. Add cooled mixture to workbowl that still contains egg whites. Pulse once or twice, just to fold in egg whites. *DO NOT OVER PROCESS*. Serve cold.

*NOTE: If any egg yolk mixes into the egg white then the white will NOT whip. If whites sit for more than 10 minutes after they are whipped they will lose their firmness and have to be redone.

NOTE: Prepare grated orange peel.** Add 1 tsp. of grated peel with eggs, if desired. Serve ORANGE PUDDING as a light, low calorie family dessert.

****CITRUS PEEL, GRATED LEMON, ORANGE, LIME
TIP: Any citrus fruit skin may be processed in the food processor to give you grated rind. Peel a thin layer from the entire fruit with a vegetable peeler. Insert METAL BLADE in clean dry workbowl for best results. With machine running drop peelings through feedtube. Process 2-3 minutes. Scrape bowl down if necessary. If peel is not fine enough add some of the sugar called for in the recipe. The metal blade can grate the peel more easily when there is a larger quantity of food in the workbowl. Use immediately or freeze.

NOTE: Some commercial baby food and pudding has modified food starch. If you feed baby from the jar the saliva from the spoon breaks the starch down and the food later becomes watery. This can cause a bacterial growth on the uneaten food.

JUNIOR AND TODDLER FOOD

Follow the same basic recipes and combinations, but chop the food rather than pureeing. To chop foods; insert METAL BLADE in workbowl, add food, pulse chop 4-8 times until desired consistency is reached. Use less liquid than what you used to make BABY pureed foods.

Baby food can only be free from sugars, salts, additives, preservatives and any chemicals and artificial color if you use food free from these. Taking a can of commercially made spaghetti and processing it to feed baby is not a good idea because it has all the products just mentioned. Stay away from commercially prepared foods for baby (and family) and you will have a much happier and healthier baby.

PLAYDOUGH   2-1/2 Cups

2 cups flour
2 Tbsp. alum
2 Tbsp. oil
1 cup water
1/2 cup salt
4-5 drops food coloring for pastel colors
10 or more drops food color for deeper shades

Insert ⬠ in workbowl, add flour and alum. With machine running add oil through the feedtube and process 10 seconds. Boil water and stir in salt until it is dissolved. Add food coloring. With machine running add water mixture through the feedtube. Process about 1 minute. Playdough should be very soft and pliable. If gooey add a little more flour. If too dry add 2-4 tablespoons more water. Keep in an airtight container and this should last 6 months.

NOTE: Mix food coloring colors for variety in shades. For example - yellow and red make orange, red and blue make purple, etc.

NOTE: PLAYDOUGH is edible, though a bit salty.

NOTE: Alum can be found in the grocery store with the spices in the baking section. It can also be found in the drug store. It keeps PLAYDOUGH fresh.

TIPS

231

233

| METAL | SHREDDING | DOUGH | SLICING | FRENCH-FRY |
| BLADE | DISC | BLADE | DISC | DISC |

Stop!!! Look no further. Here are the answers to all your questions about the food processor. The TIPS are listed alphabetically for easy reference. If any operation in the food processor is unfamiliar to you than check TIPS for suggestions to speedily show you the method. A treasure-trove of ideas for using the food processor is gathered here. Check under WORKBOWL COVER, AS AN EXTRA PAIR OF HANDS for a great idea or JULIENNE STRIPS-CARROTS for beautiful stir-fry vegetables without a julienne blade.

This fingertip food processor guide makes all your cooking fun, easy and professional-looking with just a push of the button. Use the symbol key printed on alternate pages to be sure you are using the blade or disc suggested in the TIP.

APPLESAUCE, FRESH

TIP: Add fresh peeled apples to workbowl with a little water, lemon juice and sugar. Process with METAL BLADE until apples are finely chopped. This eliminates cooking the apples. For thick applesauce, cook apples with skins on. Process cooked apples with the METAL BLADE 4-6 seconds or until desired consistency. Season.

AVOCADO, MASHED

TIP: Insert METAL BLADE. Add chunks of ripe, peeled avocado to workbowl. Pulse-chop 3-6 times for a chunky consistency. Process for 30-60 seconds for a wonderfully smooth consistency.

BABY FOOD

TIP: This is so easy to do! Insert METAL BLADE, add small, cooked pieces of food to workbowl. Pulse-chop 5-6 times. With machine running add liquid through feedtube. Process 1 minute for fine food or 30 seconds for junior food. The more liquid that is added, the creamier and smoother the consistency. See FEED BABY RIGHT for specific recipes.

BACON, CRUMBLED

TIP: Insert METAL BLADE. Place crisp cooked slices of bacon in workbowl. Pulse-chop 4-6 times or until nicely crumbled.

BANANAS, MASHED

TIP: Let the food processor mash bananas quickly and easily. Insert METAL BLADE. Add banana and pulse-chop until desired consistency. Add lemon juice to prevent darkening if desired.

BEVERAGES, PROCESSING

TIP: When making drinks in a food processor, place solid food items in first. With machine running add liquid through the feedtube. This thicker mixture will usually prevent liquids from seeping out of the workbowl.

BREAD CRUMBS, BUTTERED AND SEASONED

TIP: Butter a slice of fresh bread. If desired sprinkle on seasonings like garlic powder or salt, celery salt or parsley flakes. Insert METAL BLADE, tear or cut bread in quarters. Pulse-chop until desired consistency. You can do at least three slices at a time. If you have a larger workbowl you may do more.

BREAD CRUMBS, DRY

TIP: Break dry bread into 4 pieces. Insert METAL BLADE. With machine running drop pieces of bread through feedtube. Replace pusher. Process until fine. If some of the bread is very hard, like the heel of homemade bread, the metal blade will not cut it up; unless there is a base of crumbs in the workbowl.

BREAD CRUMBS, FRESH

TIP: Bread crumbs can easily be made out of fresh bread. Insert METAL BLADE, cut bread into 4 pieces and pulse-chop to desired fineness. Store fresh bread crumbs in refrigerator or freezer to prevent mold from forming

BREAD CRUSTS, LEFTOVER TRIMMED -
FROM TEA SANDWICHES, APPETIZERS, ETC.

TIP: Insert METAL BLADE. Add trimmed crusts. Pulse chop 4-6 times or until crusts are crumbed. Use crumbs for vegetable or casserole toppings. Freeze if you can't use that day. When ready to use it is not necessary to thaw out, just remove what you need. Gives a great flavor to casseroles, meatloaves, etc.

BREADS, QUICK

TIP: When doing quick breads in the food processor insert the METAL BLADE. Add shortening or butter, pulse-chop 3-4 times. Add eggs and sugar, process 10-15 seconds. Add any other liquid ingredients, pulse-chop 5-6 times. Add dry ingredients and pulse twice. Scrape sides of bowl, pulse 2-3 times more or just until flour disappears. More processing will produce bread with large airholes.

BREADS, YEAST—
ADDING INGREDIENTS AFTER THE FACT
TIP: If you forgot to add an ingredient to the dough, or you must add more of an ingredient just break up the dough in the workbowl and add that ingredient. Process about 15-20 seconds longer.

BREADS, YEAST—ADDING LIQUIDS
TIP: When making bread first put flour and other dry ingredients in workbowl. Then add liquids through the feedtube as machine is running. The blade will not incorporate the ingredients properly if this sequence is not followed.

BREADS, YEAST—BLADE FOR
TIP: The METAL BLADE is used when making bread with 3 to 3-1/2 cups flour. The plastic DOUGH BLADE is used with 4 or more cups of flour. Check the instruction booklet for the workbowl capacity of the model being used.

BREADS, YEAST—BLADE RISING,
TIP: Over processing the dough or overloading the machine may cause the blade to rise in workbowl. If overloading is the problem, stop the machine, remove half of the dough and process it in 2 batches instead of one.

BREADS, YEAST—DOUGH NOT RISING
TIP: If dough constantly does not rise or rises unevenly it may be because the food processor generated too much heat during processing. The dough may have overheated and the yeast was destroyed. To keep the dough cooler, add yeast to 1/4 cup water at 110°-115° and the remaining liquid needed should be at room temperature.

TIP: Be careful not to place the dough in too warm a place to rise. A spot between 75-80° is best. You may preheat the oven for ONE MINUTE ONLY at 150° to create the optimum rising place. A longer preheating time will make the oven too hot and you may have trouble with the dough not rising.

| METAL BLADE | SHREDDING DISC | DOUGH BLADE | SLICING DISC | FRENCH-FRY DISC |

BREADS, YEAST—DOUGH RISING SLOWLY

TIP: The dough may be rising in a location that has too cool a temperature. The best temperature for good rising is between 75-80°. If the dough is very rich with fat, sugar, or eggs it will take longer to rise.

BREADS, YEAST—DOUGH WITH "TOPKNOT"

TIP: If bread dough has a hard ball or "topknot" that forms around top of center post of blade and dough in bottom of workbowl is quite moist around the edges, then the liquid was either added too quickly or too slowly. Pull topknot apart in four pieces and add 2-3 tablespoons water through the feedtube as machine is running.

BREADS, YEAST—DRY DOUGH

TIP: If dough or batter is hard and dry either there isn't enough liquid or, too much flour was added. Sprinkle some water on dough or batter and pulse 5-10 seconds. If still dry, repeat until soft and pliable.

BREADS, YEAST—KNEADING TIME

TIP: Bread dough usually takes about 2 minutes total processing time from adding the liquid to the final amount of processing time needed after the dough forms a ball. Once bread dough forms a ball it is processed between 60-90 seconds. This is equal to 10-15 minutes of hand kneading or 30 seconds of processing time is equal to 5 minutes of hand kneading. As the machine is processing the dough, it is kneading it.

BREADS, YEAST—LARGE AIRHOLES

TIP: If the cooked bread is full of large air bubbles then the dough either rose too long or in too warm a place. Air bubbles may also be eliminated during shaping of the dough. Roll the dough with a rolling pin into a rectangle. You may hear some bubbles pop. Then roll the dough up jelly roll fashion. Roll up either the long or short side depending on what size bread loaf you are making. Be sure to seal the edges together or you may get an air pocket at that spot. Bake with the seam side down.

BREADS, YEAST—OVERLOADING MACHINE

TIP: When making bread in the food processor the dough should clean the sides of the workbowl. If dough is too sticky then add flour 1 tablespoon at a time while machine is running. You may also turn machine off and add flour, then pulse flour in until a ball is formed. Continue to process 30-60 seconds.

BREADS, YEAST—PROCESSING TIME

TIP: When processing sweet breads process about 30 seconds. When processing typical bread dough process about 60 seconds.

BREADS, YEAST—WARMING INGREDIENTS

TIP: No need to melt butter or margarine, or heat honey or molasses when using the food processor. The food processor will incorporate these ingredients well enough to eliminate these steps.

BROCCOLI STEMS

TIP: When a recipe calls for just the flowers of broccoli, what do you do with the stems? With the food processor you can turn the stems into a beautiful vegetable. Use the SHREDDING DISC, FRENCH FRY DISC, JULIENNE DISC or the SLICING DISC (4-6mm) and the JULIENNE TIP to make fine shreds or matchstick julienne pieces of the stems. Processing with one of these discs will make the stem more tender. You can stir fry or steam the stems. If stem is very tough peel the outside skin.

BUTTER, CREAMING OR SOFTENING

TIP: No need to worry about letting butter get soft again. Use the METAL BLADE. Cut cold butter in 4-6 equal pieces and add to workbowl. Pulse-chop 4-5 times, stop machine and scrape down sides of workbowl. Continue processing until butter is light, soft and fluffy. If preparing butter for spreading on French bread, mince garlic and parsley with METAL BLADE first; then add butter pieces and soften butter.

BUTTER, CUTTING IN

TIP: Use FROZEN butter or margarine when cutting butter into flour to make a crumb mixture. Use the METAL BLADE and pulse-chop until desired consistency.

BUTTER, ECONOMY

TIP: Extend butter by using one stick of margarine and one stick of butter. Process with METAL BLADE until light and smooth, 1-2 minutes.

BUTTER, WHIPPED

TIP: The friction of the METAL BLADE will soften butter. Add 2 tablespoons water to butter as machine is running to make whipped butter.

METAL BLADE

SHREDDING DISC

DOUGH BLADE

SLICING DISC

FRENCH-FRY DISC

BUTTERS, FRUIT

TIP: Butter and fresh fruit creamed together with the METAL BLADE is a delightful treat on toast, English muffins or breakfast pancakes. See recipes in GIFTS WITH LOVE.

BUTTERS, NUT

TIP: Insert METAL BLADE and 1 cup or more of desired nuts. Pulse-chop 6-8 times until fine, then run machine continuously until nuts become smooth and ball together. Add a small amount of oil for a smoother butter if desired.

CAKE MIX

TIP: Cake mixes require the METAL BLADE. Place the mix in the workbowl first, then add the liquid ingredients, eggs, water, or oil. Process 2 seconds, scrape down sides of the bowl, process 3 seconds more. Processing in this order prevents the batter from rising up the center shaft and onto the base causing a real mess and an unhappy food processor owner. Overprocessing will make a dry cake. Honest, 5 seconds is enough.

CAKES AND COOKIES, OVERPROCESSED

TIP: Flour mixtures are the last ingredients added to creamed mixtures in cakes and cookies. Overprocessing can occur once flour is added to the creamed mixture. Three to five pulses is all that is needed to mix flour into a creamed mixture. More than that will over process and you'll have "tough" baked products.

CAKES, SCRATCH

TIP: Cakes made from ingredients, "scratch cakes", require the METAL BLADE. Process eggs and sugar together about 1 minute. Add oil, shortening, butter or margarine and process about 1 minute, add liquid and vanilla and process 2-3 seconds. Add flour and process 3-5 seconds or just until flour disappears. This order is different than a mixer but it is much faster and easier. The cake will also be one of the very best—light and fluffy.

CANDIED FRUIT, CHOPPED

TIP: Freeze candied fruit, about 10-15 minutes. Insert METAL BLADE. Add fruit and small amount of flour from the recipe to the workbowl. Pulse-chop to desired consistency. Room temperature candied fruit can also be chopped in the batter during the final processing time.

CARROT STICKS FOR DIPPERS

TIP: One of the secrets to good carrot sticks is to purchase fat carrots. Peel carrots, remove root and stem end. Cut the carrots in three or four even lengths that will fit horizontally in the feedtube. Insert the SLICING DISC (3-4mm). Position the cutting edge of the slicing disc opposite the spot the feedtube locks in place. This produces a clean even first cut. It also gives the blade the momentum it needs to cut through the carrot. Put the cover on workbowl. Place the carrots in the feedtube with the sides resting on the disc surface. Alternate the narrow and wide ends of the carrots to make an even layer. Put pusher in feedtube and make sure cover is locked in place. Place palm of hand on pusher and press with a firm pressure. Turn the machine on and continue pressing evenly on pusher. Stop the machine when all the carrots are processed. One or two pieces may remain on the disc. This is acceptable as you don't want to process the lid. This may not be the way your mother taught you, but wasn't it fast and they make great dippers.

CARROT STICKS, DOUBLE-CUT OR JULIENNE STRIPS

TIP: See JULIENNE STRIPS - VEGETABLES SUCH AS CARROTS, etc. TIP for the method. These double-cut carrot strips in thicknesses of 2-4mm are wonderful for stir-frying or steaming. Double-cut carrot strips that are 6-8mm thick are also great for vegetable dippers or snacking.

CARROTS, SHREDDED

TIP: Insert SHREDDING DISC. Peel carrots. Cut the carrots in lengths to fit horizontally in the feedtube. Process using a firm pressure on the pusher. This gives long shreds. Pack pieces in the feedtube vertically if you want short shreds. It's O.K. if a piece remains on top of the disc. EAT IT!! You don't want the disc to shred the top of the processor cover so a piece will remain.

CELERY, DICED

TIP: Cut celery stalk lengthwise in 3 even strips but leave top of stalk whole. Insert SLICING DISC. Lock cover in place. Hold celery to side of feedtube that the disc slices toward. With machine running push celery down until fingers reach top of feedtube. Nice even diced celery and a piece the right size for lunch boxes or snacks!

METAL
BLADE

SHREDDING
DISC

DOUGH
BLADE

SLICING
DISC

FRENCH-FRY
DISC

CELERY, SHREDDED

TIP: Process large amounts of celery evenly with this technique. Insert SHREDDING DISC. Place celery in feedtube either horizontally or vertically depending on the desired length of shred. Use a firm pressure on the pusher. Great in either soups or salads.

CELERY, SLICED

TIP: Insert SLICING DISC of desired thickness. Pack even lengths of celery in feedtube. If the celery is not packed in the feedtube, it will fall over and produce irregular slices. Use a medium pressure on the pusher. If you want only a few slices see SLICES—EVEN SLICES OF SLENDER VEGETABLES OR "DANCING" TIP.

CELERY, SLICED DIAGONALLY

TIP: See SLICING DIAGONALLY CUT VEGETABLES TIP.

CHEESE, CRUMBLED BLUE

TIP: Insert METAL BLADE. Place inch cubes of well chilled or partially frozen blue cheese in workbowl, pulse-chop 2-3 times until cheese is crumbled. If cheese is at room temperature it will cream together instead of crumbling.

CHEESE, SOFTENING CREAM

TIP: Cream cheese does not need to be at room temperature when using a food processor. In fact, the cream cheese may break down into a liquid if too soft and over processed. Cut cold cream cheese into 6-8 even pieces and using METAL BLADE pulse-chop 6-8 times until creamy. Scrape down the sides of the workbowl and pulse-chop until all cheese is soft and fluffy. Remember the colder the cream cheese the longer it will take to process. The friction of the blade against the cream cheese does the softening.

CHEESE, MOZARELLA SHREDDED

TIP: Place cheese in freezer for 20 minutes to insure good shredding results. Use this idea with any soft cheese like mozzarella, Monterey jack or muenster. Be sure to use the press-release technique in the CHEESE, SHREDDED TIP.

CHEESE, PARMESAN
TIP: Parmesan cheese can be grated finely in the food processor. Place METAL BLADE in a dry workbowl. Cut the parmesan cheese in 1 inch pieces. Room temperature cheese is easier to cut. If you can not cut it with a knife then the food processor can't either. With the machine running add the pieces one at a time through the feedtube. Cover feedtube with hand or replace pusher to eliminate small pieces of cheese from coming out. After adding all cheese continue to process until cheese is finely grated, about 30-60 seconds more.

CHEESE, PUSH-RELEASE METHOD
TIP: Place piece of very cold cheese into the feedtube. Set pusher in feedtube and lock cover. Turn machine on, press moderately on the pusher, release pressure by pulling up on the pusher. Repeat pressing and releasing of pusher until last piece is processed.

CHEESE, SHREDDED
TIP: Cheese should always be processed cold from the refrigerator. Some soft cheeses like mozzarella and muenster process better if frozen for 20 minutes. Cut a piece of cheese to fit the feedtube and place in the feedtube resting on the SHREDDING DISC. Place cheese in feedtube with long side down if you want long shreds or short side down for short shreds. Always use a light pressure when shredding cheese. DO NOT push hard with the pusher. Let the machine shred the cheese. "Push-release" is the very best technique to keep the cheese from getting gummy and not shredding properly. Turn the machine on, press on the pusher—release (pull-up), press pusher—release, press and release to let the last little piece of cheese bounce through. Four ounces of cheese processed makes one cup shredded. Use this technique for any cheese that is semi-frozen or firm like cheddar, Edam, Gouda or Swiss. Too much pressure on the cheese and pusher could cause the stem to snap. Use this technique every time for shredded cheese without any problems.

CHEESE, SHREDDING POORLY
TIP: The pusher creates friction between the cheese and the SHREDDING DISC making the cheese warm and giving poor shredding results. This is why it is so important to have cold or semi-frozen cheese to process.

| METAL BLADE | SHREDDING DISC | DOUGH BLADE | SLICING DISC | FRENCH-FRY DISC |

CHEESECAKE

TIP: The METAL BLADE does all the work for you. First, see GRAHAM CRACKER CRUST TIP. Remember it is not necessary to have the cream cheese at room temperature. In fact, the cream cheese may break down into a liquid if too soft and over processed. Pulse-chop cream cheese with METAL BLADE until creamy, add eggs and liquid to help process more quickly. Add any remaining ingredients and process until combined. You're done! (See INDEX for a cheesecake recipe.)

CHOCOLATE CHIPS, ADDING TO COOKIE DOUGH

TIP: Chocolate chips should be poured onto the dough and not around the shaft of the metal blade. If the chips fall to the bottom of the workbowl, the metal blade will chop them. If the metal blade is covered with dough and the chips rest on the dough, they will blend into the dough in 1-2 pulses, without being cut-up.

CHOCOLATE, MELTED

TIP: Instead of melting unsweetened chocolate squares break squares into halves. Insert METAL BLADE, place chocolate in workbowl and pulse-chop chocolate 6-10 times. Add sugar from recipe and process 1-2 minutes more until chocolate is as fine as sugar. Continue with remaining recipe directions.

CHOCOLATE, SHREDDED

TIP: Save your knuckles!! Insert SHREDDING DISC in a cool, dry workbowl. Have chocolate at room temperature. Use either milk chocolate or baker's chocolate. Place chocolate in feedtube, shred using light pressure on the pusher.

CHOPPING, EVENLY

TIP: Insert METAL BLADE. Cut food into 4-6 equal pieces, even if it is only a small piece of a food and add to workbowl. The food will chop more evenly than if you added one large piece. Pulse-chop 2-3 times. Check the contents of workbowl, if the food is too coarse pulse-chop 2-3 times more or until desired consistency. If you are getting "mush", you are running the machine too long. A pulse-chop is only a second. Four to six pulses will chop a medium onion or potato easily. If you do not like this method of chopping then see the FRENCH FRY DISC-CUBING TIP.

CHOPPING, LARGE QUANTITIES EVENLY

TIP: When chopping fruits or vegetables with the METAL BLADE it is better to fill the workbowl loosely and only half full. Process two half filled bowls instead of one very full bowl. ALWAYS pulse-chop to avoid over processing and to achieve a more even consistency.

CHOPPING, VARYING CONSISTENCIES

TIP: The order ingredients are added to the workbowl when chopping with the METAL BLADE will give different consistencies. For example, three vegetables pulse-chopped all together will be the same fineness, while chopping celery and green pepper first and onions last will produce coarser onions. The other variable is the hardness of the vegetable or fruit. In the above example if celery and carrots had been chopped together the carrots would be a little coarser then the celery. If the same consistency is desired for a hard and soft vegetable first pulse-chop the hard vegetable a few times and then add the softer vegetable. Pulse-chop to desired consistency.

CITRUS PEEL: GRATED LEMON, ORANGE, LIME

TIP: Any citrus fruit skin may be processed in the food processor to give you grated rind. Peel a thin layer from the entire fruit with a vegetable peeler. Insert METAL BLADE in clean dry workbowl for best results. With machine running drop peelings through feedtube. Process 2-3 minutes. Scrape bowl down if necessary. If peel is not fine enough add some of the sugar called for in the recipe. The metal blade can grate the peel more easily when there is a larger quantity of food in the workbowl. Use immediately or freeze.

CLEANING FOOD PROCESSOR

TIP: See FOOD PROCESSOR, CLEANING

COCONUT, FRESH CHOPPED

TIP: Insert METAL BLADE. Add peeled coconut pieces to workbowl. Lock cover, pulse-chop 4-5 times, depending on the desired consistency.

| METAL BLADE | SHREDDING DISC | DOUGH BLADE | SLICING DISC | FRENCH-FRY DISC |

COCONUT, FRESH SHREDDED
TIP: Insert SHREDDING DISC. Pack fresh peeled coconut in the feedtube. Process using medium pressure on the pusher. You will get beautiful long shreds of coconut.

COLESLAW
TIP: The way coleslaw is prepared is as varied as our American heritage. A very thinly sliced slaw is best prepared using a 1-2mm SLICING DISC. Coleslaw can also be prepared by chopping with the METAL BLADE or shredding with the SHREDDING DISC. Use the FRENCH FRY DISC or JULIENNE DISC for a different consistency too. Each family has it's own favorite style so experiment with the methods given to find the one your family likes best. Check SALADS for complete directions.

COOKIES
TIP: Insert METAL BLADE. Cookies are processed in a flash in the food processor. Add dry ingredients to workbowl, except sugar. Pulse 3 seconds to combine and set aside on wax paper. Add butter or shortening, pulse-chop 4-6 times, add eggs and sugar, process until creamy. Add any other liquid called for in the recipe and process until smooth. Add flour mixture and pulse-chop 4 times, just until blended. Do not overprocess. If nuts are desired see NUTS, CHOPPING DURING MIXING TIP.

CRANBERRIES, CHOPPED
TIP: Fresh or frozen cranberries can be pulse-chopped to the desired consistency with the METAL BLADE. See SALADS for a recipe.

CREAMY CONSISTENCY
TIP: When processing thick mixtures (like baby foods, purees, ice cream, sherbets, milk shakes, sauces and gravies) use the METAL BLADE. Place the food in the workbowl and pulse-chop 3-4 times. Add the liquids through the feedtube while the machine is running to produce a light, creamy texture.

CRUMBS, COOKIE, CRACKER AND POTATO CHIP
TIP: Insert METAL BLADE. Place cookies, pieces of crackers or chips in workbowl. Pulse-chop 3-4 times. Let machine run until desired consistency. See GRAHAM CRACKER CRUST TIP also.

| METAL BLADE | SHREDDING DISC | DOUGH BLADE | SLICING DISC | FRENCH-FRY DISC |

CUBING

TIP: Use the FRENCH FRY DISC for more than just making French fries. It is great for cubing fruits and vegetables like tomatoes, potatoes, apples, zucchini, etc. The placement of the food in the feedtube will determine the size of the cubes. Cut an initial slice off the bottom for a flat surface. Cut whole fruits and vegetables in 3 even vertical sections. Place the 3 sections as a whole in the feedtube, so the French fry disc cuts across the short wedges. The feedtube must be packed tightly so food will not fall over. Use a medium pressure on pusher to process. A piece of food will remain on the top of the French-fry disc. The machine may move because of the food left on the disc. Stop machine as soon as food is processed to avoid this movement. See FRENCH FRY DISC TIP for more complete directions for various foods.

CUCUMBER HALF MOONS

TIP: Insert SLICING DISC (3-4mm). Use quantity of cucumber desired and peel if you wish. Cut cucumbers in half vertically so you get half circles which are easier to eat. Pack the feedtube so the cucumbers won't fall over. Process using medium pressure on pusher.

CUCUMBER SLICES

TIP: Insert SLICING DISC. Stripe cucumber skin with a fork or citrus stripper for a decorative effect. Check to see if cucumber fits in the feedtube. Cut cucumber in half vertically if necessary to fit small feedtube. Cut whole cucumber across center to fit two pieces side by side in a large feedtube. Use a medium pressure on pusher. If you don't use a continuously firm pressure on the pusher you will get slices of various thicknesses.

EGG, HARD COOKED— CHOPPED AND SLICED

TIP: Use the METAL BLADE to pulse-chop hard cooked eggs in the food processor. Hard cooked eggs do not slice well in a food processor because the yolks are very soft.

EGG WHITES, FOLDING IN WHIPPED

TIP: Whipped egg whites can be folded into a mixture with a food processor. Add whipped egg whites to mixture in workbowl. Pulse-chop 1-4 times depending on amount being folded into mixture. It is important not to overprocess or the egg whites will break down.

EGG WHITES, WHIPPED

TIP: Insert METAL BLADE in clean workbowl. Add 3-7 egg whites and sugar, if required. Room temperature whites process best. There CANNOT BE ANY yolk mixed with the whites or the whites will not whip properly. Process 8 seconds. With machine running, add a mixture of 1 tablespoon water and 1 tablespoon white vinegar slowly through the feedtube. Process 1-2 minutes or until desired consistency. Be ready to incorporate the egg whites into a recipe as they will start to break down after 5-10 minutes.

FEEDTUBE, SIZE

TIP: Some processors have a large feedtube and then a small feedtube within the large feedtube. Other food processors have just one feedtube opening. The feedtube openings of most food processors are larger at the bottom than at the top openings. Try inserting food from the bottom of the feedtube if it won't go through the top of the feedtube.

FOOD PROCESSOR CLEANING

TIP: It's no problem to clean the food processor. When opting to use the food processor instead of a knife, don't let the washing of the food processor keep you from using it. When making foods like breads, cookies, or cakes; leave the METAL BLADE in the workbowl after you are finished and fill the workbowl immediately with water. You could even make a loaf of bread after making a cake. Scrape excess batter from bowl and blade. No need to wipe them. The bread dough will clean the workbowl and blade. Besides it will make the best loaf of bread even if you have processed a chocolate cake. Go ahead and try it!

Process fruits first and then vegetables and eliminate washing in-between processing. Just wipe out the workbowl and the cover with a paper towel, if necessary. There isn't any need to wash the workbowl until all processing is done. Process the garlic and onions last as they have the only flavors that may transfer to other foods. The time for washing the food processor parts is minimal when you consider the time it saves you. Remember, all the parts are dishwasher safe too.

Try to process as many items as you can when you are working with the food processor. Package foods like shredded cheese, chopped onion and green pepper, chopped meat, sliced fruits and vegetables for future use. Freeze or refrigerate, as appropriate. When you open these packages it will almost feel as if the cook's helper has been in.

FOOD PROCESSOR EYE
TIP: Try to buy food that will fit in the feedtube. For example, if you need round whole lemon slices buy a smaller lemon that you're sure will fit the feedtube. If it's too big you will have to cut it in half.

FOOD PROCESSOR MOVING
TIP: Some firm vegetables like carrots, rutabagas, and potatoes may move the machine after the vegetable has been sliced, shredded or French-fried. There is usually a piece of vegetable remaining on the top of the disc creating friction between the cover and the disc, forcing the machine to move. Stop the processor immediately after processing these vegetables.

TIP: Heavy yeast doughs also cause the processor to move. If the machine seems too strained or "jumpy" divide the dough in half and continue with the necessary processor kneading time.

TIP: When adding more flour to a yeast dough pulse-chop machine to blend in the flour and keep machine from moving. When flour is blended in, then run machine continuously to finish kneading.

| METAL BLADE | SHREDDING DISC | DOUGH BLADE | SLICING DISC | FRENCH-FRY DISC |

FOOD REMAINING ON THE SLICING, SHREDDING, FRENCH FRY, OR JULIENNE DISC

TIP: A piece of food will remain on the disc after processing with one of the above discs because there is a space between the cover and the disc. This space prevents the cover from being cut by the disc. There is no pressure from the pusher when food is in this space so a piece of food will always remain on top. That piece of food is just a little treat for the cook to eat!

FRENCH FRY DISC

TIP: So you bought the FRENCH FRY DISC to make carrot sticks and it doesn't work. Read on to find many novel uses for this disc. Use the FRENCH FRY DISC to make long, even strips of potato, zucchini, jicama, apple, pear, daikon radish, canteloupe, or cooked beets. The disc will not French-fry most hard uncooked root vegetables like carrots, turnips or rutabaga. Partially cook these vegetables to process them with a French-fry disc. Insert the FRENCH FRY DISC. Place food in feedtube horizontally and process using a medium-firm pressure. A piece of food will remain on the disc.

The FRENCH FRY DISC is wonderful to use for CUBING many fruits and vegetables. There are specific directions for many foods given below. Use your imagination after reading these examples.

APPLES, PEARS—Cut off blossom end of fruit. Cut in 4 quarters and core. Pack tightly and upright in feedtube and process using quick firm pressure on pusher. These are delightful for fruit salads.

BANANAS—Fill feedtube with bananas placed upright. Process using light pressure on the pusher. Use in fruit salads, desserts and combine with whipped cream for a crepe filling.

CARROTS, RADISHES, PARSNIPS—Pack vegetable tightly and upright in feedtube. Process using quick, firm pressure on pusher. Use in soups, salads, or vegetables dishes.

CABBAGE, LETTUCE—For a coarser slaw or lettuce texture, place a wedge of desired vegetable in feedtube. Process using a quick, firm pressure on the pusher.

CUCUMBERS, ZUCCHINI, YELLOW SUMMER SQUASH— Slice vegetable in half vertically. Pack vegetable halves tightly, upright and across the width of the feedtube. Process using quick firm pressure. Use in salads, vegetable dishes or as a garnish for gazpacho. See following TIP also for another method.

EGGPLANT, JICAMA, POTATOES, RUTABAGAS, SWEET POTATOES, TURNIPS, YAMS—For "picture perfect" cubes process as directed. Insert SLICING DISC of desired thickness. Use at least a 4-8mm thick blade. The thicker blade will, of course, make larger cubes. Slice the vegetable using a firm pressure on the pusher. Remove disc, take slices out of workbowl like a deck of cards. Insert FRENCH FRY DISC. Pack slices upright, tightly and across the width of the feedtube. If slices are packed parallel to the length of the feedtube, you will produce French fries. Process using a quick, firm pressure on pusher.

GREEN PEPPER—Slice the top and bottom off the green pepper and then cut it into fourths. Stand up in the feedtube so the round side of the pepper is across the width of the feedtube. The feedtube must be tightly packed. In a large feedtube it takes 2 green peppers to pack the feedtube. Process using a quick firm pressure on the pusher.

MELONS LIKE CANTELOUPE, HONEYDEW, CASABA— Seed and peel melon. Cut melon in wedges. Pack wedges tightly, upright and across the width of the feedtube. Process using quick, firm pressure. Use in fruit salads or freeze cubes of fruit on tray to use in fruit sherbets. See TIP: SHERBET for details.

ONIONS— Cut off root and stem end of onion. Place whole peeled onion in the feedtube, flat side on the FRENCH FRY DISC. Make sure the feedtube is packed, process using a medium pressure. Since an onion grows in layers, it makes even cubes out of each layer.

TOMATOES—Depending on the size and firmness of the tomato make three or four vertical cuts not quite through the tomato. If the cuts are made all the way through the tomato will not cube nicely. Place the tomato, cut side down, with the cuts going across the width of the feedtube. Process using a quick, firm pressure on pusher.

FRUITS FOR JAMS OR JELLIES

TIP: Reduce jelly making time by coarsely pulse-chopping pre-measured fruits for jam and jelly recipes. Use the METAL BLADE for the chopping.

FRUIT AND VEGETABLE CARTWHEELS

TIP: Use a citrus stripper and remove five to six evenly spaced strips of peel from food or use a fork and draw deeply along the peel. Process, using SLICING BLADE of desired thickness.

FRUITS, SLICING SOFT

TIP: When slicing soft fruits (such as bananas and strawberries) in a food processor use a quick light pressure on the pusher. Use SLICING DISC of desired thickness.

TIP: Soft fruits and vegetables (such as strawberries, bananas, mushrooms) will slice well in a food processor as long as they are firm and not over ripe.

TIP: When fruits and vegetables become too soft to slice use METAL BLADE to process them and to mix in other foods. For example, ripe bananas are great in milk shakes, cakes, or pancake batter. Soft tomatoes can go in meatloaf, chili, or sloppy joes. Soft strawberries are wonderful in milkshakes, pureed for toppings for ice cream or cake, and can also be made into STRAWBERRY BUT-TER. See GIFTS WITH LOVE.

GARLIC, MINCED

TIP: Insert METAL BLADE. Trim off each end of garlic clove, peel. If garlic skin is difficult to remove let the processor do it. With the machine running drop garlic clove through the feedtube. Stop machine immediately and remove skin that has collected on sides and bottom of workbowl. Replace pusher. Continue processing until garlic is finely minced. Process the entire ball of garlic at one time if you desire. Place remaining minced garlic in a jar of salad oil and keep refrigerated for future use. The oil can be used for salads or frying and has a lovely garlic flavor.

GINGER ROOT, MINCED

TIP: Insert METAL BLADE. Peel ginger root if desired. Cut ginger root into several pieces. With machine running add pieces of ginger root through the feedtube. Cover feedtube opening with hand in between additions of ginger. Process all ginger root and store in covered jar of sherry. Keep refrigerated for later use. Use the sherry for sauces and other cooking needs.

GRAHAM CRACKER CRUST

TIP: Insert METAL BLADE. Break 14 graham cracker squares into the workbowl. Pulse-chop 6-8 times. Add 1/4 cup butter cut in several pieces and 1/4 cup sugar. Pulse-chop 6-8 times more or until crumbs are finely chopped and well combined with butter and sugar. Wasn't that simple? No more beating with a rolling pin. Press into 8-9 inch pie pan, bake at 375° for 6-8 minutes or refrigerate for 30 minutes.

TIP: Cinnamon and nuts can be added to the above recipe as a variation for CINNAMON NUT GRAHAM CRACKER CRUST. Add 1/2 cup nuts and 1/4 teaspoon cinnamon with the butter and proceed with the previous directions for GRAHAM CRACKER CRUST.

TIP: Use vanilla or chocolate wafers in place of the graham crackers for a delightful COOKIE CRUMB CRUST. Crumb enough wafers to make about 1-1/3 cup crumbs. Then add butter and reduce sugar by 2 tablespoons. Continue with recipe as directed in GRAHAM CRACKER CRUST. Use the nuts or cinnamon variation also if you desire.

GRATING

TIP: Grating (like Grandma's hand grater) can be achieved in a food processor by inserting the METAL BLADE and pulse-chopping to the desired consistency. The finer the consistency you desire the larger quantity of food you can put in the workbowl and still have good results. Of course, you will pulse-chop longer for a finer consistency. Fill the workbowl no more than two thirds full. Use this method for carrots, apples, potatoes, cabbage, etc.

GRAVY, LUMPY

TIP: If gravy is lumpy, the food processor will take out the lumps. Insert METAL BLADE, add gravy and process until smooth. Use this trick to smooth out any mixture from gravy to wallpaper paste.

GREEN BEANS, FRENCH-CUT

TIP: Use the SLICING DISC, preferably a thin (2 mm) slicing disc. Cut the beans in lengths to fit horizontally in the feedtube. Stack them horizontally in the feedtube and apply medium pressure on pusher. Green beans may be blanched before processing. The blanching makes it easier for some processors to slice the beans.

| METAL BLADE | SHREDDING DISC | DOUGH BLADE | SLICING DISC | FRENCH-FRY DISC |

GREEN PEPPERS, CHOPPED
TIP: Green peppers can be pulse-chopped to the desired fineness by using the METAL BLADE. Be careful not to overprocess. Processing green peppers too long will turn them into mush as they have a high water content and get mushy very quickly.

TIP: Even size pieces of chopped green pepper can be produced by first slicing the pepper in rings with the SLICING DISC. Leave green pepper in workbowl. Insert the METAL BLADE, pulse chop 2-3 times to get desired size pieces.

TIP: See FRENCH FRY DISC -GREEN PEPPERS, CUBING TIP also .

GREEN PEPPERS, RINGS
TIP: Insert SLICING DISC of desired thickness. Cut off stem. Remove seed pod, but don't cut pepper. If the whole pepper doesn't fit in the feedtube then cut off the blossom end and cut through one side of the pepper. Roll this pepper piece like a jelly roll to fit the feedtube. Place the whole pepper, cut side down, or the prepared pepper roll standing up in the feedtube and process using medium pressure.

HASH BROWN POTATOES
TIP: See POTATOES, HASH BROWNS TIP.

HERBS, FRESH CHOPPED
TIP: Insert METAL BLADE. For best results, add clean dry herb to clean, dry workbowl. Pulse-chop stems first 6-8 times, then add leaves or flowers and pulse-chop 4-6 times more or until fineness desired. Freeze in small quantities. Use frozen to sprinkle on foods. If you wish, microwave herbs between 2 paper towels on HIGH until nicely dried. Use for basil, parsley, cilantro, sage, etc.

HORSERADISH, FRESH GRATED
TIP: Insert METAL BLADE, add peeled horseradish root pieces. Pulse-chop 5-6 times. Continue processing until desired consistency. Make the LO-CAL SOUR CREAM; add this freshly grated root to taste, for a great lo-cal HORSERADISH DIP.

HOT FOODS
TIP: Hot foods (such as cooked vegetables to be pureed) may be placed in the workbowl for processing without causing any damage to the workbowl or the machine.

ICE CREAM

TIP: This is a great recipe to prepare with very ripe fruits or just to enjoy the fresh summer fruits. Packaged frozen fruit may also be used. Peel, pit or seed fruit, as desired. Insert (4-8mm) SLICING DISC. Fill feedtube with prepared fruit pieces. Slice, using a medium pressure on the pusher. Freeze two cups sliced fruit, whole berries or fruit chunks in a single layer on a cookie sheet. Insert METAL BLADE, add 2 cups frozen fruit and pulse-chop 6-8 times. Add 2-3 tablespoons sugar; pulse-chop until fruit is finely chopped, about 6-8 times. With machine running, add 1/2 cup whipping cream through feedtube and process until smooth and creamy. Serve immediately or keep in freezer up to 3 hours. If frozen longer, reprocess and serve. Use strawberries, peaches, raspberries, plums, bananas, etc. May double amounts for larger capacity food processors.

ICE CUBES, CRUSHED

TIP: Ice cubes can be crushed in a food processor. Processing ice cubes may dull your blade and scratch your bowl. It is best to use home prepared ice cubes. Insert METAL BLADE, with machine running add ice cubes through the feedtube one at a time. Replace pusher and process for 30-60 seconds depending on amount of cubes used and desired fineness.

If making a drink with a slush-like consistency add no more than one cup liquid to the crushed ice in the workbowl. Prepare crushed ice. With machine running add liquid to the crushed ice through the feedtube. Replace pusher and process 5-10 seconds or until slush-like consistency.

INSTANT PUDDING MIX

TIP: Insert METAL BLADE. Add pudding mix, then milk. Pulse 3-4 times. Let machine run until thick, about two minutes.

INSTANT WHIPPED TOPPING

TIP: Chill bowl and METAL BLADE. Insert METAL BLADE. Add topping mix. With machine running pour milk and vanilla slowly through the feedtube. Continue processing until nicely whipped, one to two minutes.

| METAL BLADE | SHREDDING DISC | DOUGH BLADE | SLICING DISC | FRENCH-FRY DISC |

JULIENNE DISC

TIP: Some processors have a 2-3mm square julienne disc available. Use this disc to process apples, pears, peeled coconut, zucchini, etc. Root vegetables like beets, carrots, parsnips, rutabagas, etc. must be precooked before processing. Insert JULIENNE DISC. Place food in feedtube and process using medium pressure on pusher. A piece of food will remain on the disc after processing. The machine may also move when processing is completed. Use julienne strips for salads, garnishes and vegetable dishes. If you would like a fine even dice then use this disc in the same way the FRENCH FRY DISC is used for CUBING. See FRENCH FRY DISC-CUBING TIP.

JULIENNE STRIPS - CHEESE

TIP: Buy presliced cheese from the deli department or use prepackaged cheese slices that are at least 1/8 to 1/4 inch thick (10-12mm). Place in freezer for 1 hour to firm for julienning. Insert SLICING DISC (4-6mm). Roll cheese slices together or pack slices of cheese vertically in feedtube. Make sure the cheese fills the feedtube completely. If necessary, cut the stack of slices in half or thirds to make a wedge thick enough to fill the width of the feedtube. Process using a medium pressure on the pusher.

JULIENNE STRIPS
- LUNCHEON MEATS LIKE BOLOGNA, HAM, TURKEY

TIP: Buy presliced luncheon meats from the deli department or use prepackaged meat that is sliced at least 1/8 to 1/4 inch thick. Freeze meat for 1-2 hours or until firm. Insert SLICING DISC (4-6mm). Roll meat jelly roll style to fit the feedtube or pack stack of meat slices upright. Make sure the width of the feedtube is well filled. Process using a medium pressure on the pusher.

JULIENNE STRIPS - VEGETABLES SUCH AS CARROTS, ZUCCHINI, BROCCOLI STEMS, BEETS, POTATOES

TIP: Insert the SLICING DISC. The thickness of the julienne will be decided by the thickness (2-8mm) of the slicing disc used. To achieve "picture perfect" julienne strips, first place the food horizontally and cut one side flat. Cut the food in lengths to fit the feedtube. Fill the feedtube with one layer of food that has the flat side on the slicing disc. Process using medium to firm pressure on the pusher, depending on the firmness of the vegetable. Repeat first three steps until all vegetables are processed. Take slices out of workbowl and stack them like a deck of cards. Replace the SLICING DISC. Pack the slices in the feedtube vertically so they are standing on edge. Make sure the feedtube is TIGHTLY packed. Use up the slice you cut off by hand, if necessary, to pack the feedtube tightly. If the feedtube is only half full the slices will fall over and not julienne correctly. The final length of the julienne depends on whether you slice the width or the length of the food.

LENGTH   WIDTH

KIBBEE

TIP: This is a Lebanese dish with uncooked lamb and bulgar wheat that can be made easily and quickly in the food processor. Insert the METAL BLADE. Add cold lamb, cut in pieces, and seasonings. Pulse-chop until almost desired fineness. Add wheat and pulse twice more to blend.

LENGTH OF SHRED - CHEESE, VEGETABLES, FRUITS

TIP: Insert SHREDDING DISC. For longer shreds of carrots, zucchini, potatoes, cheese, apples, etc. lay the food or vegetable horizontally in the feedtube. Shorter shreds are produced by standing the vegetable vertically in the feedtube.

METAL   SHREDDING   DOUGH   SLICING   FRENCH-FRY
BLADE   DISC   BLADE   DISC   DISC

LETTUCE, SHREDDED

TIP: Lettuce is shredded in a food processor by slicing it. A thin SLICING DISC will produce long thin strands while a thick SLICING DISC will produce slices that are good for tossed salads. Using the shredding disc will produce lettuce puree. Break iceberg lettuce into a piece to fit the feedtube, insert SLICING DISC of desired thickness and process using medium pressure.

LETTUCE, SLICED

TIP: See LETTUCE, SHREDDED TIP.

LIQUIDS, ADDING TO MIXTURES

TIP: Insert the METAL BLADE. It is better to add liquids to solid food in the workbowl, than to add food to liquids in the workbowl. If the liquid is added to the food it forms a thicker mixture. This will usually prevent any leakage through the shaft that the blade rests on. This also allows larger quantities to be processed as the leakage is eliminated. See MILK SHAKES and LIQUIDS, PROCESSING TIPS also.

LIQUIDS, PROCESSING

TIP: After processing hold the middle of the metal blade in place with a finger tip until you pour the liquid into another container. Leaving the blade in place keeps the liquids from running out through the center of the workbowl.

TIP: Some processors have openings in the bottom of the METAL BLADE. Insert the index or middle finger through the outside center of the workbowl into this opening while the METAL BLADE is in the workbowl. Hold tightly with the finger and place thumb around bottom outer side of workbowl. Fan out the rest of the fingers over the bottom of the workbowl. Then pour out the liquid while holding onto the blade. You may find this a convenient way to hold the workbowl whether or not it has liquid in it.

TIP: Remove the pusher from the feedtube in order to add liquids through the feedtube as the machine is running.

TIP: Process no more liquid than to the top of the metal blade when making juice concentrates or other liquids which have no solids added to them.

TIP: Use only half the liquid in a recipe if the processor workbowl has a small capacity. The remaining liquid, like milk or water, can usually be stirred in easily by hand.

LIQUIDS, PROCESSING SMALL AMOUNTS

TIP: Insert METAL BLADE. Use this tip for vinagrettes, sauces or other small quantity liquid mixtures. Insert METAL BLADE, process ingredients as directed. While machine is running, slightly tip the machine. This allows the METAL BLADE to pass through the mixture instead of the blade skimming over the liquid.

MAYONNAISE, THICK

TIP: The secret to thickening mayonnaise is to add oil VERY SLOWLY to egg mixture in workbowl at the beginning while the machine is running. If the oil is added all at once or too quickly the mayonnaise will not thicken. If the pusher has a tiny hole in it, place pusher in the feedtube. With the machine running pour 1/4 cup of oil in the pusher and it will drizzle slowly into the workbowl. When that oil is added; remove the pusher, add the remaining oil in a slow steady stream through the feedtube, or add the remaining oil through the opening in the pusher. When all the oil has been added process an additional 30 seconds. You should have perfect mayonnaise every time.

MEAT, ECONOMY SLICES

TIP: A less tender cut of meat like round steak can be used for stir-fry because the meat is sliced so thinly that it is tender without any special preparation. Use a 3-6mm SLICING DISC.

MEAT, FRESH GROUND

TIP: Meat that is partially frozen (30-60 minutes) will chop more evenly than meat that is cold from the refrigerator. Use the METAL BLADE. Cut meat in even 2-3 inch squares. Pulse-chop 8-10 times or until chopped to desired consistency. Do not fill the workbowl more than half full. Too much meat in the workbowl will result in an uneven chop or overprocessing. Check the instruction booklet for the amount of meat that is best for the model you are using. Over processed meat is not NICE!!

| METAL BLADE | SHREDDING DISC | DOUGH BLADE | SLICING DISC | FRENCH-FRY DISC |

MEAT, GRISTLE IN GROUND

TIP: The gristle in meat will not chop when processing meat in the food processor. Remove the gristle before chopping. If the gristle is not removed before chopping it will form long strings. You can pick it out of the chopped meat after processing.

MEAT, SLICING COOKED

TIP: Rare and medium rare cooked meats must be frozen but partially thawed so the meat surface can be pierced with the tip of a knife. Rare cooked meat is not firm enough to slice well unless frozen. Medium and well done cooked meats are firm enough when refrigerated to slice but some freezing time will improve the slicing ease. Insert SLICING DISC of desired thickness. It is best to use a slicing disc of 4mm or thicker when slicing cooked meat. Pack feedtube firmly and slice using a medium-light pressure.

MEAT, SLICING RAW

TIP: Insert SLICING DISC (4-8mm). In order to slice meat in the food processor it must be frozen but slightly thawed. Thaw the meat enough so the point of a knife can go into the meat. If you cannot cut through the meat with a knife then neither can the food processor. If the meat is too soft the meat will not slice properly. The meat should be firmly packed into the feedtube. It should also be set in the feedtube so it will slice against the grain. Process using medium-light pressure on the pusher. The machine may make loud noises when slicing partially thawed meat.

METAL BLADE, CLEANING

TIP: To easily remove creamy, sticky dips, spreads or batters from the blade, first scrape most of the mixture from the workbowl. Put METAL BLADE and workbowl back on base, cover and lock machine. Pulse machine 2-3 times. The food clinging to the blade will spin off leaving a clean blade. Then remove the clean blade and scrape out any remaining mixture from the workbowl. Most blades have a knob or special notch to hold onto when the blade is soiled or slippery.

MILK SHAKES

TIP: Insert METAL BLADE and place ice cream in the workbowl, pulse-chop 2-3 times. With machine running add milk and flavorings through the feedtube. This order of food placement prevents the liquid from "running out" the center workbowl opening. This makes a super creamy shake. See BEVERAGES for recipes.

MOTOR, STRAINED FOOD PROCESSOR

TIP: Some food processors, when overloaded, have a circuit breaker which will shut off the motor. This happens when you are using the METAL BLADE or DOUGH BLADE. The motor overheats due to a dough or batter that is too sticky. When this happens, let machine cool down 5-10 minutes. See TIP about STRAINED FOOD PROCESSOR MOTOR-WHILE PROCESSING DOUGHS. The dough or batter MAY be processed enough to continue with recipe.

MOTOR, STRAINED FOOD PROCESSOR-WHILE PROCESSING DOUGHS

TIP: If the food processor slows down and sounds strained, the dough is too sticky because it contains too much liquid or the quantity of dough may have exceeded the capacity of the food processor. If the dough is sticky, add 1-2 tablespoons more flour. Let stand a few minutes. Scrape sides of workbowl, pulse-chop 4-5 times. If blade still revolves slowly, turn off food processor and remove some dough. Process in two batches.

MUSHROOMS, CHOPPED

TIP: Insert METAL BLADE. Add mushrooms to workbowl. Pulse-chop 4-8 times depending on the fineness desired. BE careful not to overprocess.

| METAL BLADE | SHREDDING DISC | DOUGH BLADE | SLICING DISC | FRENCH-FRY DISC |

MUSHROOMS, SLICED

TIP: Picture perfect slices can be obtained by cutting one side of the mushroom cap flat. Put flat side down on the SLICING DISC (1-8mm). Alternate stem and cap ends so they are firmly packed in feedtube. Sometimes it is easier to place several mushrooms on the SLICING DISC and then "capture" them with the feedtube. Process one layer at a time for "picture-perfect" slices. Use light pressure on the pusher. If appearance is not important then just lay mushrooms on sides in feedtube and process.

NUTS, CHOPPED

TIP: Chop nuts by pulse-chopping using the METAL BLADE or by using the SHREDDING DISC.

SHREDDING DISC—The shredding disc will chop a large quantity of nuts evenly without needing to empty the workbowl. There is never any worry of overprocessing the nuts when you use the shredding disc and the nuts are always chopped finely and evenly. Place nuts in the feedtube and process using medium-firm pressure on the pusher. Great for nut rolls and dessert toppings!

METAL BLADE—With the METAL BLADE you can vary the consistency by pulse-chopping more or less. For best results pulse-chop about one cup at a time to the desired consistency. Pulsing 4-5 times is usually enough to chop the nuts coarsely. If the pulse action is not used it is very easy to produce a nut butter even though that is not what you planned. Nuts can also be chopped within the body of a recipe and this is the easiest way to chop nuts when preparing a mixture. See NUTS, CHOPPED DURING MIXING TIP for further help.

NUTS, CHOPPED DURING MIXING

TIP: Recipes calling for chopped nuts in this book have the time needed for chopping as part of the recipe. If you omit the nuts, then pulse twice more since the pulsing for nuts was eliminated. If using a recipe that has not been adapted to the food processor use the following general method. In cookie, cake and quick bread mixtures add the nuts after the flour mixture has been pulsed twice. Add the nuts and pulse-chop twice more. By adding whole, shelled nuts to the batter you can eliminate chopping as a separate step. The four pulses are enough to blend in the flour and chop the nuts at the same time. Other examples of the nuts being chopped with other ingredients could be a cheese ball or appetizer recipe. Remember pulsing 2-3 times is all that is needed to chop nuts coarsely in the food processor.

NUTS, CHOPPED FINE FOR TORTES, NUT COATING

TIP: Insert METAL BLADE. Chop nuts very finely without turning into nut butter by adding 1-2 tablespoons of flour or sugar called for in the recipe. The flour or sugar will absorb the oil from the nuts to prevent nut butter. Pulse-chop 10-12 times or until fineness desired.

NUTS, CHOPPED FINELY

TIP: Processing more than one cup of nuts at a time gives a very fine chop. If a chunky texture is desired chop one cup or less.

OLIVES, CHOPPED

TIP: Insert METAL BLADE. Add pitted olives to workbowl adding a few more olives than desired as the quantity will decrease in volume as you chop. Pulse-chop 3-6 times depending on the fineness desired. Drain off any olive liquid.

OLIVES, SLICED

TIP: Insert (2-6mm) SLICING DISC. Put cover in place. Pack the feedtube with one layer of pitted olives, standing the olives upright for perfect slices. Larger olives are easier to handle. Insert pusher and process using quick light pressure.

ONIONS, CHOPPED

TIP: Insert METAL BLADE. Cut onion in 4-6 even pieces. Pulse-chop 4-6 times. Count out each second for each pulse. Pause for 1 second after each pulse so that you DO NOT OVERPROCESS or you will have onion mush!!

ONIONS, CUBED

TIP: See FRENCH FRY DISC-CUBING TIP.

ONIONS, SLICED

TIP: Insert SLICING DISC. Cut off both ends of onion evenly. Cut onion in half vertically, if necessary, to fit feedtube. Place end surface on slicing disc. Be sure onion is firmly packed in feedtube. Slice using a medium pressure on pusher.

METAL BLADE   SHREDDING DISC   DOUGH BLADE   SLICING DISC   FRENCH-FRY DISC

PANCAKES

TIP: Mix pancake batter in the food processor with the METAL BLADE for a very light and fluffy batter. Add fresh fruit to the batter such as soft bananas and process while you are blending the ingredients. Pulse-chop 5-6 times for best results. See WORKBOWL COVER, KEEPING CLEAN TIP for a helpful idea.

PARSLEY, CHOPPED

TIP: Parsley and workbowl must be very dry. Dry parsley using salad spinner or place washed parsley in a plastic bag with several paper towels to absorb the moisture. Insert METAL BLADE. The stems may be chopped also. If doing both stems and flowers, add stems first and pulse-chop 8-10 times. Add flowers and pulse-chop until fine. Don't forget that all the vitamins are in the stems so don't be so quick to throw them out. Refrigerate parsley in covered container for about 1 week or store in a small brown bag in refrigerator almost indefinitely. Try freezing in small portions for use in recipes. You may also dry it. See HERBS, FRESH CHOPPED for drying method TIP.

PASTA

TIP: Insert METAL BLADE, add 1-1/2 cups flour, 2 eggs, 1 teaspoon salt and 1 tablespoon oil. Pulse-chop 3-4 times to combine. Continue processing for 30 seconds while pasta is forming into a ball. Check the consistency of the dough. If the dough is too soft, add 1 tablespoon flour at a time, check consistency after each addition. Process pasta another 30 seconds. Pasta should be firm, shiny and not sticky. Let dough rest 30 minutes or more before rolling out and cutting. Use this recipe for hand rolling or a hand crank pasta machine. Follow the manufacturer's directions for pasta if you have an electric pasta machine or attachment.

PATES

TIP: Insert METAL BLADE. Pulse-chop cooked meat until coarse. Add seasonings, onions, bacon, etc. that are in recipe. Pulse-chop until well blended. With machine running pour liquid ingredients slowly through the feedtube. Process until smooth. See also APPETIZERS—PATE UNDER ASPIC.

PEANUT BUTTER

TIP: Insert METAL BLADE, add nuts to workbowl. Pulse-chop 4-5 times. Let machine run continuously for about 1-2 minutes. The nuts will form a ball. Continue processing until smooth. Chunky peanut butter is made by adding more nuts after peanut butter is smooth and pulse-chopping 3-4 times more. No oil is needed to make peanut butter but adding 1/4-1/2 teaspoon per cup of nuts will produce creamier peanut butter. Dry roasted nuts may be used or a combination of dry roasted and cocktail peanuts may be used. Add oil if desired. Refrigerate 2-3 months or at room temperature for 1-2 weeks. If desired, warm peanut butter to spreading temperature in the microwave.

PEPPERONI, CHOPPED

TIP: If the food processor has a hard time slicing pepperoni then chop it with the METAL BLADE. Cut pieces of pepperoni and place in workbowl. Pulse-chop until desired consistency. This can be used on pizza, salads, or in AUNTIE'S PEPPERONI BREAD in BREADS.

PEPPERONI, SLICED

TIP: Pepperoni must be frozen for successful slicing because of the high fat content. Remove the casing before freezing, if desired. If you cannot cut through the pepperoni then neither can the food processor. Use a thin SLICING DISC (1-3mm) for best results. Make two or three short even lengths instead of one tall length if the pepperoni is very slender. Pack the pepperoni very tightly into the feedtube. Make sure the slicing edge of the disc is opposite the feedtube when the cover is locked in place for best slicing results. Do not push hard with the pusher when processing the pepperoni. The processor will be noisy when slicing pepperoni.

| METAL BLADE | SHREDDING DISC | DOUGH BLADE | SLICING DISC | FRENCH-FRY DISC |

PIE CRUST

TIP: See DESSERTS for a pastry recipe or use a favorite recipe of yours. Insert METAL BLADE. For best results, use FROZEN fat. Process fat and flour for 8-10 seconds until mixture is consistency of coarse meal. Add ice cold water to fat-flour mixture while machine is running. DO NOT let dough form into a ball or it will be over-processed and not flaky. Stop machine when dough is just starting to come together. Scrape dough mixture onto a sheet of plastic wrap. Bring four corners together with pastry inside and form into a ball. Roll out immediately, refrigerate, or freeze for later use. Perfect crust every time!!

NOTE: Process the pastry mixture just until it looks like popcorn in the workbowl.

PIE CRUST, GOOEY

TIP: Fat must be frozen to insure that it will cut into flour correctly. Room temperature fat (butter, shortening, lard etc.) will become too warm in the processor and make a gooey pie crust.

PIE CRUST, OVERPROCESSED

TIP: When pie crust dough balls together it WILL be over processed and tough when eaten. RASPBERRY FOLDOVERS is a great recipe to make if you happen to over process the pie crust. See DESSERTS.

PIE CRUST, TOUGH

TIP: Processing the pastry into a ball will overprocess the flour resulting in a tough crust. Any pie crust that is overhandled by rolling and rerolling will also become tough.

PIES, CREAM OR FRUIT

TIP: Cream or fruit pies are easily made with the help of the food processor. Prepare crust first using the BASIC PASTRY DOUGH or the GRAHAM CRACKER CRUST. Using the METAL BLADE, process together the ingredients for the cream pie. Check the INSTANT PUDDING TIP if using instant pudding.

For fruit pies, peel, core, or seed fruits. Insert SLICING DISC (4-8mm). Place fruit in feedtube upright or on sides, but pack feedtube tightly for best results. The way the fruit is loaded will determine the shape of the slices. Apply medium pressure on pusher. Stop machine, refill feedtube and repeat processing until all fruit is processed. Workbowl can be filled to within 1/2 inch of the top.

| METAL BLADE | SHREDDING DISC | DOUGH BLADE | SLICING DISC | FRENCH-FRY DISC |

PLACEMENT OF FOOD IN FEEDTUBE

TIP: The placement of food in the feedtube of the food processor is the secret to success when slicing fruits, vegetables, etc. If circular slices are what you want then vegetables and fruits should be placed vertically, evenly, and tightly in the feedtube so each piece is holding the next one up. If the food is not tightly packed in the feedtube, it will fall over and the processor will produce irregularly shaped slices. Always use the pusher to guide the food through the feedtube and be ready to push BEFORE you start the machine.

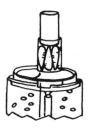

POSITION OF SLICING DISC

TIP: The slicing edge of the SLICING DISC must be opposite the feedtube when the cover is locked in place. This allows the machine to build up momentum when it is turned on before contacting the food that is being sliced. This is especially important with very firm or hard foods like carrots, frozen meat or pepperoni, turnips, etc. This positioning will also give you more even slicing results as the slice is started perfectly.

POTATO PANCAKES

TIP: It's so easy to make potato pancakes in the food processor. Insert METAL BLADE. Add chunks of potatoes to workbowl. Pulse-chop until fairly fine, about 6-10 times. Add egg, flour, and chunks of onions to potatoes in workbowl. Pulse-chop until onions are fine, about 6-10 times. When you have reached the desired consistency, remove METAL BLADE and pour batter from workbowl. Only 20 seconds work for delicious potato pancakes!

Some people like the potatoes shredded. If that is the case insert METAL BLADE, process egg, flour and onion. Remove blade and insert SHREDDING DISC to shred potatoes. Mix ingredients together and cook. See VEGETABLES for a recipe.

POTATOES, CUBED

TIP: See FRENCH FRY DISC-CUBING, POTATOES TIP.

POTATOES, HASH BROWNS

TIP: There are two schools of thought on processing potatoes for hash browns. One is to shred the potatoes with the SHREDDING DISC, then shred an onion with it for a nice flavor. The second is to slice the potatoes using the SLICING DISC. Then change to a FRENCH FRY DISC. Pack the potatoes in the feedtube standing up and crosswise. Process using a firm pressure on the pusher. This will give you cubes. For better nutrition and a country flavor leave the skins on when processing the potato.

POTATOES, MASHED

TIP: Cook and skin potatoes. Insert SHREDDING DISC, process potatoes. Heat milk and butter in a saucepan or microwave. Stir into potatoes in bottom of workbowl. Pulse with METAL BLADE twice. Too much processing will give potatoes "gluey" consistency. If this happens, stir in by hand more warm milk until potatoes become creamy. For 1 medium potato you may need as much as 1/2 cup milk depending on desired consistency. Season.

PROCESSING SINGLE ITEMS

TIP: The SLICING DISC in a food processor operates in a counter clockwise direction. To keep single items from falling over place them by the side of the feedtube that the blade will push the food towards. See SLICES-EVEN SLICES OF LONG SLENDER VEGETABLES TIP also.

PROCESSING TIME

TIP: Remember, when using the METAL BLADE the longer food is processed in a food processor the finer it becomes.

TIP: Because food is mixed so quickly in a food processor with the METAL BLADE, it only takes seconds to process food items, NOT minutes.

PULSE, PULSE-CHOP

TIP: When using the METAL BLADE each pulse or pulse-chop in a recipe is equal to 1 second. If a recipe says pulse-chop 3-4 times you will be pulsing for 3-4 seconds. There are two reasons for pulse-chopping. The first reason is you stop the machine to check the consistency of the food. Checking makes you aware of how fast the chopping takes place. The other reason is each time you start and stop the machine the larger pieces are thrown into the METAL BLADE and a more even consistency is achieved.

PUREES

TIP: Insert METAL BLADE. Fill workbowl half full of soft cooked fruits or vegetables. Pulse-chop 4-6 times. With machine running add one cup liquid, taken from the recipe, through the feedtube; process until smooth, 20-30 seconds. More than one cup liquid can be added to the puree depending on the liquid capacity of the workbowl. Empty workbowl into another container and repeat process if necessary.

PUSHER, OPENING ON THE SIDE

TIP: In the large pusher assembly of the Cuisinart® food processor there is a hole in the sleeve. It is put there to enable you to pick up the cover and the pusher assembly with one hand. Grasp the pusher assembly and your fingers will go over the hole enabling you to hold onto the cover. It is not used to put food into the processor. When using any SLICING or SHREDDING disc all large foods must be put in the large feedtube BEFORE locking on the pusher-sleeve assembly. The pusher will expand upward to accommodate the piece of food and then you will be able to lock the sleeve onto the bowl. This large assembly does NOT pull apart. It is unsafe to operate the food processor if this happens.

PUSHER, PRESSURE ON

TIP: Always use the palm of the hand when pushing on the pusher and keep pushing down continuously until all the food in the feedtube is processed. It is very important to guide the food with the pusher. Generally, the pressure needed is matched to the softness or firmness of the food being processed. When slicing you can vary the thickness of the slices somewhat by changing the pressure. A very light, slow pressure on the pusher will produce thinner slices. If the feedtube is firmly packed it will also help produce thinner slices along with a light pressure.

PUSHER, TINY HOLE

TIP: In some food processors there is a tiny hole in the pusher. This hole will allow oil to drip slowly into the workbowl to make a nice thick mayonnaise. Use it for the butter when making a hollandaise sauce or any other liquid you want to add slowly.

RADISHES, SHREDDED

TIP: Insert SHREDDING DISC. Place cleaned radishes in the feedtube. Process using firm pressure on pusher. Some radish pieces may remain on the disc after processing. Use shredded radishes in vegetable and salad dishes to add color.

REFILLING THE FEEDTUBE

TIP: When slicing, shredding, French frying, or julienning you fill the feedtube, then process the food using the pusher to guide the food through the feedtube. STOP the machine and then refill the feedtube. Continue until all the desired amount of food is processed or until the workbowl is full.

RUTABAGA HALF MOONS

TIP: Try it first before you turn up your nose. It's better uncooked! Peel and cut in half vertically. Be sure to cut both ends flat. The flat surface starts the slices evenly and the pusher presses evenly on the upper flat surface. Insert the SLICING DISC. Process both half pieces together if the feedtube is big enough or one half at a time. Use a firm pressure on the pusher.

SALAD, EASY ONE BOWL

TIP: Insert METAL BLADE, add 1 clove garlic, 1/4 cup red wine vinegar, 1/2 cup salad oil, 1 tablespoon water, 1/2 tsp. salt, 1/2 tsp. oregano, and 1/4 tsp. pepper. Process until well blended and garlic is chopped. Pour half of VINAGRETTE DRESSING in a container for another salad. Leave remaining dressing in workbowl. Remove METAL BLADE. Process only the amount of vegetable desired as it is difficult to stop the processor halfway through a vegetable. Insert SHREDDING DISC and process desired vegetables. Remove shredding disc and insert SLICING DISC. Slice vegetables desired. Finish by slicing thick slices of lettuce or spinach. Each ingredient will be left in the workbowl as it is processed unless the workbowl becomes full. Invert workbowl over serving dish, toss and serve.

SAUCES, CREAM

TIP: If cream sauce gets lumpy, process in the food processor with the METAL BLADE until smooth.

SHERBET, FRUIT

TIP: This is a good recipe for using left over fruits from a picnic or party, etc. Use your imagination and try any fruit combination you enjoy— bananas and strawberries, watermelon and raspberries, peaches and apricots. Let your imagination and your fruit basket guide you. It will serve four. Use 2 cups frozen fruit (watermelon or peaches), 1/2 cup berries (raspberries), 2-3 tablespoon whipping cream and 2 tablespoons orange or almond base liqueur (optional). Seed or peel fruit as desired and freeze in 1 inch chunks on a baking sheet. Insert METAL BLADE, add half the frozen fruit and pulse-chop 6-8 times. With machine running add remaining fruit cubes and the berries through the feedtube. Replace pusher. When fruit is finely chopped, remove pusher. Add the cream and liqueur through the feedtube while machine is running. The texture should be smooth. Serve immediately or store in freezer up to three hours. If frozen over three hours, reprocess and serve.

SIFTING CONFECTIONERS' SUGAR

TIP: Use METAL BLADE in a clean, dry workbowl and add confectioners' sugar. Pulse-chop 4-6 times until lumps disappear. Now you can throw the flour sifter away!

SIFTING INGREDIENTS

TIP: Pulsing all dry ingredients together in the workbowl using the METAL BLADE combines them evenly just as sifting does.

SLICES, DIAGONALLY CUT VEGETABLES

TIP: Vegetables that are not quite tightly packed in the feedtube will process on the diagonal when using the SLICING DISC. If they are too loosely packed they will fall on their sides.

TIP: You may also cut even lengths of vegetables on the diagonal. Pack slices in feedtube with diagonal surface flat on SLICING DISC. Pack feedtube full enough to keep pieces from falling over. Process using medium-light pressure on the pusher.

| METAL BLADE | SHREDDING DISC | DOUGH BLADE | SLICING DISC | FRENCH-FRY DISC |

SLICES—EVEN CIRCULAR SLICES OF CARROTS, CELERY, RHUBARB ETC.

TIP: To slice long slender fruits or vegetables evenly be sure the feedtube is packed tightly or the produce will fall over and slice diagonally. Cut the produce in short even lengths to pack the feedtube rather than using long pieces in an unpacked feedtube. Use the palm of hand with an even pressure on the pusher to guide the food through the feedtube.

SLICES—EVEN SLICES OF LONG SLENDER VEGETABLES OR "DANCING"

TIP: This tip applies especially to celery and green onions. Insert SLICING DISC. Lock cover in place. Hold onto UNTRIMMED tops and insert food in feedtube. With the machine running move the vegetable up and down in the feedtube and stop slicing when the tops of the vegetable reach the top of the feedtube. DO NOT try to process your fingers.

SLICES, "PICTURE PERFECT"

TIP: Always cut the ends of fruit, vegetables, meat, etc. flat for a more even slice. Place cutting edge of disc opposite the feedtube when the cover is locked in place. Lay the food flat side down on the SLICING DISC. Pack the feedtube evenly and as fully as possible. Place pusher in feedtube. Use the palm of hand with an even pressure on pusher to guide the food through the feedtube. Be ready to push BEFORE the machine is started for "picture perfect" slices. Start the machine, pressing pusher through with palm of hand. Always stop the machine to refill the feedtube. If the feedtube is refilled while the machine is running when using the slicing, shredding or French fry disc it could be dangerous and the processed food will be uneven and unattractive.

SLICES, THIN

TIP: Not all machines have thin SLICING DISCS or you may not have this disc for the processor. To produce thinner slices pack the feedtube very tightly and apply a light pressure on the pusher. The slices should be thinner. Use this technique for thin slices of carrots, celery, cabbage, cucumber, potatoes, etc. It is the next best technique to owning a 1-2mm slicing disc.

SOUPS, CREAMED

TIP: Cook vegetables for soup. Insert METAL BLADE. Fill workbowl half full of cooked vegetables. Pulse-chop 6-8 times. With machine running add soup liquid until the level of food is even with the top of the metal blade. Adding liquids to solids keeps the liquid from spilling out of the workbowl. Fill workbowl no more than half full of liquid. When emptying the workbowl, hold onto the METAL BLADE with a fingertip on top or with a finger underneath the workbowl through the bottom of the METAL BLADE. This keeps the cream mixture from running out of the center workbowl opening. See TIP: WORKBOWL, HOLDING also. Repeat processing method with any remaining vegetables. The thickening (like flour or cornstarch) can be added to cold milk or cream and processed with the vegetables also. Return all the ingredients to the soup kettle and heat until thickened, but do not boil.

STEAK TARTARE

TIP: Steak tartare can be made so easily in the food processor. The METAL BLADE will chop the fresh tenderloin to the desired consistency in just seconds. Add a little fresh parsley, tarragon or dill and an onion to the raw meat. Pulse-chop until the meat is nicely chopped and seasonings are blended. Season with salt and pepper. Serve with raw egg, small capers and Melba toast.

STREUSEL TOPPING

TIP: This streusel topping recipe can be used for any fruit filling. You may substitute 1/2 cup packed brown sugar for 1 cup granulated. Use 1 cup sugar, 3/4 cup flour, 1/4 tsp. nutmeg, dash of salt, 1/2 tsp. cinnamon and 1/2 cup butter, FROZEN. Insert METAL BLADE, add dry ingredients and pulse 2-3 times. Cut butter in six pieces. Add to workbowl. Pulse chop 5-6 times or until mixture is crumbly. Sprinkle over filling and bake at 375° for 30-40 minutes or until topping is crisp and brown. To produce a crumbly mixture be sure to use FROZEN butter or margarine. The mixture will ball if room temperature fat is used.

METAL
BLADE

SHREDDING
DISC

DOUGH
BLADE

SLICING
DISC

FRENCH-FRY
DISC

SUPERFINE SUGAR

TIP: No more searching for superfine sugar at the grocery store when you own a food processor. Insert METAL BLADE, add 1-2 cups sugar and process until very fine about 1-2 minutes. Use this sugar in desserts and drink recipes. Store and label any sugar not used.

TOMATO, FRESH PULP

TIP: Use SHREDDING DISC. Remove stem end of tomato. Place tomato in feedtube with cut end on SHREDDING DISC, process. The juice and pulp shred through and the skin stays at the top of the disc. Works great on soft tomatoes that are very juicy.

TOMATO, SLICING

TIP: Insert SLICING DISC. Apply quick, medium pressure on pusher when processing soft vegetables and fruits like tomatoes. Some machines have sharper slicing discs and will produce better slices than others.

TIP: Use a moderately firm tomato. Core tomatoes, cut in half vertically if desired. Insert SLICING DISC of desired thickness. Process the whole or half tomato depending on the feedtube size. Use quick, medium pressure on pusher.

WALLPAPER PASTE

TIP: If making a non-food item like wallpaper paste and there are lumps in the mixture try this. Insert METAL BLADE, fill workbowl half full with paste and process until smooth. Repeat until all paste is smooth and lump free. There will be some air bubbles but they will smooth out when you apply the wall paper.

WASHING BLADES AND DISCS

TIP: The METAL BLADE, SLICING and SHREDDING DISCS are very sharp. Treat them with care. If washing by hand use a dishwashing brush and brush with the cutting edge so you do not dull it. If the stems detach from the DISCS leave the stem attached to the disc to hold onto as you wash the DISCS. The METAL BLADE has a plastic post to hold when you wash it by hand. The DISCS may be washed in a dishwasher but place the cutting surfaces down so family members won't cut themselves. Put the METAL BLADE where it will not bang into another dish or the dishwasher. It is not the hot water or detergent in a dishwasher that dulls the blades but the bumping and hitting of non-food items.

WHIPPING CREAM, WHIPPED

TIP: A clean cold bowl and cold blade speed the processing. Insert METAL BLADE. With machine running, add cream slowly through feedtube. Process 1 minute. With machine running slowly add sugar and vanilla,if desired, through the feedtube. Process an additional minute or until stiff. Do not overprocess unless you want to make butter!

WORKBOWL COVER, AS AN EXTRA PAIR OF HANDS

TIP: The feedtube on a food processor cover will hold a sandwich size baggie so you can easily fill it with chopped, sliced, or shredded food. Place baggie into feedtube and turn the rim of the sandwich baggie around the outside edge of the feedtube just as you would line a wastebasket. It will hold the baggie as you clean out the workbowl freeing both hands to hold and scrape.

WORKBOWL COVER, KEEPING CLEAN

TIP: When you only want to process with the METAL BLADE and not use the feedtube, keep the cover clean the following way. Use a sheet of plastic wrap large enough to lay over the top of the workbowl. Add the cover and lock it on in the usual manner. The plastic wrap is thin and won't interfere with locking the cover but it will shield the cover from any spatters. No need to wash the cover and pusher!

WORKBOWL, CAPACITY

TIP: When using the METAL BLADE, you achieve better chopping results if you fill the workbowl half full with food. The bowl can be filled to within one inch of the top when using the SHREDDING, SLICING, or FRENCH FRY DISCS. When using these discs the food will also pile higher in one spot. The food is processed from the top when using the DISCS and that is the reason for the difference in capacity between chopping with the METAL BLADE versus DISC operations.

| METAL BLADE | SHREDDING DISC | DOUGH BLADE | SLICING DISC | FRENCH-FRY DISC |

WORKBOWL, CLEANING BETWEEN STEPS

TIP: Often all that is necessary is to wipe out the workbowl with a paper towel between steps. Plan your steps to work from dry to liquid ingredients and leave odorous items like onion and garlic until last if possible. Processing this way eliminates constant washing of the workbowl.

WORKBOWL, HOLDING

TIP: Some processors have openings in the bottom of the METAL BLADE. Insert the index or middle finger through the outside center of the workbowl into this opening while the METAL BLADE is in the workbowl. Hold tightly with the finger and place thumb around bottom outer side of workbowl. Fan out the rest of the fingers over the bottom of the workbowl. Then pour out the contents while holding onto the blade. You may find this a convenient way to hold the workbowl whether or not it has liquid in it.

WORKBOWL, LEAKY

TIP: Prevent liquids from "running out" by adding the dry ingredients first and then adding the liquid ingredients. This keeps the mixture from seeping out of the workbowl through the center workbowl opening. The thicker mixture forms a seal and is less likely to seep out the opening. If too much liquid is added first it will run out the center workbowl opening onto the machine base. It won't hurt the machine but it is certainly messy!

WORKBOWL, WASHING

TIP: All the parts, except the motor base, of most food processors may be washed in a dishwasher. Check the instruction booklet.

ZESTING CITRUS USING THE PROCESSOR

TIP: This works best with a processor that has a large feedtube. Insert the SHREDDING DISC (FINE if available). Wash fruit and remove stem if necessary. Place small citrus fruit in feedtube. Do NOT use the pusher. Turn machine on, the fruit will bounce around. The SHREDDING DISC will cut little pieces of skin off the fruit producing the cut zest of the fruit. Stop machine when white pith of skin shows.

BASIL, CILANTRO, AND MINT—FREEZING FRESH

TIP: Wash and shake herbs to remove excess water. Insert METAL BLADE. Pulse-chop 4-6 times, add oil (about 1-1½ tablespoons per cupful of chopped herbs) and continue processing until desired consistency. The herb, water (clinging to the leaves) and the oil will make a pesto-like consistency. Freeze in ice cube trays. Package cubes and store 6-8 months. Use cubes to flavor soups, sauces, salad dressings and gravies for a garden fresh flavor all year long.

DATES, CHOPPED

TIP: This tip is used when a recipe calls for chopped dates and nuts. Insert SHREDDING DISC. Place cover on workbowl. Place a layer of nuts in the feedtube, add pitted dates and finish with another layer of nuts. Insert pusher. Process with medium-light pressure on pusher until dates and nuts are processed. The nuts keep the dates from getting stuck in the shredding disc.

DATES CHOPPED, MUFFINS

TIP: Insert METAL BLADE. Add pitted dates to the bottom of the workbowl. Add all other ingredients and pulse-chop 5-6 times. Or first place all ingredients in workbowl except dates. Add dates to workbowl last. Pulse-chop 5-6 times. This will give a coarser chopped date.

ICE, SHAVED

TIP: Insert SHREDDING DISC. Place ice cubes (not commercially frozen) in feedtube. Insert pusher, turn processor on and push lightly on pusher until all ice is processed. Work quickly. Drain any water that remains on bottom of workbowl. Store shaved ice in freezer until ready to use.

LIVER, CHOPPED CHICKEN

TIP: Cook chicken livers. Refrigerate until well chilled. Insert SHREDDING DISC. Place cover on workbowl and add liver to feedtube. Insert pusher and process with a medium pressure. This method avoids overchopping and does not make a paste consistency which can happen when using the metal blade.

281

SUBSTITUTIONS

INGREDIENT	AMOUNT	SUBSTITUTE
Baking Powder	1 tsp.	1/4 tsp. baking soda + 1 tsp. cream of tartar or 1/4 tsp. baking soda + 1/2 tsp. baking powder
Broth	1 cup	1 bouillon dissolved in 1 cup water
Butter	1 lb.	Pour 2 cups evaporated milk in food processor. Process until butter forms. Chill.
Chocolate	1 oz. unsweetened	3 Tbsp. cocoa + 1 Tbsp. fat
	1 oz. semi-sweet	3 Tbsp. cocoa + 1 Tbsp. fat + 3 Tbsp. sugar
Cornstarch	1 Tbsp.	2 Tbsp. flour
Cream, Coffee	1 cup	7/8 cup milk + 3 Tbsp. butter
Cream, Heavy	1 cup	3/4 cup milk + 1/3 cup butter
Cream, Sour	1 cup	7/8 cup sour milk + 3 Tbsp. butter or 1 cup cottage cheese processed with 2 Tbsp. milk and 1 tsp. lemon juice
Cream, sour (con't.)	1 cup	6 oz. cream cheese + milk to equal 1 cup or 1 cup yogurt or 1 cup evaporated milk + 1 Tbsp. vinegar
Cream, Whipping	1 cup	Chilled evaporated milk + 1 tsp. lemon juice Processed until whipped

SUBSTITUTIONS

INGREDIENT	AMOUNT	SUBSTITUTE
Egg	1 whole	2 yolks
Flour	1 cup	1 cup + 2 Tbsp. sifted cake flour or 7/8 cups cornmeal or 1 cup rolled oats
Flour, cake	1 cup sifted	1 cup minus 2 Tbsp. sifted all-purpose flour
Flour, for thickening	1 Tbsp.	1/2 Tbsp. cornstarch or 2 tsp. tapioca
Garlic	1 clove	1/8 tsp. garlic powder or 1/8 tsp. minced garlic
Honey	1 cup	1-1/4 cups sugar + 1/4 cup liquid
Milk, sour or buttermilk	1 cup	1 cup milk + 1 Tbsp. lemon juice or vinegar. Let stand 5 minutes.
Milk, Buttermilk	1 cup	1 cup yogurt
Milk, whole	1 cup	1/2 cup evaporated + 1/2 cup water
Mustard	1 Tbsp.	1 tsp. dry mustard + 1 Tbsp. vinegar
Nuts	1 cup	1 cup grapenuts
Sugar	1 cup	1 cup brown sugar packed or 1-3/4 cups confectioners' sugar
Sugar, carmelized	1 tsp.	1 Tbsp. commercial gravy coloring
Syrup, corn	1 cup	1 cup sugar + 1/4 cup liquid
Soy Sauce	1/4 cup	3 Tbsp. Worcestershire + 1 Tbsp. water
Worcestershire	1 Tbsp.	1 Tbsp. soy sauce + 1 dash liquid red pepper seasoning

Need Additional Copies? Use this order form.

Please send _____ copy/copies of
SO NOW YOU OWN A FOOD PROCESSOR   @ $9.95 each $_____

POSTAGE AND HANDLING $2.00 each $_____

TOTAL ENCLOSED (U.S. FUNDS ONLY) $_____

Please make check or money order payable to:
EAST-WEST PUBLISHING CO.

Name _____

Address _____

City/State/Zip_____

Send to: East-West Publishing Co.,

East-West Publishing Co.
Dona De Santis-Reynolds
563 Shoreham
Grosse Pte. Woods, MI 48236

Need Additional Copies? Use this order form.

Please send _____ copy/copies of
SO NOW YOU OWN A FOOD PROCESSOR   @ $9.95 each $_____

POSTAGE AND HANDLING $2.00 each $_____

TOTAL ENCLOSED (U.S. FUNDS ONLY) $_____

Please make check or money order payable to:
EAST-WEST PUBLISHING CO.

Name _____

Address _____

City/State/Zip_____

Send to: East-West Publishing Co.,

East-West Publishing Co.
Dona De Santis-Reynolds
563 Shoreham
Grosse Pte. Woods, MI 48236

Need Additional Copies? Use this order form.

Please send _____ copy/copies of
SO NOW YOU OWN A FOOD PROCESSOR   @ $9.95 each $_____

POSTAGE AND HANDLING $2.00 each $_____

TOTAL ENCLOSED (U.S. FUNDS ONLY) $_____

Please make check or money order payable to:
EAST-WEST PUBLISHING CO.

Name _____

Address _____

City/State/Zip_____

Send to: East-West Publishing Co.,

East-West Publishing Co.
Dona De Santis-Reynolds
563 Shoreham
Grosse Pte. Woods, MI 48236